Critical Thinking

A Concise Guide

Second edition

Tracy Bowell

and

Gary Kemp

Routledge
Taylor & Francis Group

LONDON AND NEW YORK

First published 2002
by Routledge
2 Park Square, Milton Park, Abingdon, Oxon OX14 4RN

Simultaneously published in the USA and Canada
by Routledge
270 Madison Avenue, New York, NY 10016

Second edition 2005

Reprinted 2006 (twice), 2007

Routledge is an imprint of the Taylor & Francis Group, an informa business

© 2005 Tracy Bowell and Gary Kemp

Typeset in Aldus, Akzidenz Grotesk and Tekton by
Florence Production Ltd, Stoodleigh, Devon
Printed and bound in Great Britain by
TJ International Ltd, Padstow, Cornwall

British Library Cataloguing in Publication Data
A catalogue record for this book is available from the British Library

Library of Congress Cataloging in Publication Data
Bowell, Tracy, 1965–
   Critical thinking: a concise guide/Tracy Bowell and Gary Kemp.
   – 2nd ed.
     p. cm.
   Includes bibliographical references and index.
   1. Critical thinking. I. Kemp, Gary, 1960 Oct. 15– II. Title.
   B809.2.B69 2005
   160–dc22   2004023944

ISBN 10: 0–415–34312–7 (hbk)
ISBN 10: 0–415–34313–5 (pbk)
ISBN 13: 978–0–415–34312–1 (hbk)
ISBN 13: 978–0–415–34313–8 (pbk)

■ Contents

Contents

■ Preface to the first edition

Like all authors of texts on critical thinking or critical reasoning, we have tried to write a book that is genuinely useful. But our conception of what is useful differs somewhat from that of most of those authors.

On the one hand, we have avoided formal logical methods. Whereas the application of formal methods is justified primarily by its value in coping with complex logical structure, the logical structure of everyday argumentation is very seldom so complex that an argument's validity, or lack of it, cannot be revealed to ordinary intuition by a clear statement of the argument in English. Yet no formal means short of the first-order predicate calculus is sufficient to represent the logic of the majority of everyday arguments. Rather than compromise by presenting less comprehensive formal methods that are useful only in a narrow range of cases, we have avoided them entirely.

On the other hand, we have discussed and employed the *concepts* of logic more thoroughly than is customary in texts that avoid formal methods. We have defined them as accurately and in as much detail as we could, without superfluous refinement or inappropriate theoretical elaboration. We have done this for three reasons. First, it is only by grasping those concepts clearly that the student can achieve a stable and explicit understanding of the purposes of presenting and analysing arguments. Second, facility with those concepts enables the student to think and to talk about arguments in a systematically precise way; it provides a common currency in terms of which to generalise about arguments and to compare them. Third, experience, including our teaching experience, suggests that the concepts of logic themselves, when they explicitly appear in argumentative contexts, are amongst the most persistent sources of confusion. A symptom of this is the relativism that is so often encountered and so often lamented. At the root of this, we assume, are certain equivocations over the word 'truth'. We have tried to clear these up in a common-sense

Preface to the first edition

and non-dogmatic way, and thereby to clarify further concepts that depend on the concept of truth, such as validity, probability, inductive force, soundness, justification and knowledge. We hope that clarity about these concepts, and the ability to use them with confidence in analysing arguments, will be among the most valuable accomplishments to be acquired by studying this book.

We do not entirely accept the view that examples in a book on critical thinking should be real, or even that they should be realistic. Of course, the aim is that students should be able to deal with real arguments. But whereas real examples typically call for the exercise of several strategies and the application of various concepts at once, those strategies and concepts have to be learned one at a time. Unrealistic, trumped-up examples are often much more useful for illustrating isolated concepts and points of strategy. We have tried to vary the realistic with the artificial as the situation recommends.

Thanks to Lee Churchman and Damien Cole, both of whom updated earlier versions of this text for us in preparation for teaching, and thereby provided many helpful examples. Thanks also to all those who have provided ideas either as teaching assistants or students of our Critical Reasoning course at the University of Waikato: especially Paul Flood, Stephanie Gibbons, Andrew Jorgensen, Dawn Marsh, Alastair Todd, Louis Wilkins and Tim Wilson. We also thank the Philosophy Department at the University of Waikato for giving Bowell time to stop in Glasgow to work with Kemp in October 1999.

Tracy Bowell, University of Waikato
Gary Kemp, University of Glasgow
January 2001

■ Preface to the second edition

The second edition has benefited enormously from teachers using the book who have been kind enough to pass along comments and suggestions. Largely in response to these, we have: expanded the range of exercises; included answers to selected exercises; discussed the relation between formal logic and our informal approach; expanded the use of argument trees; added further instructions and tips for removing rhetoric and clarifying the logical structure of an argument; included a completely worked example, illustrating the form that a complete written argument analysis might take; thoroughly revised the final chapter linking critical reasoning to theoretical issues in epistemology. Along the way, we have streamlined and clarified in sundry smaller ways. We have many tutors, teachers and other readers to thank, but we would especially like to single out Helen Beebee, Lawrence Goldstein, Chris Lindsay and Anne Pittock. We thank the Faculty of Arts and Social Sciences, University of Waikato for funding Kemp's visit to Waikato in Spring 2004, and the study leave granted to Bowell in 2004 partly for work on the book.

Tracy Bowell, University of Waikato
Gary Kemp, University of Glasgow
7 January 2005

■ Introduction and preview

We are frequently confronted with *arguments*: these are attempts to *persuade* us – to influence our beliefs and actions – by giving us *reasons* to believe this or that, or to act in this way or that. This book will equip you with concepts and techniques used in the identification, analysis and assessment of arguments. The aim is to improve your ability to tell *whether* an argument is being given, exactly *what* the argument is, and whether you ought to be persuaded by it.

Chapter 1 introduces the concept of argument as it should be understood for the purposes of critical thinking. Argument is distinguished from other linguistic means of getting people to do and to believe things. We introduce a method for laying out arguments so as to understand them more clearly, and we discuss various ways in which language can obscure an arguer's intended meaning.

Chapter 2 introduces validity and soundness, the main concepts required for the analysis and assessment of deductive arguments. These are arguments whose premises, if true, guarantee the truth of the conclusion. We discuss the assessment of validity and soundness, and explain the meaning and use of the principle of charity.

Chapter 3 continues our coverage of the concepts central to this book, this time for the analysis and assessment of inductive arguments: inductive force and inductive soundness. We also discuss inductive inferences and degrees of probability.

Chapter 4 is a detailed discussion of rhetorical ploys and fallacies, two species of what we call 'sham-reasoning'. Common species of each are considered, and using the concepts and techniques covered in previous chapters, we provide a method for exposing fallacious reasoning and explaining what is fallacious about it.

Chapter 5 covers in more detail the techniques required for reconstructing arguments and discusses specific issues that tend to arise in practice. We demonstrate techniques for deciding which material is relevant to an argument; for dealing with ambiguous and vague language; for uncovering an argument's hidden premises; for adding connecting premises; for dealing with practical reasoning and for dealing with causal arguments.

Chapter 6 is concerned with further concepts and techniques for argument assessment. We introduce the concept of rational persuasiveness, and introduce further techniques for assessing arguments and for refuting them. We also include a complete worked example, applying and illustrating the analytical techniques and concepts developed during the course of the book.

Finally, in Chapter 7 we consider some of the philosophical issues underlying the concepts and techniques used here. We discuss truth and its relationship to belief and knowledge, and relate these issues to the concept of rational persuasiveness. We sketch some connections to philosophical questions in the theory of knowledge.

Each chapter concludes with a chapter summary and exercises; answers to selected exercises are at the end of the text. Where appropriate, the reader is encouraged to look outside the book for further examples to serve as exercises.

Chapter 1

Why should we become critical thinkers?

The focus of this book is written and spoken ways of persuading us to do things and to believe things. Every day we are bombarded with messages apparently telling us what to do or not to do, what to believe or not to believe: buy this soft drink; eat that breakfast cereal; vote for Mrs Bloggs; practise safe sex; don't drink and drive; don't use drugs; boycott goods from this country or that; vivisection is murder; abortion is murder; meat is murder; aliens have visited the earth; the economy is sound; capitalism is just; genetically modified crops are safe; etc. Some messages we just ignore, some we unreflectively obey and some we unreflectively reject. Others we might think about and question, asking 'why should I do, or refrain from doing that?', or 'why should I believe that, or not believe it?'.

Why should we become critical thinkers?

When we ask the question 'why?' we're asking for a **reason** for doing what we are being enjoined to do, or for believing what we are being enjoined to believe: Why should I vote for Mrs Bloggs, or eat this particular breakfast cereal? Why should I believe that meat is murder, or that the economy is sound? When we ask for a reason in this way we are asking for a **justification** for taking the action recommended or accepting the belief – not just a reason, but a good reason – that ought to motivate us to act or believe as we are recommended to do. We might be told, for example, that Wheetybites are a nutritious, sugar-free, low-fat breakfast cereal; if this is so, and we want to eat a healthy breakfast, then we've been given a good reason to eat Wheetybites. If, on the other hand, we are given only state-of-the-art marketing techniques – for example, images of good-looking people happily eating Wheetybites with bright red strawberries out of fashionable crockery – then, although an attempt has been made to persuade us to buy Wheetybites, it would not appear that any attempt has been made to provide good reasons for doing so.

To attempt to persuade by giving good reasons is to give an **argument**. We encounter many different types of attempts to persuade.[1] Not all of these are arguments, and one of the things that we will concentrate on early in this book is how to distinguish attempts to persuade in which the speaker or writer intends to put forward an argument, from those in which their intention is to persuade us by some means other than argument. Critical thinkers should primarily be interested in arguments and whether they succeed in providing us with good reasons for acting or believing. But we also need to consider non-argumentative attempts to persuade, as we must be able to distinguish these from arguments. This is not always straightforward, particularly as many attempts to persuade involve a mixture of various argumentative and non-argumentative techniques to get readers and listeners to accept a point of view or take a certain course of action.

You may find it surprising to think of an 'argument' as a term for giving someone a reason to do or believe something – telling them why they should boycott certain products or disapprove of pornography for instance. Perhaps in your experience the word 'argument' means a

---

1   Not all attempts to persuade use language, often they use images or combine images with language, most advertising, for instance, involves a combination of images and text or speech aimed to persuade us by non-argumentative means to buy stuff. Although the persuasive power of images is an interesting issue, here we are interested only in attempts to persuade that use written or spoken language. But images can also occur in argumentative attempts to persuade. We see on television, for example, a shot of dead fish in a dirty pond; a voice says, 'This is why we must strengthen the anti-pollution laws'. In this sort of case, we can think of the image as *implicitly* stating a premise, in the sense to be described below (pp. 15–18).

disagreement – shouting the odds, slamming doors, insults, sulking, etc. In fact in some of those situations the participants might actually be advancing what we mean by an argument, putting forward a well-argued case for washing up one's dishes for example, but in many cases, they will not be arguing in the sense that we have in mind here.

The sort of argument we have in mind occurs frequently in ordinary, everyday situations. It is by no means restricted to the works of Plato, Descartes and other scholars famous for the arguments they put forward. You and your acquaintances give each other reasons for believing something or doing something all the time – why we should expect our friend to be late for dinner, why we should walk rather than wait for the bus and so on. Open a newspaper, and you'll find arguments in the letters section, editorials and various other discussion pieces. In television and radio broadcasts (especially current affairs shows) and in internet discussions you'll find people arguing their case (though they may well also resort to other persuasive techniques as well). The same thing occurs in a more elevated form at university and college. Throughout your time as a student you will hear lecturers and other students arguing for a point of view, and in set readings you will encounter attempts to persuade you of various claims about all manner of issues. In the workplace you may find yourself having to argue for a particular course of action or argue on behalf of a client or associate.

If you develop your ability to analyse people's attempts to persuade so that you can accurately interpret what they are saying or writing and evaluate whether or not they are giving a good argument – whether, for example, they are providing you with a good reason to believe that pornography should be banned – then you can begin to liberate yourself from accepting what others try to persuade you of without knowing whether you actually have a good reason to be persuaded.[2]

But then, you may ask, why is it liberating to demand reasons before you are persuaded to adopt new beliefs? Isn't it less trouble to go through life unreflectively, doing more or less as you please and not worrying too much about whether you have good reason to do or believe something,

---

2   Although this book emphasises the value of reason and the benefits of using techniques of persuasion that are rational, we should also bear in mind that what is claimed to be rational is not always rational, and certainly does not always have positive consequences. Historically, for example, those who wield power have often granted themselves authority over what counts as 'rational', condemning as 'irrational' what threatens the status quo. The correct response to that sort of rhetorical manoeuvre, however, is not to say 'so much the worse for rationality, then!'; the correct response is to question whether the charge of irrationality is justified, or whether the term is merely being abused or manipulated. Rationality in itself is a neutral force, independent of anyone's particular interests or beliefs.

beyond whether or not you want to? Well, it may often be easier in the short run, but it might lead to a life dominated by bad decisions and discontentment. Socrates, the ancient Athenian philosopher famously argued that 'the unexamined life is not worth living'.[3] While this may or may not be true, the only way to find out is to approach the issue in a critical and rational manner. Paying attention to arguments gets you, eventually, to the truth of a matter, thereby making the world and the people in it easier to comprehend and to deal with.

Even if a desire to discover the truth does not seem a sufficiently strong reason for being concerned about having good reasons to justify your actions and beliefs, there are various life situations in which the ability to interpret and evaluate a person's case properly may be crucial to that person's well-being, or even to their remaining alive. For example, in a court trial the jury is instructed to convict an alleged murderer if the prosecution has proved their guilt beyond reasonable doubt. The jury is being asked to consider the prosecution's case (which, ideally, is an argumentative attempt to persuade them of the guilt of the accused), and the evidence they offer at each step of making that case. It has to consider whether there is good reason to accept the argument or whether some faults in it mean that there must be some doubt about its truth. The skills of evaluation and interpretation involved in argument analysis are what we use (or ought to use) in determining the strength of the prosecution's case in such situations. In fact in any situation in which we have to make decisions, be they about our lives or the lives of others, there is no substitute for the ability to think logically and to detect errors in the thinking of others.

It is a good reflection of the importance of the skills you are developing that those in power sometimes fear the effects of those who can think critically about moral, social, economic and political issues. The ability to think critically, then, is essential if one is to function properly in one's role as a citizen. It is not for nothing that Socrates, the most famous of critical thinkers, was sometimes referred to as 'the Gadfly'.

Beginning to think critically: recognising arguments

We do many things with language – state a fact, ask a question, tell someone to do something, insult someone, praise someone, promise to do something, swear an oath, make a threat, tell a story, recite a poem, sing a song, say a character's lines in a play, cheer on a football team.

---

3   Plato, *Apology* , 38a (Harmondsworth: Penguin, 1969), p. 72.

In this book we write about 'attempts to persuade' – by argument and by other means. As we've mentioned, not all attempts to persuade (using language) are attempts to persuade by argument. Others are attempts to persuade by means of rhetorical devices. In Chapter 4 we discuss the most common of these devices in detail. For the time being we'll just make some remarks about rhetoric in general. For our purposes rhetoric is defined as follows:

Rhetoric
Any verbal or written attempt to persuade someone to believe, desire or do something that does not attempt to give good reasons for the belief, desire or action, but attempts to motivate that belief, desire or action solely through the power of the words used.

The crucial thing to understand here is that an attempt to persuade by argument is an attempt to provide you with **reasons** for believing a claim, desiring something or doing something. Arguments appeal to your critical faculties, your reason. Rhetoric, on the other hand, tends to rely on the persuasive power of certain words and verbal techniques to influence your beliefs, desires and actions by appeal to your desires, fears and other feelings.

Threats and bribes are special cases that may appear to count as rhetoric according to our definition. In fact they are closer to argument; for they work by announcing to the recipient that they have a good reason to act as suggested. For example, if Smith attempts to persuade Jones to lend him her car by threatening to inform the police that she uses a fake driver's licence, then he is implicitly giving her a reason to lend him her car – if she doesn't do so, the police will find out about the driver's licence; since she doesn't want that to happen, she has a reason to lend him the car. Although threats and bribes may be immoral and may motivate partly by appeal to our fears and desires, among other feelings, they do motivate through force of reason and for that reason do not count as rhetoric.

Rhetorical techniques can be manipulative and coercive; their use should generally be avoided by those who aspire to think critically and to persuade by reason. That is not to say that rhetoric is always undesirable. Often it is used to great effect for good causes. Consider this excerpt from Sir Winston Churchill's famous speech to Parliament during the Second World War in which he attempts to rein in a sense of celebration at the success of the evacuations of British troops from Dunkirk, and to remind parliamentarians, and the public generally, that there was still a long way to go in defeating the Nazis and their allies. Churchill uses some remarkably effective rhetoric for a good cause and he might well be admired as a talented rhetorician. But his speech does not amount to an attempt to persuade by argument:

> The British Empire and the French Republic, linked together in their cause and in their need, will defend to the death their native soil, aiding each other like good comrades to the utmost of their strength. Even though large tracts of Europe and many old and famous States have fallen or may fall into the grip of the Gestapo and all the odious apparatus of Nazi rule, we shall not flag or fail. We shall go on to the end, we shall fight in France, we shall fight on the seas and oceans, we shall fight with growing confidence and growing strength in the air, we shall defend our Island, whatever the cost may be, we shall fight on the beaches, we shall fight on the landing grounds, we shall fight in the fields and in the streets, we shall fight in the hills; we shall never surrender, and even if, which I do not for a moment believe, this Island or a large part of it were subjugated and starving, then our Empire beyond the seas, armed and guarded by the British Fleet, would carry on the struggle, until in God's good time, the New World, with all its power and might, steps forth to the rescue and the liberation of the old.

On the other hand, those who try to persuade you of not such good causes might also be effective, persuasive rhetoricians. European dictators of the last century – Hitler, Mussolini, Franco, Stalin – provide good examples of this.

Of attempts to persuade that are arguments, not all are good arguments. So when analysing attempts to persuade we have to perform three tasks:

- The crucial first stage involves distinguishing *whether* an argument is being presented. We need to **identify** the issue being discussed, and determine whether or not the writer or speaker is attempting to persuade by means of argument.
- Once we have established that the writer/speaker is presenting an argument, we can move to the task of **reconstructing** the argument so as to express it clearly, and so as to demonstrate clearly the steps and form of the argument's reasoning.
- A clear reconstruction makes our third and final stage – **evaluating** the argument, asking what's good about it and what's bad about it – much easier to perform and to justify.

In subsequent chapters we explain in detail what we mean by reconstruction, and explain what makes an argument a good one. Our aim is not to help you acquire the basic comprehension skills that you need to work out what a passage or speech is about. We assume that you already have that skill, though working through this book might help you to hone it more finely. So we will begin with the first step, by considering how to distinguish arguments from other ways of putting forward opinions and persuading people to act.

When we put forward an argument we are either advancing an opinion (a claim that we think is true) or recommending an action. In either case we give a number of claims intended to support the claim or the recommendation. However, these two types of arguments can be collapsed into one. For we can think of an argument that recommends an action as advancing a claim to the effect that the hearer or reader should, or ought to, do such-and-such. For example, an argument whose aim is to get you to buy Wheetybites can be understood as advancing the claim: 'you ought to buy Wheetybites.'

Thus all arguments can be understood as attempting to provide reasons for thinking that some claim is **true**. The nature of truth is a deep and controversial philosophical issue that we do not need to contemplate here. We are working with an ordinary, non-theoretical concept of truth – one which says that to label a person's claim as true is to say that what it states is how things really are. For example, if a person makes the true claim 'Moscow is further from London than Paris', then according to our intuitive conception of truth, it is true just because Moscow *is* further from London than Paris. Our working definition of truth then, is as follows:

> To say that a claim is *true* is to say that what is claimed is how things actually are.

A single claim, however, does not constitute an argument. An argument needs more than one claim: it needs the claim of which the arguer hopes to convince his or her audience, plus at least one claim offered in support of that claim. To illustrate the difference between arguments and claims, consider these **unsupported claims**:

- It's going to rain later.
- The Labour Party is making a better job of running the country than the Conservative Party ever did.
- Philosophers are odd, unworldly people.
- The world is facing environmental catastrophe.

Why should we become critical thinkers?

The following examples, by contrast, attempt to give some **support** for these claims. Whether they provide adequate support is something we will look at later. The important point is to see the difference between this set and the first set:

- It's going to rain later; I know because I heard the weather forecast on the radio and it's usually reliable.

- The Labour Party is making a better job of running the country than the Conservative Party ever did. Unemployment is down, prosperity is up and the Pound remains strong. These are the crucial signs that the country is doing well.

- I've met a few philosophers in my time and they've always been strange people, heads in the clouds, not really in touch with the real world. Philosophers are odd, unworldly people.

- Climate scientists predict that the world is facing environmental catastrophe, and they are the experts on these issues.

There are special terms for the two parts of arguments: the primary claim, the one we are trying to get others to accept, is the **conclusion**. The supporting claims, the ones intended to give us reasons for accepting the conclusion, are the **premises**. As with the word 'argument', we are using the word 'premise' here in a restricted way, not necessarily corresponding to all the ways in which the word is ordinarily used. People might respond to an expression of opinion by saying, 'that's just your premise, but no one knows that *for sure*'; they do so to cast doubt on the truth of the claim being made. That is not the sense of the word 'premise' used in the discussion and analysis of arguments: for this purpose, a premise is simply any claim put forward as support for the conclusion of an argument, however certain or uncertain that claim may be.

We can now give a working definition of **argument**:

An argument
A set of propositions of which one is a conclusion and the remainder are premises, intended as support for the conclusion.

And what exactly do we mean by a **proposition**?

A proposition
The factual content expressed by a declarative sentence on a particular occasion. The same proposition may be expressed by

---

different sentences. For example, on a given occasion, 'The Government has decided to hold a public enquiry into the affair' would express the same proposition as 'It was decided that the Government would hold a public enquiry into the affair'.

One outcome of this is that different *sets of sentences* could express the *same argument*.

Aspects of meaning

Depending on how we use a sentence, it may express aspects of meaning additional to its factual, propositional content.

Rhetorical force

This is the rhetorical aspect of a sentence's meaning. It is not part of the propositional content that it expresses; rather, it is the emotive or other-wise suggestive window-dressing surrounding the proposition, which may be used to persuade us. The sentence in question can reasonably be taken to express this rhetorical message given the linguistic conventions according to which the words involved are normally used. The point is best grasped when we consider sentences that express the same proposition but have different rhetorical force. The sentence 'She is bringing up her children on her own' expresses the same proposition as the more rhetorically charged 'She's a single mum'. But while the former merely expresses a fact about the person's family arrangements, the second, by its use of the emotive and politically significant term 'single mum', might function not only to inform us of a fact, but also to manipulate our sympathies concerning the person in question (depending upon our beliefs and feelings about parenthood).

Implicature

Implicature is meaning, which is not *stated*, but which one can reasonably take to be *intended*, given the context in which the sentence is written or uttered (it is known more generally in linguistics as *conversational implicature*). Unlike rhetorical force, implicature cannot typically be interpreted according to conventions covering our ordinary use of the words in the sentence used. In order to recognise implicature, if there is any, we need to know the *context* in which a statement is made. Contextual factors include who the speaker is, who she is addressing and the circumstances surrounding the particular use of the sentence. Suppose, for example, that a student's parent asks one of her lecturers how she is progressing in her studies and he replies: 'Well she hasn't been thrown out for missing classes.' The lecturer doesn't actually state 'she's not doing very well', but the implicature is that she's not. Implicature can serve as a source of rhetorical power when the unsaid, implied aspect of a sentence's meaning is employed to stimulate responses motivated by emotion or prejudice (we discuss this rhetorical ploy on page 124). It is also a way of *communicating* something without incurring the responsibility of having explicitly *said* it. Note that a statement cannot implicate something merely because the speaker *intends* to convey it. A statement implicates a given proposition only if a listener who is fully aware of the relevant context would *reasonably take that proposition to have been intended*. For the same reason, something can be implicated even when the speaker does *not* intend it. If a given proposition is indeed what a fully informed listener would reasonably take to have been implicitly intended by a statement, then that proposition is implicated even if the speaker did not intend it. Thus our responsibility for what we say – our responsibility to choose the right words – goes beyond what we explicitly state.

Standard form

An argument may be about any subject and have any number of premises, but it will always have only one final conclusion. This argument has just one premise:

> Bart has two sisters.
>
> Therefore, Bart is not an only child.

This has two:

> Helping someone to commit suicide is the same as murder.
>
> Murder is wrong.
>
> Therefore, helping someone to commit suicide is wrong.

And this one three:

> Car use is seriously damaging the environment.
>
> Reducing car journeys would reduce damage to the environment.

We should do what we can to protect the environment.

Therefore, we should use cars less.

As you can see, arguments for analysis are set out in a particular style with the premises listed in the order that they occur in the reasoning process and the conclusion appearing at the bottom. We can refine this style and further clarify the argument by numbering the premises P1, P2 and so on, and drawing a line between the last premise and the conclusion, which we mark with a 'C'. The line between premises and conclusion is called an **inference bar**, and its purpose is to distinguish steps in reasoning. The bar should be read as standing for 'therefore' This style of setting out arguments is called **standard form**. The purpose of setting out arguments in this manner is to maximise clarity. Using this method helps us to see the stages of reasoning clearly and to make comparisons between arguments of similar form. When dealing with arguments as they are ordinarily presented, distinguishing the exact conclusion from the premises, the premises from each other, and the premises and conclusion from other, irrelevant, material can be difficult. Writing the argument in standard form provides us with the most comprehensive and clearest possible view of it, ensuring that while discussing the argument and attempting to evaluate it, we do not lose track of exactly what the argument is.

A number of the exercises included in this book require you to set out arguments in standard form. To do this is to **reconstruct** the argument, and the end product – the argument set out in standard form – is called a **reconstruction** of the argument, or an **argument-reconstruction**. In reconstructing arguments you should follow the example below by taking these steps:

- Identify the conclusion.
- Identify the premises.
- Number the premises and write them out in order.
- Draw in the inference bar.
- Write out the conclusion, placing C) in front of it.

Thus the previous example looks thus in standard form:

P1) Car use is seriously damaging the environment.
P2) Reducing car journeys would reduce damage to the environment.
P3) We should do what we can to protect the environment.

C) **We should use cars less.**

Why should we become critical thinkers?

Identifying conclusions and premises

The question of whether a passage or speech contains an argument is the question of whether the speaker or writer is attempting, by means of that passage or speech, to persuade his or her audience of some conclusion by offering premises in support of it. This is a question about the intentions of the writer or speaker – 'What does this person intend to do with these words here?' – that cannot always be answered unless we know something of the **context** – the circumstances in which the passage or speech appeared or took place. But even when we've determined that an argument is being advanced, its premises and conclusion are often buried deep among the other elements of a speech or text, and there are no hard and fast rules for distinguishing the propositions that form an argument from those that perform some other function in a text or speech. Identifying arguments is largely a matter of determining what the author or speaker intends by interpreting her words (spoken or written), and this comes with practice. Often writers and speakers leave some of their premises unstated because they assume that readers or listeners will know what they have in mind. So in reconstructing arguments we often have to add premises to make their structure and content complete. Further, people do not always express their arguments in very clear language, so we have to clarify each proposition before we can command a clear view of the argument as a whole (we look at difficulties with linguistic meaning later in this chapter).

Identifying conclusions

Once you have determined that a text or speech contains an attempt to persuade by argument, it is easiest to proceed first by identifying its conclusion. Determining whether a passage contains an attempt to persuade by argument and identifying the conclusion of that argument do not always occur independently however. Sometimes you will identify the conclusion in the process of working out that a passage does indeed contain an argument. On other occasions you may have already worked out that a passage contains an argument by paying careful attention to the writing style and the context without yet having identified the conclusion. We will, in any case, treat these processes as independent steps in argument analysis.

The conclusions of the following examples are probably clear from the first reading:

> Since Jo Bloggs is a politician and politicians are always corrupt,
> I guess Jo Bloggs is corrupt.

I'm anti-hunting because I believe that hunting foxes is wrong.
After all, it's wrong to kill simply for pleasure and fox-hunting
involves the killing of innocent animals for pleasure.

Before moving on, make sure that you can identify the conclusions in
each of these examples.

Several points make the identification of conclusions an easier task

1 Once you have decided that a passage or speech contains an attempt
to persuade by argument, try to see what the main point of the passage
or speech is. Ask what point the speaker or author is trying to establish;
that point will be the conclusion. Once you come to re-construct an argument for analysis, paraphrasing the main point as one simple proposition
will make the argument easier to handle. Bear in mind that a writer or
speaker may make the same point in a number of different ways, so you
may have to settle upon one particular way of expressing it.

2 Any proposition on any topic can be a conclusion. It is possible to
attempt to argue for any claim, from the highly theoretical to the most
mundane. So the type of subject-matter of a proposition – religion, morality, science, the weather, politics, sport – is not in itself a guide to
identifying whether or not that proposition is intended as the conclusion
of a passage's argument. The premises and conclusions of arguments
should ideally be expressed in declarative sentences, but in real-life arguments they may be expressed otherwise. When reconstructing arguments,
we may need to rewrite premises and conclusions as declarative sentences
in order to clarify the propositions expressed. For example, the apparent
question, 'Aren't all socialists idealists?' might be used to express a
premise that all socialists are idealists. The types of linguistic phenomena
that need to be rewritten for clarity's sake are discussed in detail later in
this chapter.

3 A single text or speech may contain several arguments for several different but connected conclusions. Sometimes we argue for one point, then
a second, and then use those conclusions as premises in an argument for
a third and final conclusion. These chains of arguments are known as
extended arguments and we look at them in more detail shortly.

4 A helpful guide to recognising arguments are words that usually indicate that a writer or speaker is putting forward an argument. For example,

if someone says, 'Given the facts that A, B and C, **it follows that D**', you can be sure that D is the conclusion of the intended argument (and that A, B and C are the premises). Other common **conclusion indicators** are:

- Therefore . . .
- Hence . . .
- Thus . . .
- It can be concluded that . . .
- So . . .

Usually (though not always) these words or phrases follow the sentences that express an argument's premises. Another way of expressing an argument is to include the premises and conclusion in a single sentence with an indicator word separating them. For example, in the sentence 'The fact that John Plunkett is a politician proves that he has a very big ego' the conclusion that Mr Plunkett has a very big ego is separated from the premise that states that he is a politician by the indicator '**proves**'. Other words that serve the same function are:

- . . . implies . . .
- . . . establishes . . .
- . . . shows . . .

Commonly, a writer or speaker will state the conclusion of their argument before stating the premises. There are indicator words that are typically placed after the conclusion in these cases. For example, in the sentence 'Gordon Brown must be a very important man since he is Chancellor of the Exchequer', the conclusion that Mr Brown must be a very important man is separated from the premise stating that he is Chancellor of the Exchequer by the indicator word 'since'. Other words and phrases that serve the same function are:

- . . . because . . .
- . . . for . . .
- . . . follows from the fact that . . .
- . . . is established by . . .
- . . . is implied by . . .

These indicators are not foolproof and should not be treated as a substitute for careful identification and interpretation of attempts to persuade by argument. Not all arguers will help the critical thinker out by making use of indicator words. The fact that a text or speech does not include an indicator word is not a reliable reason for thinking that it does not express an argument. If a passage does not appear to have any conclusion indicators then an alternative way of identifying the conclusion is to try inserting conclusion indicators at appropriate places in sentences that appear to be good candidates for the conclusion. Then see if the passage or speech still reads or is heard smoothly and if its meaning is unchanged. There are no conclusion indicators in the following speech, but it is still an attempt to argue:

> I think that Dinnah should sue the local council. They have admitted that they were negligent in not mending the cracked pavement that she tripped over when she broke her ankle and that's sufficient grounds for compensation.

Here if we try placing the conclusion indicator 'therefore' at the beginning of the second sentence ('They have admitted that they were negligent . . .'), it becomes clear that it is not the conclusion of the intended argument. Inserting 'because' between the first and second sentence (and thereby joining them to make one sentence), on the other hand, leaves the meaning intact and makes it clear that the conclusion – the claim that the speaker wants us to accept – appears at the beginning of the speech. Of course, when we write out the argument in standard form we change the order of the sentences and place the conclusion at the end preceded by the inference bar. Notice that the second sentence contains two premises so that in standard form the argument would be written thus:

P1)   The local council has admitted negligence.
P2)   An admission of negligence is sufficient grounds for compensating an injured party.

C)   **The local council should compensate Dinnah.**

5 **Indicator words** are not *parts* of the propositions that the argument comprises; rather they *introduce* or *frame* the conclusion and premises. So when we write arguments in standard form so as to reconstruct them, we omit the conclusion indicator words from our reconstruction.

6 So far we have only discussed **explicit conclusions** in which a writer or speaker expresses her conclusion directly and more or less clearly. However, conclusions sometimes remain unexpressed. These are **implicit conclusions**. They are only *implied* or *suggested* by the actual text or speech content, not *explicitly expressed* by it. This usually happens when the speaker or writer thinks that the context is sufficient to make the conclusion obvious so that it literally 'goes without saying'. This is often a bad idea as the conclusion is not always as obvious to those whom one is trying to persuade as it is to the persuader. It can also be a way of concealing one's uncertainty as to exactly what one is arguing for. In the name of clarity and explicitness, try to avoid implicit conclusions in your own writing and speech. It isn't clear, for example, what (if any) conclusion is implicit in the following:

> There's so much pornography available via the internet these days and young people are so easily influenced, it's bound to result in a social collapse into an orgy of rape, abuse and indecency.

Identifying premises

As you go through the process of identifying an argument's conclusion, it is likely that you will also spot some or all of its premises. Thus the stages of identification are not entirely separate in practice. The identification of an argument's premises is a search for reasons given by the writer or speaker to think that their conclusion is true. Like the identification of conclusions, much of the process of identifying premises amounts to close and charitable reading of what a writer or speaker says; but again there are some helpful guides:

1   Ask yourself what the writer's or speaker's reasons for believing their conclusion are. What evidence does the writer or speaker give to think that the conclusion is true? The propositions that you come up with in response to these questions are likely to be the premises of the intended argument.

2   Like conclusions, premises can have any subject-matter whatsoever. It does not matter whether a proposition is controversial or unanimously agreed, it can still be a premise.

3   In most real examples of writing and speech arguments are embedded within other language that is not intended as part of the argument itself, although some of this language may be used in what we call **sham-reasoning** in Chapter 4. Again, it helps to work out the overall structure of the passage when trying to identify the premises. Consider the following:

> I really think the Government should reconsider its policies on higher education. Education is such a complicated topic, and their policies are just more poll-driven nonsense; Blair and his cronies

> are so image-oriented with their expensive suits and so on, they
> invite pop stars to their parties and behave as if they too were
> pop stars, just out to sell themselves really.

In this example the speaker gets side tracked into commenting upon the
Prime Minister's suits and party guest-lists, and fails, beyond the vague
charge that the Government's policies are 'poll-driven nonsense', to offer
a substantive criticism. Most of what is said is at best only obliquely relevant to the issue.

4   As with conclusions, there are certain words that usually (but not
always) indicate the presence of premises – **premise indicators**. We
have already seen some of these because they mark the speaker or writer's
move from premises to conclusion or from conclusion to premises ('since',
'because', 'is implied by' and so on.) There are other words and phrases
that introduce sentences stating a premise or premises. A speaker or writer
might state their conclusion and then begin the next proposition with
such phrases as:

- ▶ My reason is . . .
- ▶ My evidence for this is . . .
- ▶ This is so because . . .

For example:

> I put it to you that Ms White killed Colonel Mustard in the
> ballroom with the candlestick. The reason I make this claim is that
> on the night of Colonel Mustard's death Lady Scarlet saw Ms
> White in the ballroom beating Colonel Mustard over the head with
> the very candlestick that was later found to have Ms White's
> fingerprints and Colonel Mustard's blood on it.

Other premise indicators may occur at the beginning of a sentence
containing both the premise and the conclusion. For example:

> On the basis of the fact that they have promised big tax cuts, I
> conclude that the Conservative Party will probably win the next
> general election.

5   Again, when writing out the premises of an argument in standard
form, take care not to include the indicator words as they are not part of
the propositions that make up the argument. When indicator words such
as 'since' and 'because' are not functioning to indicate premises or conclusions, however, but are used *within* an argument's propositions, then they

should be included in the reconstruction. This is particularly important when 'because' is used in a proposition used to express an explanation. See the next section, discussing the distinction between arguments and explanations.

6 Again, as with conclusions, a text or speech may not include specific premise indicators. Context is the best means of identifying premises in such cases. It may also help to try adding premise indicators to propositions to see if the passage or speech still runs smoothly.

7 Ordinary language can make identifying arguments more difficult than it might otherwise be because people do not always express all of their premises explicitly. Thus many attempts to persuade by argument rely on implicit premises: these are propositions assumed or intended by the arguer as reasons in support of the conclusion, but which are not actually expressed by any sentence provided by the arguer. Sometimes this happens out of oversight; other times because the arguer assumes that, in the given context, the premise may already be taken for granted. In Chapter 5 we will discuss the interpretation of hidden premises and the reconstruction of arguments to include them.

Arguments and explanations

Words that function as **indicator words** can be used for other purposes. The sentence, 'Since 2004 I have been a student at the University of Anytown' contains the word 'since'; but in this case the word merely designates the beginning of a period of time, and does not indicate a premise of an argument.

A trickier case is the use of words such as 'since' and 'because' – especially 'because' – in **explanations**. The distinction between *arguments* and *explanations* is important, but not always easy to make because arguments and explanation often have a very similar structure. In some cases we have to think hard about the context in order to determine which is intended. We need to work out whether they are telling us that such-and-such event occurred as a result of some other event – that is, whether they intend to assert a relation of cause and effect. For in that case, 'because' is being used to introduce an **explanation**, not an argument.

The best way to appreciate the distinction between arguments and explanations is to consider an example. Consider this proposition:

The tap is leaking.

Someone might advance an explanation for this by saying something like:

The tap is leaking because it needs a new washer.

On the other hand, we can imagine someone advancing an argument for that very same proposition, reasoning as follows:

There is sound of dripping water coming from the bathroom.
Therefore, the tap is leaking.

What exactly is the difference? The difference is that when giving the explanation, the speaker assumes that his or her audience *already accepts the proposition that the tap is leaking*, or at least that the speaker has no need to *persuade* the audience of this fact. Given this fact, the speaker is *asserting* that the *cause* of that fact is the faulty or worn-out washer. By contrast, when giving an argument, the speaker does not assume that the audience accepts or will accept that the tap is leaking outright; the arguer intends to persuade the audience that this is so by giving the audience a good reason to believe it.

This example of an explanation uses the word 'because' – the word here indicates a causal relationship instead of a logical connection between premise and conclusion. As demonstrated by the following examples, 'since', 'therefore', 'thus' and 'so' may also be used in explanations that are not intended to provide reasons for acting or believing something:[4]

▶ Since we forgot to add yeast, the bread didn't rise.
▶ We forgot to add yeast, therefore the bread didn't rise.
▶ We forgot to add yeast, thus the bread didn't rise.
▶ We forgot to add yeast, so the bread didn't rise.

The distinction between arguments and explanations can be confusing where the explanation of actions is concerned (that is, things that people *do*). This confusion arises because in the case of actions, reasons *are* causes! That is, the *explanation* of an action normally involves specifying the *reason* for it: a person does something *because* he or she had a certain *reason*. Thus, in asking about reasons for actions – asking 'Why are you doing that?' – we are sometimes looking for a **justification** – that is, we want the person to give us an argument for why the action is reasonable or acceptable – and other times we simply want an explanation, in the

---

4   While reading this book you may also have noticed a further use of 'thus'. 'Thus' can be used to mean 'in this way' and often proceeds an example or a quotation.

sense of wanting to know the cause. Nevertheless, the distinction between arguments and explanations still holds.

Suppose you are driving fast and your passenger asks, 'Why are you driving so fast?'. You assume your passenger is not in any way suggesting that you shouldn't drive so fast. You think they don't mind in the slightest. You assume they are merely curious as to why you're driving fast – whether it's because you're late, being chased by the police or perhaps testing the limits of your new car. Your reply, however, is simply 'Because I enjoy it'. This would be an explanation: you are telling your passenger why you're driving fast, not trying to persuade them of anything.

But suppose, when your passenger asked 'Why are you driving so fast?', you think maybe they do mind. So you take the question as demanding a justification for your driving so fast. If you now say 'Because I enjoy it', then you would be arguing, roughly, that it is all right to drive at such a speed on the grounds that you have a right to do what you like. In that case 'Because I enjoy it' would be a premise of an argument, which might initially be expressed thus:

> It's OK for me to drive as fast as I like, because I like driving fast. I think we should be free to do anything that we enjoy.

It might be rewritten thus in standard form:

> P1)   I enjoy driving fast.
> P2)   It is acceptable for me to do anything I enjoy.
> _____
> **C)   It is acceptable for me to drive fast.**

In such a case, your enjoying it might both a *reason* for driving fast *and* a cause of it.

Intermediate conclusions

The conclusion of one argument may serve as a premise of a subsequent argument. The conclusion of that argument may itself serve as a premise for another argument and so on. A simple illustration:

> Fido is a dog. All dogs are mammals, so Fido is a mammal. And since all mammals are warm-blooded, it follows that Fido is warm-blooded.

In this argument, an **intermediate** conclusion – that Fido is a mammal – is used as a premise for a further argument, whose conclusion is that Fido is warm-blooded. We represent **extended arguments** of this kind like this:

P1)   Fido is a dog.
P2)   All dogs are mammals.

C1)   Fido is a mammal.

P3)   All mammals are warm-blooded.

C2)   Fido is warm-blooded.

We give the two conclusions numbers: C1 is the conclusion of an argument whose premises are P1 and P2; C2 is the conclusion of an argument whose premises are C1 and P3. So C1 is both the conclusion of one argument and the premise of another.

Normally, in such cases, the last conclusion reached (the one with the highest number) is the proposition that the arguer is most concerned to establish. It is the ultimate target. So we call this simply *the* conclusion of the argument, whereas any other conclusions, reached as steps along the way, are called **intermediate conclusions**.

We sometimes want to concentrate for a moment on a particular part of an extended argument. In the above case, for example, we might be particularly interested either in the first part of the argument, or in the second. We will sometimes speak of the argument *from* P1 and P2 to C1, or of the argument *from* C1 and P3 to C2. We can also speak of the **inference** from P1 and P2 to C1, and the **inference** from C1 and P3 to C2.

The use of the word 'inference' in logic and critical thinking is another case where a word is used in a somewhat restricted sense in comparison with ordinary language. All reasoning consists of inferences. In the logician's sense of the word each step of reasoning, each move from premise or premises to conclusion, is an inference. Contrary to the way the word is often ordinarily employed, there need be nothing doubtful about an inference. We sometimes say, 'but that's just an *inference*', meaning to cast doubt upon whether a given proposition should really be accepted on the basis of others. But in our sense of the word, an inference may be completely certain, not subject to doubt. For example, it is an inference, in our sense, to go from 'John is a classical musician' to 'John is a musician' – despite the fact that there can be no doubt that if the first proposition is true, then so is the second (in the terminology to be introduced in Chapter 2, it is a **valid** inference).

Linguistic phenomena

As we've seen, once we've determined that a text or a speech contains an attempt to persuade by argument, the remainder of argument-reconstruction is largely a matter of interpreting the speech or text as accurately as possible. Here we are trying to work out what the speaker or writer intends readers or listeners to understand, and consequently do or believe, on hearing or reading their words. Phenomena in ordinary language sometimes make this task more difficult because they obscure speakers' and writers' intended meanings and therefore make it difficult to tell which proposition their sentences are supposed to convey. So aspirant critical thinkers need to be aware of the ways in which language can work to hide writers' and speakers' meanings and must practise spotting potentially problematic sentences. At this stage you should aim to be able to recognise these sentences and to be able to give the possible interpretations of them; that is, the propositions that they could be used to convey.

Ambiguity

A sentence is **ambiguous** in a given context when there is more than one possible way of interpreting it in that context – that is, if there is more than one proposition it could plausibly be taken to express in that context. There are two types of ambiguity.

Lexical ambiguity

This is a property of individual words and phrases that occurs when the word or phrase has more than one meaning. The set or group of things to which an expression applies is called its **extension** (it helps to think of an extension as all the things over which the word or phase extends or spreads itself). Thus the extension of the word 'student' is the set of all students. An ambiguous word or phrase, then, has two or more separate and different extensions – it picks out two or more different sets of things. Ambiguous words and phrases can bring their ambiguity into sentences, making those sentences capable of having more than one possible interpretation. The word 'match' is one such word. The sentence 'He is looking for a match' could be intended to mean any of the following propositions:

> ❭ He is looking for a small stick of wood with an inflammable tip.
> ❭ He is looking for another one the same [as this one].
> ❭ He is looking for [wants] a game of tennis (or some such).

Words that are potentially lexically ambiguous are not necessarily ambiguous in every context. Suppose you know that the person 'looking for a match' in the example above is trying to light a fire, then there would be little reason to interpret him as looking for anything other than a small stick of wood with an inflammable tip. Notice that it is not only nouns that can be lexically ambiguous. Suppose you are going to meet someone for the first time and all you've been told about them is what a friend has told you – 'She's a hard woman'. This could mean: She's a difficult person; She's an aggressive person; She has a very well-toned muscular body. Whichever interpretation you adopt will have an important effect on your expectations of the woman in question. When interpreting sentences that are lexically ambiguous, we have to focus on the context in which they are written or said and the consequent probability of each of the possible interpretations being the correct one. For instance the sentence 'A visitor to the zoo was attacked by the penguins' is lexically ambiguous because the preposition 'by' has two possible meanings in this context. The sentence could express either of the following propositions:

▶   The penguins attacked a visitor.
▶   A visitor was attacked beside the penguins' enclosure.

However, in the absence of any information about a vicious penguin, and given what we know about the usually non-aggressive behaviour of penguins towards zoo visitors, it would probably be reasonable to interpret the sentence as intended to express the second proposition.

There are a few words that are not really ambiguous but may seem so when we hear them, though not when we see them written. This is because the words, though spelt differently, sound the same. For example, when heard, as opposed to read, the question 'Are you a mussel (muscle) man?' could be either an enquiry as to a person's taste in seafood or as to his physique. Of course, once we see the question written, we are in no doubt as to its meaning.

The examples considered so far are relatively simple to understand because the alternative meanings of words such as 'match' and 'hard' are very different. However, instances of lexical ambiguity also occur when a word has alternative meanings that are much closer together. Such cases are much harder to interpret and we need to pay a lot of attention to the context in which the word is being used and to the probability of the speaker or writer's intending one interpretation rather than the other.

Suppose someone reports that 'The average mortgage has doubled in six years'. The speaker or writer might mean to say that the average existing mortgage has doubled its value in the past six years, so people with mortgages owe twice as much now as they did six years ago, which would be a pretty worrying situation because so many people would have increased their debts in such a short space of time. On the other hand, the speaker or writer might have intended to claim that the average mortgage taken out now is twice as big as the average mortgage taken out six years ago, which would simply be a reflection of increasing property prices.

Syntactic ambiguity

This occurs when the arrangement of words in a sentence is such that the sentence could be understood in more than one way (as expressing more than one proposition). You will probably be familiar with examples of syntactic ambiguity as it is often the basis of jokes and newspaper headlines that appear odd. For example, '33-year old Mrs Jones admitted to dangerous driving in Leeds Crown Court yesterday' could mean either of the following:

- In Leeds Crown Court yesterday Mrs Jones admitted to dangerous driving.
- Yesterday Mrs Jones admitted to driving dangerously inside Leeds Crown Court itself.

The sentence is syntactically ambiguous because it could, consistently with English grammar, be used to express either proposition. But since the second interpretation is extremely unlikely, it is unlikely that an actual use of this sentence would be ambiguous. But consider this case:

US President Bush has cancelled a trip to Scotland to play golf.

We can easily imagine a real context in which this sentence is ambiguous as to whether the purpose of the cancelled trip was to play golf or whether the trip was cancelled so that the president could play golf.

Once we decide the most likely interpretation, we should always rewrite the ambiguous sentence so as to eliminate the ambiguity. For example, we might rewrite the above sentence thus:

In order for him to play golf, US President Bush's trip to Scotland has been cancelled.

Notice that in cases such as this we have to change the sentence quite radically to rid it of the syntactic ambiguity and clarify its meaning. Consider a further example:

The Government will announce that the electricity supply is to be cut off tomorrow.

The sentence leaves ambiguous the question of when the announcement will be made and when the electricity supply is to be cut off:

▶ Tomorrow, the Government will announce that the electricity supply is to be cut off. (The announcement will be made tomorrow.)

▶ The Government is going to announce that, tomorrow, the electricity supply will be cut off. (The announcement will be made now, the electricity will be cut off tomorrow.)

Syntactic ambiguities are sometimes more difficult than lexical ones to interpret on the basis of context. Also, the possible interpretations of a sentence may be closely related so that there may not appear to be a very wide difference in meaning. Often we assume that one interpretation is intended without giving any consideration to alternatives. But such differences can be very significant indeed. Suppose someone were to claim:

We should not tolerate those homeless people living on our streets.

They might be saying that we should be intolerant of homeless people themselves. Or they might be saying that the people who do live on the streets should not be allowed to live on the street. On the other hand, the intended proposition might be that we should not tolerate the fact that there are homeless people living on our streets. That is to say, the view expressed might be critical of a society in which people are forced to live on the streets rather than critical of such people themselves.

Vagueness

Vagueness is a property of words and phrases. It is *not* the same as ambiguity, but it is often mistaken for it. For instance, when former US President Clinton famously said, 'I did not have sexual relations with that woman . . .' he was not (as alleged) hiding behind the *ambiguity* of the phrase 'sexual relations', but rather behind its *vagueness*. As we saw when considering lexical ambiguity, a word is ambiguous when it has two or more possible and *different* meanings – thus two or more separate extensions. The particular meanings might themselves be perfectly clear and precise. The vagueness of a word, on the other hand, is really a feature of its meaning: the meaning of a word or expression is vague if it is indefinite or uncertain what is conveyed by the word. Thus a word may be ambiguous without being vague – as in 'ball' (round play-thing, formal dancing-party) – or vague without being ambiguous, as in 'sexual relations' (what exactly constitutes sexual relations?).

Sometimes, someone aware of the weakness of their own position will deliberately leave their meaning vague in order to camouflage that weakness and to evoke strong feelings of approval or disapproval in their readers or listeners. Many highly charged words that wield rhetorical power in public discourse are used vaguely. Examples include: 'rights', 'liberal', 'harassment', 'racism', 'sexism'. It is hard to discern one perfectly exact meaning for each of these words and it would be unrealistic to expect them to have such a meaning. Their extensions tend to include a cluster of objects, beliefs or actions that are not necessarily unified in any precise way. Take 'liberal', for instance. This word conveys various characteristics including:

- Belief in a permissive society.
- Belief in freedom of speech, of association, of choice.
- Belief that certain restrictive laws should be relaxed (e.g. against drugs).[5]
- Belief that the state should interfere as little as possible in citizens' lives.
- Belief in laissez-faire economic policies.
- Supports the Liberal Democratic Party.
- Not strict.
- Politically left-wing.
- Wishy-washy.
- Soft on crime.

One might be a liberal and not hold all of these beliefs or have all of these characteristics. Indeed, a person might have some or even many of them and *not* be a liberal.

Here is a whole passage infected with vagueness of the kind we have in mind:

Make no mistake, the researchers involved in the highly controversial project to map the human genome are involved in a radical project of unprecedented gravity and spiritual significance.

---

5   As you may have noticed the word 'drugs' is used vaguely in this claim. Although in the context of most arguments about legislation and criminality it means illegal drugs, it could also include alcohol, prescription medicines, pain-killers, nicotine and so on. Deliberately vague use of words in such a way constitutes either the rhetorical ploy of trading on an equivocation (see pp. 122–4) or the fallacy of equivocation (see pp. 154–5).

Do they venture there with appropriate caution and humility? What they are doing is not even comparable to the research that made the atomic bomb possible, for it goes right to the essence of what we are as human beings. Like Dr Frankenstein, they are tinkering with life; they are travelling into unknown and sacred regions as no scientist previously has ever dared. The secret wellsprings of life, of our very being as homo sapiens, have ever remained shut up, concealed by aeons of either blind but cunning and ultimately unfathomable natural processes, or, as some continue to believe despite the showy displays of science and technology, concealed by the very hand of its Author, the Author of Nature Himself.

What is the writer of this rather over-excited dose of hyperbole trying to argue? Clearly they think that there is something dangerous or otherwise ill-advised about the project to map the human genome. But they have not begun to make it clear what the danger is. The research is distinguished from atomic research by its concern specifically with life, but nothing is said as to why this is peculiarly dangerous beyond the use of extremely vague verbiage such as 'sacred', 'radical', 'gravity', 'spiritual significance' and so on. In a context such as this, with so much at stake, we need to have precise reasons why, despite the promise of medical benefits, the project is dangerous.

Words can also be vague in another, more philosophically technical respect. Philosophers of language use the term 'vague' to apply to words that have a clear meaning, but which have an indefinitely demarcated extension. Obvious cases are colour-words like 'orange': there is no precise division between orange things and yellow things, for example. Things can often be precisely *compared* with respect to such attributes, however. For example, X may be more bald, or fatter, sleepier, taller or faster than Y, even if it is not definite whether or not X is bald, fat, sleepy, tall or fast. Borderline cases can also arise in the case of nouns. In fact vagueness occurs in many more cases than we might at first think. Take 'city': York is normally said to be a city, but is it really? Is it not merely a town? What about Doncaster? Lancaster? Harrogate? Carlisle?

To a great extent, we take these sorts of vagueness in our stride, having become used to interpreting these phenomena unreflectively in ordinary language. But even the simplest cases can cause misunderstandings. Suppose your boss promises that you're going to receive a 'big pay rise' this year. When you receive the pay increase you discover that the rise is only 10p an hour. When you complain, your boss defends their promise by saying that the rise is bigger than last year's and therefore big in comparison (see the section on implicit relativity, pp. 30–1, for further discussion of such cases).

Primary and secondary connotation

The rich secondary connotation of some words provides a further source of vagueness. Every ordinary noun and every adjective – 'elephant', 'immoral', 'company', 'stupid' – has a range of things to which it applies: the **extension** of the term. The set of all bananas constitutes the extension of 'banana'; the set of all square things constitutes the extension of 'square'. A given thing falls within a word's extension if, and only if, it fits a certain *rule* associated with the use of that word. For example, the rule for the noun 'ram' is 'male sheep'. This rule is called the **primary connotation** of the term. This will be some set of characteristics, in this case being male and being a sheep which, by definition, everything to which the word applies must have. All of a term's primary connotation must apply to an object for that term to apply to it. The notion of a female ram, for example, is a logical impossibility, a contradiction.

Thus when we are told that something is a B, for some general term B, we know that the thing must exemplify the primary connotation of the term; if we're told it's a ram, then we know it's a male sheep. However, when we are told that something is a ram, we tend to assume other things about that thing that are not included in the primary connotation: that it is woolly, has horns, lives on a mountainside or in a field, eats grass. . . . So if you know that something is a ram, it is reasonable to suppose that it has these additional characteristics. These further characteristics that the term 'ram' also conveys make up its **secondary connotation**. Things that fall under the term will generally exhibit these characteristics, but there is no logical contradiction in supposing there to be a thing that falls under the term but lacks a characteristic included under the secondary connotation. For instance, there is no logical contradiction in supposing that a thing might count as a ram – that is, fulfil the demands of the primary connotation – yet lack some or, indeed, all of these characteristics. It is not logically impossible that there could be a bald, hornless male sheep that lives in a barn and whose diet consists of potatoes.

Why should critical thinkers be interested in the distinction between primary and secondary connotation? The most immediate relevance was demonstrated in our examination of vagueness. It is difficult to pin down the precise meaning of a word such as 'liberal' because, on the one hand, its primary connotation is very difficult to pin down, and on the other, its secondary connotation is so rich. In fact, in the case of vague words, the distinction between primary and secondary connotation tends to break down, or be difficult to draw. Take a look back at the list given earlier of characteristics conveyed by 'liberal': it is difficult to say which are part of its primary connotation, and which are only part of its secondary connotation.

A further reason for us to concern ourselves with this distinction is that it is the secondary connotation of many words that gives the sentences in which they occur their rhetorical force. Consider the noun 'feminist'. Its primary connotation is difficult to pin down and it is full of secondary connotations that can be used to the rhetorical advantage of both those who support and those who oppose feminism. Here are just some of the characteristics our critical thinking students have come up with when asked what the word 'feminist' conveys to them:

- Man-hating
- Lesbian
- Dungarees
- Unshaven
- Strong
- Political

- Fighter
- Staunch
- Left-wing
- Pro-abortion
- Pro-women

When interpreting speakers and writers we should also be aware of the role of secondary connotation in **metaphorical** uses of language. **Metaphors** often function by bringing only the secondary connotation of a word into play. In most cases the primary connotation is in fact false of the object or person in question. When someone insults another person by calling them a 'pig', the claim is literally false, but they are attempting to ascribe some of the characteristics of the secondary connotation of 'pig' – the way it eats, the way it smells, its penchant for mud, for instance. In the course of interpretation, we should take care not to treat metaphors as literal claims and not to confuse a metaphorical use of a word with an ambiguous one. When Shakespeare's Romeo attempts to express the beauty of his lover, Juliet, he says, 'My love is a rose'; this is intended as a metaphor that ascribes some of the characteristics of the secondary connotation of 'rose' to her – its beauty, fragility and sweetness – and is not ambiguous between literal and metaphorical meanings of 'rose'.

Rhetorical questions

Rhetorical questions take the form of a question but indirectly assert a proposition (like a declarative sentence does). That is, they are not really used to ask a question, but to make a point in an indirect way. Speakers and writers often use rhetorical questions when they're making a point they assume to be obvious, so the answer to the question 'goes without saying'. However, in many cases the point is neither obvious nor universally agreed. Rhetorical questions obfuscate speakers' and writers' intended meanings because they make it more difficult to interpret whether or not a speaker/writer really does support a given claim. Rhetorical questions are common in polemical newspaper articles and in readers' letters to editors. If you encounter rhetorical questions in texts and speech that you are analysing, try to rewrite the question as a declarative sentence. For instance, if someone were to write:

> Should my right to freedom of speech be limited just because you disagree with me?

they probably wish to convey the proposition that their freedom should not be so curtailed, so they are not genuinely asking a question. They expect that the reader's response will be an automatic 'No, of course not'. To convey the proposition that seems to be intended, we could rewrite the rhetorical question as a declarative sentence:

> My right to freedom of speech should not be limited just because you disagree with me.

You should resist the temptation to employ rhetorical questions in your own arguments.

Irony

Speakers and writers sometimes express their claims using irony. This takes the form of language that, taken literally, would convey the opposite of what they wish to convey, or something otherwise very different from it. Consider the following instance:

> It is pouring with rain, very windy and cold. Mr I. Ronic says, 'Mmm lovely weather today'.

Mr Ronic is probably being ironic, and intends to comment that the weather is lousy.

It is important to be aware of the possibility of irony. In order to ridicule a position they are opposed to, speakers and writers sometimes sarcastically pretend to espouse that position; but it isn't always obvious that they are doing so.

Implicitly relative sentences

Consider the following examples:

- ▶ She earns an above average salary.
- ▶ He is of average intelligence.

- ▶ Great Aunt Edie is a fast runner.
- ▶ Taxes are high.
- ▶ The rent on our flat is low.

Sentences such as these represent another potential problem for the critical thinker striving to work out exactly what a speaker or writer intends to convey by their words. The sentences are **implicitly relative**. They make a comparison with some group of things, but that comparison is not explicitly mentioned. For instance, to understand what it is for a person to earn an 'above average salary', we need to know of what group the average to which it is compared is. Or consider the one about Aunt Edie? Does the speaker intend to convey that Great Aunt Edie is a fast runner such that she runs at world record pace or that she is a fast runner for a woman of her age? Or something in between, such as that she is faster than the average person? If such sentences are interpreted without the recognition of their implicit relativity, then there is the possibility that they will be interpreted as making a comparison with a group other than that intended by the writer or speaker. Great Aunt Edie is not a fast runner when compared with Paula Radcliffe and thus interpreted the claim would be false. But when compared with other ninety-four-year-olds, many of whom haven't broken into a run for many years, she is a fast runner and the claim is true. Once we recognise such claims as implicitly relative and interpret them accordingly, they are more likely to have a definite truth value. But not always. Implicit relativity is often compounded by other sources of vagueness. For example, even if we do know what comparison class is being invoked in the case of Aunt Edie, it is by no means clear just how much faster a person must be than the average person of that class in order to be fast relative to it.

Problems with quantifiers

Quantifiers are words that tell us how many/much of something there are/is, or how often something happens. As you will see, not all quantifiers specify an exact quantity of the thing, rather they provide a rough guide. In the following examples the quantifiers are underlined (this is not an exhaustive list of quantifiers):

- ▶ All men drive <u>too</u> fast.
- ▶ Members of Parliament are <u>often</u> self-serving.
- ▶ <u>Few</u> doctors support the health reforms.

Why should we become critical thinkers?

- The lecturer awarded <u>almost all</u> the assignments an A grade.
- <u>Nearly all</u> the students passed the course.
- She likes <u>hardly any</u> of her fellow students.
- <u>No</u> examiner should take bribes.
- <u>Lots of</u> computers develop faults.
- <u>Nine</u> hospitals will close at the end of this year.
- She <u>never</u> closes the door behind her.
- There are adequate computing facilities in <u>fewer than half</u> of the country's schools.
- He <u>always</u> writes his own speeches.
- <u>Most</u> women would choose to stay at home with their children if they could afford to.

There are four potential problems with quantifiers:

1 Speakers and writers don't always use quantifiers with sufficient precision, so that the proposition they intend to convey is unclear and open to misinterpretation and rhetorical abuse. Suppose your friend says: 'Premiership footballers all earn massive payments from sponsorship deals.' You don't agree and you mention an exception – Fergie Footballer receives only his footballer's salary, with no extra money from endorsing sports shoes or shirts. Suppose your friend defends her claim by saying that she didn't really mean that every single player in the Premiership earns big money from endorsements and sponsorship, but only that *most* or *nearly all* of them supplement their earnings in this way. Now that her claim is clear, you see that it is one with which you are more likely to agree.

2 Some quantifier-words are themselves vague. Suppose, for instance, that someone claims:

Some Members of Parliament support the decriminalisation of cannabis use.

What does '**some**' mean here? It could mean that only a handful hold the view described, it could mean that a larger minority of members hold that view. Without a more precise understanding of how many Members of Parliament are intended to be conveyed by 'some', it is difficult to know how to respond to the claim. Moreover, the claim is open to abuse from people who hold views on both sides of such a debate. Advocates of decriminalisation can use it in support of their cause; their opponents can use it to back up their anti-decriminalisation stance (the latter might say, 'Only some Members of Parliament support. . .').

3 Often people simply *omit* quantifiers. For instance, someone might protest:

Lecturers don't give students a chance to complain.

At face value this might appear to convey the proposition that:

No lecturer (ever) gives a student a chance to complain.

Yet it is likely that what the speaker really wants to say is something like:

Most of the lecturers I've encountered haven't given students enough chance to complain.

Notice that once the appropriate quantifier is made explicit, the claim applies to a much smaller group of lecturers than one might have supposed when the quantifier remained implicit.

Consider another example:

Today's students are dedicated to their studies.

If we interpret this as expressing this proposition:

All of today's students are dedicated to their studies.

we are likely to want to challenge the claim as we will be able to cite exceptions to the generalisation. If, however, we interpret the claim as it is more likely to be intended, then the quantifier that we make explicit should be 'most' or 'almost all', thereby exposing the proposition really intended as:

Most of today's students are dedicated to their studies.

and this proposition has a greater likelihood of being true. Cases that we use to challenge the truth of a generalising claim are known as **counter-examples**. (The process discussed here should not be confused with that of refuting a complete argument by counterexample, which is dealt with in Chapter 6.)

Quantifiers and generalisations

It is a commonplace for people to say that you can never really generalise. However, this is certainly not true just as it stands. When someone says this they might be understood as claiming, 'all generalisations are false'. But this is itself a generalisation; so if the claim is true, the claim is false! So that can't be what it means. In any case, it is obvious that some generalisations are true (even if they are not very interesting ones). That is, there are counterexamples to the claim that all generalisations are false. For example, 'All cities in the UK have a bus service' is obviously true and no case could really be raised to undermine its truth.

What exactly is a **generalisation**? In fact, the ordinary term 'generalisation' is a bit vague; it means, roughly, 'statement about a category of things'. A generalisation is not simply any statement that includes quantifiers, since 'there are five eggs in the refrigerator' contains the quantifier-phrase 'there are five', but is not a generalisation. But we need not be too precise about this. For our purposes we will reserve the term for 'categorical' statements involving quantifiers such as 'all', 'every', 'always', 'no', 'never' and so on, but also 'most', 'usually' and the like.

To get a better grasp of which types of generalisations may cause problems during the analysis and assessment of arguments, the main thing we need is to distinguish between **hard** and **soft** generalisations. Consider the following generalisations (note that few of them have explicit quantifiers):

- Private schools attain better examination results than state schools.
- Traffic congestion is bad in Glasgow.
- Regular exercise benefits your health.
- Labour voters support a ban on hunting with hounds.
- People play less sport when they get older.

No doubt the counterexample fanatic will be able to provide us with plenty of exceptions – congestion-free short cuts across Glasgow; labour voters who are keen fox-hunters; the person who had a heart attack while doing their regular work-out at the gym. And they can cite this as a reason to accept the claim that all generalisations are false because one can always find an exception to them. However, to do so would be to misinterpret what people usually intend to convey when they say or write such things. It's rare for someone to mean that these sorts of generalisations are true without exception. The quantifier they intend to imply is probably one that is not synonymous with 'all' or 'every', but one such as 'in most cases', 'usually', or 'almost all'. These generalisations are **soft generalisations**. We use soft generalisations when we want to express the idea that such-and-such is true of certain things **normally**, **typically**, **generally**, **usually**, **on average**, **for the most part**.[6] In the examples above, the speaker/writer could make her intended meaning much clearer by adding one of these words or phrases; for example:

> Private schools generally attain better examination results than state schools.

On the other hand, someone using a **hard generalisation** does intend it to apply without exception. Such a generalisation is rightly conveyed by a quantifier such as '**all**', '**every**', '**no**', '**always**', '**never**'. For example:

▶ Every passenger must hold a valid passport.

▶ No doctor who helps a patient to die should consider themselves to be above the law.

If someone makes a claim that is intended as a hard generalisation and we can find a counterexample to it, then we have refuted their claim. But quantifier-free generalisations are not typically intended as hard generalisations. If the fanatical anti-generaliser does have a point, we believe, it is a point about rhetoric, not truth. What the anti-generaliser is justifiably worried about are generalisations about groups defined by race, ethnicity, nationality, gender, class and sexuality. Suppose that there are two social classes amongst Martians: the Zormons and the Ringons. And suppose the generalisation 'Ringons are more violent than Zormons' is true when taken as a soft generalisation, but false when taken as a hard generalisation. A Ringon anti-generaliser might object to someone's saying this. But we've seen that the point cannot be that the generalisation is not true, in spite of the fact that not every Ringon is more violent

---

6   Care should be taken interpreting and using 'usually' to express soft generalisations because it is ambiguous in some contexts. For instance, the sentence, 'British universities usually have a mathematics department' could be intended to mean that most or almost all British universities have a mathematics department, or that they have them most or almost all of the time, but at some times they have no such department. If 'usually' could be ambiguous in a context, it is better to use 'typically' or 'generally' instead.

than every Zormon. This generalisation is, it must be admitted, true when taken as a soft generalisation.

However, it might be argued, it is rhetorically dangerous. There are two reasons. The first reason is that many people are not very clear about the possible ambiguities of such a statement. It might wrongly be taken as a hard generalisation, and furthermore it might wrongly be taken as asserting something about the innate or genetic qualities of Ringons. In itself, it does not do this. So unless these possible misinterpretations are deflected by making the exact intended meaning perfectly explicit, this generalisation will remain very provocative and a likely cause of ill-feeling. The second reason is the brute fact that, even if these ambiguities are resolved, generalisations (even soft ones) about groups of people do often cause people to take offence. There are times when people take offence at a generalisation about a group and are simply irrational in doing so; no amount of explaining the difference between a soft generalisation and a hard one, or the difference between a generalisation about actual facts and one about alleged genetic qualities will change this. Like many kinds of irrationality, this is a natural kind of irrationality that cannot easily be overcome. No matter how factually true a generalisation may be, it is natural to feel that there is something dehumanising about it. So we cannot reasonably expect that people will always be able to overcome that feeling. Morality requires us to consider the consequences of our actions, and, since speech and writing are types of action, natural (though irrational) responses to what we say and write must sometimes be taken into account in deciding what we ought to say. We should not say what is false, but that a proposition is true is not always enough to justify expressing it. This, we believe, is the grain of truth in the anti-generaliser's position.

CHAPTER SUMMARY

Critical thinking enables us to ensure that we have **good reasons** to believe or do that which people attempt to persuade us to do or to believe. Attempts to persuade may be **argumentative** or **non-argumentative**. Most of the latter count as **rhetoric**, which is any attempt to persuade that does not attempt to give good reasons for the belief, desire or action in question, but attempts to motivate that belief, desire or action solely through the power of the words used. The former, on the other hand, persuade us by giving reasons for us to accept a claim or take the action suggested. Not all arguments are good arguments. Good arguments are those that provide us with **good reasons** to act or to accept a claim.

An argument consists of a **set of propositions**. The proposition expressed by a statement is its factual content, and should insofar as possible be distinguished from the rhetorical force of the sentence. Propositions may **implicated** by an utterance without being explicitly stated: a proposition is implicated by an utterance when it would reasonably be taken to have been intended. Among the propositions that constitute an argument, one is its **conclusion** – the proposition argued for – and rest are its **premises** – the reasons given to accept the conclusion. Once we have determined that a text or a speech contains an argument, we must work out which sentence is intended to express the argument's conclusion and which are intended to express its premises. Words that serve as **conclusion indicators** and **premise indicators** offer a helpful (but not foolproof) guide to doing so successfully. We should also pay close attention to the context of the text or speech. Setting out arguments in **standard form** is a five-stage process that enables us to see the form of arguments better and hence, to compare, analyse and assess them more easily. Arguments must be distinguished sharply from **explanations**: arguments attempt to provide reasons for believing a proposition whose truth is not assumed already to be accepted; explanations assume a certain proposition is already accepted as fact, and attempt to specify the cause.

There are various **linguistic phenomena** that can make the task of identifying and interpreting arguments more difficult. In the case of **ambiguity**, **vagueness**, **metaphor**, **rhetorical questions** and **irony**, these can be problematic because they obscure speakers' and writers' intended meanings. In the case of **implicitly relative sentences** and sentences that use **quantifiers** inappropriately, they can be problematic because they fail to convey speakers' and writers' intended meanings in their entirety. Quantifying sentences can also cause problems for the interpretation of arguments when they are used inaccurately to express **generalisations**. There are two types of generalisation: hard and soft. **Hard generalisations** are true only if they are true without exception. To avoid misinterpretation they should be expressed in sentences that use quantifiers such as **all**, **every**, **no**, **none**, **always**, **never**. **Soft generalisations** are only true of the majority of the class that is the subject of the generalisation. They should be expressed in sentences that use quantifiers such as **most**, **almost all**, **in most cases**, **generally**, **typically**, **usually**. In all cases linguistic phenomena prevent the intended meaning from being explicit, we should pay careful attention to context in order to render the most plausible interpretation of the attempt to persuade. Where appropriate we should **rewrite** sentences to make their meaning explicit.

EXERCISES

1 Decide whether each of the following cases contains an argument. If it does not, write 'N/A'. If it does, identify its premises and conclusion by underlining the appropriate propositions and writing 'C' under the conclusion and 'P' and the appropriate number under the premises. Remember that premise and conclusion indicators are not part of those propositions:

Example

    <u>Bob is a dog</u> and <u>all dogs are black</u>. So <u>Bob is black</u>.

✎   P1   P2   C

Notice that we have not underlined the words that connect or introduce the propositions, only the propositions themselves:

a   It follows from the fact that all cats are pests that this cat is a pest.

b   I'll never get to work if this traffic keeps up.

c   Whenever a person drinks instant coffee they end up with stomach ache and Jack is going to have stomach ache since he just drank a cup of instant coffee.

d   There is going to be a frost in the morning because the temperature has fallen below zero.

e   The biscuit tin is empty because the children ate all the biscuits.

f   Christians take care of the needy. Tony Blair's social and economic policies discriminate against the needy. He can't be a Christian.

g   Since this animal is a fish, it can't be a mammal.

h   The American-led invasion of Iraq has set the cause of world peace back by centuries.

i   Leeds is north of Birmingham and Birmingham is north of Brighton. So Leeds is north of Brighton.

j   My ex-partner was always telling me to change my appearance, so I changed my partner.

k   If those chemicals are released into the river, thousands of fish will die.

l   Since inflation is increasing, the price of mortgages is sure to go up.

m   Everyone at the lecture is bored. No one who is bored is listening. Therefore no one at the lecture is listening.

n   He's been on crutches since he was injured in the accident.

o   On the basis of the fact that it includes scenes depicting drug abuse, the film should not be shown on prime-time television.

p   If we don't do something to control the level of car traffic now, air pollution will become so bad that our grandchildren will not be able to walk the streets for fear of asphyxiation.

q   The Government proposes to reform the benefits system. Whenever such reforms occur someone loses out, so the Government's proposals are unfair.

r   Something must be done to regulate the cultivation of genetically manipulated foodstuffs. Uncontrolled production of these crops will lead to a collapse of the ecosystem.

s   If we hit our children, they will learn that violence is acceptable, so we shouldn't physically discipline our children.

t   It is, therefore, an impractical solution to the problem of homelessness.

2   Write out the following arguments in standard form. You need not supply missing premises or change the words used unless it is absolutely necessary to retain the sense of a sentence, but you should omit indicator words:

Example

The Government should ban fox-hunting. Fox-hunting causes suffering to animals and anything that causes suffering to animals should be banned.

✎   P1)   Fox-hunting causes suffering to animals.
   P2)   Anything that causes suffering to animals should be banned.

———————————————————————————

   C)   **The Government should ban fox-hunting.**

a   If Manchester Utd win against Arsenal, Chelsea will go to the top of the Premier League. Manchester Utd have beaten Arsenal so Chelsea will be top of the league.

b   Children should not watch television programmes that lack educational merit. *Pokemon* fails to promote linguistic and cognitive development and programmes only have educational merit in so far as they promote linguistic and cognitive development. Children should not watch *Pokemon*.

c   I put it to you that Ms White killed Colonel Mustard in the ballroom with the candlestick. The reason I say this is that on the night of Colonel Mustard's death Lady Scarlet saw Ms White in the ballroom beating Colonel Mustard over the head with a candlestick, which was later found to have Ms White's fingerprints and Colonel Mustard's blood on it.

d   The team manager should be sacked. Whenever the team manager is sacked, team spirit is revitalised and this team's spirit certainly needs revitalising.

e   Excessive consumption by consumers in the developed world causes poverty and disease in the developing world and that's simply unjust. So if we care about the rest of the world, we should curb our consumption.

f   History will show President Bush to have been a successful president after all. The reason is that he has managed to maintain the USA's reputation as a super-power and that's the most important criterion by which to judge a US president.

3   Without looking back at the relevant section, write a paragraph explaining the difference between lexical and syntactic ambiguity, then give a plausible example of each and explain their possible interpretations.

4   In the following sentences indicate the words or phrases that are lexically ambiguous and explain their possible meanings:

a   The last time I saw them they were sitting beside the bank.

b   Happiness is the end of life.

c   Archbishop of Canterbury praises organ donor for his humanity.

d   Museum visitor attacked by mummy.

e   Stolen car found by statue.

f   British left waffles on Ireland.

g   Iraqi head seeks arms.

h   An intense depression swept over the British Isles today.

i   Blair leans further to the right.

j   Chancellor wins on budget, but more lies ahead.

5   The following sentences are syntactically ambiguous. Rewrite them so as to give the most plausible interpretation. If two or more interpretations are equally plausible, give them all. You may need to rearrange the word order and/or add words:

Example

A former professional dancer was accused of assaulting a
33-year old woman with her daughter.

✎ **A former professional dancer and her daughter were
accused of assaulting a 33-year old woman.**

a   The two suspects fled the area before the officers' arrival in a red Ford Escort driven by a woman in black.

b   I was invited to go to the movies yesterday.

c   Mary left her friends depressed.

d   People who use cocaine often die early.

e   Smith had a pair of boots and a pair of slippers that he borrowed from Jones.

f   Wanted: A bay mare, suitable for a novice with white socks.

g   Jones left the company in a better state.

h   Glasgow's first commercial sperm bank opened last Friday with semen samples from twenty men frozen in a stainless steel tank.

i   They were exposed to someone who was infected with the virus a week ago.

j   The police would like to speak to two women and a van driver who fled the scene of the accident.

6   Without looking back at the relevant sections, write a paragraph explaining the difference between vagueness and ambiguity. Give examples to illustrate your explanation.

7   For each of the following identify the quantifier and say whether the generalisation is soft or hard:

Example

Almost all students have contemplated cheating in an
examination.

✎ **Almost all**
   Soft generalisation

a   No one may leave the room until the culprit owns up.

b   Few of the applicants are sufficiently qualified for the job.

c   Most Members of Parliament are committed to their constituents.

d   A majority of our members are prepared to go out on strike in support of their pay claim.

e   All passengers must fasten their seatbelts for take-off and landing.

f   Generally birds can fly.

g   Almost all of the patients are ready to be discharged.

h   Hardly any of the people surveyed were in favour of the proposed law change.

i   Every doctor must abide by the Hippocratic Oath.

j   Almost none of the candidates have the charisma to succeed in politics.

8   Each of the following sentences expresses a generalisation, but its quantifier is missing. For each sentence, if it is true as a hard generalisation, add an appropriate quantifier to make it a hard generalisation. If it could only be true as a soft generalisation, add an appropriate quantifier to make it a soft generalisation:

Example

Passengers must hold a valid ticket before boarding the train.

✎ **All passengers must hold a valid ticket before boarding the train.**

a   Cats have tails.

b   Children like to eat ice cream.

c   Voters voted for Labour Party candidates at the last general election.

d   Owls are mammals.

e   Cars run on petrol or diesel.

f   Citizens of a democratic country should be free to come and go as they please.

g   Members of Parliament are male.

h   Universities in the UK have a vice chancellor.

i   People care enough about the environment to change their lifestyles.

j   British people can speak a foreign language.

Chapter 2

Logic: deductive validity

Our attempts to engage in critical thinking are sometimes frustrating. Often, even when we feel certain that there is something wrong with an argument, we find it hard to explain exactly what it is that's wrong with it. Sometimes this is frustration with ourselves; but it can easily look like frustration with the person giving the argument (it can certainly be interpreted as such by that person!). One of the primary aims of training in critical thinking is to learn concepts and techniques that will help us to express clearly what is wrong with an argument, thereby dispelling that frustration. By helping us to assess arguments more efficiently, this helps us in the pursuit of truth. But also, by becoming more articulate in our criticisms, we become less frustrated, and thereby less bad-tempered. This can help to smooth out our relationships with other people (whereas you might have thought that improving your skill at critical thinking would make you into a disagreeable quibbler).

This frustration derives from two sources: First, confronted with an argument, we find it hard to hold the whole thing clearly before our mind's eye, and find it hard to say exactly what the argument *is*. Second, even when we do succeed in laying the argument out before us clearly, we find it hard to describe or explain what is wrong with it:

- The first issue is addressed by techniques and strategies for **argument-reconstruction**: the representation of arguments in standard form, so as to give us a clear and comprehensive view of them.
- The second issue is addressed by techniques and concepts of **argument assessment**: the determination of whether or not arguments provide good reasons for accepting their conclusions.

We discuss practical details of argument-reconstruction in Chapter 5. This chapter and the next are mostly concerned with argument assessment. Ordinarily, we speak of arguments as being good or bad, strong or weak, valid or invalid, sound or unsound, persuasive or unpersuasive, intelligent or stupid, without having a clear idea of what we mean by these terms, and without clearly distinguishing their meanings. So not only are we vague when we use one of these terms to criticise the argument; our attempts to explain ourselves by means of the others are still vague. Thus our primary task in this chapter and the next is to explain the basic logical concepts in terms of which assessment is carried out – **validity**, **soundness** and **inductive force**.

You may be surprised that detailed discussion of argument assessment precedes the detailed discussion of argument-reconstruction in Chapter 5; surely you have to reconstruct an argument before you can assess it? In fact, it is slightly less straightforward than that: although the final assessment of an argument must await its reconstruction, good reconstruction-practice must be informed by a good grasp of the concepts used in assessment. The purpose of the next section is to explain this important point.

The principle of charity

An argument is a system of **propositions**: a set of premises advanced in support of a conclusion. People succeed in expressing the propositions they have in mind with varying degrees of clarity. In addition, an argument may depend upon premises that the arguer does not state at all, but which he or she is implicitly assuming.

For example, if someone argues: 'Sally is taking drugs; therefore she is breaking the law,' the arguer is probably using the rather vague term 'drugs' in the narrow sense of 'unlawful recreational drugs', or perhaps in the sense of 'narcotics'. In the wider sense of 'drugs' that includes medicinal drugs, this would obviously be a bad argument. Furthermore, the arguer is assuming, without explicitly stating, that it is illegal to take such drugs. So two sorts of thing are left implicit in this argument: first, the arguer assumes a more precise meaning than is explicitly expressed by the word 'drugs'; second, the arguer fails to make explicit all the facts from which he or she infers the conclusion. A premise is left implicit.

Since the purpose of argument-reconstruction is to determine exactly what argument has been given, it follows that part of the task of argument-reconstruction is to **clarify** what the arguer actually said, and to **supplement** what the arguer actually said (to make *explicit* what was merely *implicit* in the arguer's statements). That is, we try to represent the argument in such a way as to create a perfect match between the propositions that actually constitute the argument and the sentences which represent the argument in standard form.

Two important consequences follow from this:

- The sentences we use in a reconstruction of the argument need not be the very same sentences used by the arguer in giving their argument. We may employ sentences that more clearly or precisely express the propositions that constitute the argument.
- Our reconstructed version of the argument may contain premises that are not expressed by any of the sentences actually used by the arguer.

Argument-reconstruction is essentially a task of **interpretation**. What we are trying to reconstruct, to represent as clearly as we can, is a certain train of thought, of reasoning – however well or badly the arguer may have succeeded in expressing it. This cannot be an exact science. It cannot be mechanical or foolproof. It calls for judgement, a critical but sympathetic eye or ear and even a certain degree of intuition, of understanding of people – of the ways people tend to think in given sets of circumstances, and of some typical ways in which people fail to express themselves clearly.

Nevertheless, the process can be undertaken in a systematic way, and there are general guidelines to follow. One of the most general of these is what we call the **principle of charity**, which we now explain.

We have just said that argument-reconstruction of is often a task of surmising what the arguer had in mind, and was trying to express. Our primary evidence for this, naturally, is the specific words actually used by the arguer. Beyond this, we look to various sorts of facts about the **context** or **circumstances** in which the person employed the words that he or she did. For example, consider this argument:

But he is still in Paris! Therefore, he cannot possibly be in
St Petersburg by tomorrow.

Of course nowadays St Petersburg is only a few hours from Paris by
aeroplane. In the context of today, a person's being in Paris today would
not prevent their being in St Petersburg tomorrow. If someone were to
give a similar argument regarding some presently living person – the
Russian president Vladimir Putin for example – then we would be puzzled.
Since everyone is aware of air travel, nobody thinks that it is impossible
to get from Paris to St Petersburg in one day. So in the context of today,
we would have to inquire further to discover what the arguer thinks is
preventing Mr Putin's journey. But suppose these words were given by
someone in 1807, referring to Napoleon. Then surely the arguer would
be assuming that it is not possible to get from Paris to St Petersburg at
such a speed. That assumption would obviously have been correct in
Napoleon's day. Indeed it would have gone without saying, which is
precisely why the arguer need not have expressed it explicitly. The fastest
way to travel then was by horse.

Such facts pertaining to the context in which the argument is
given, together with the specific words used by the person, will constitute the total evidence you have for reconstructing the argument. In
some cases, the context is known, and makes it obvious what the arguer
was implicitly assuming. In other cases, we may have to learn more
about the context; this happens especially when interpreting historical
documents.

In other cases, however, we may learn all the relevant contextual
factors, yet it remains possible to represent the person's argument in more
than one way. And it may happen that one reconstruction represents
the argument as a good one, another as a bad one. In such a case, which
reconstruction should you prefer? Which should you advance as *the*
reconstruction of the argument?

It depends upon your purpose. If you are hoping to convince others
that the person is wrong, you are most likely to succeed if you represent
it as a bad one. Indeed, this is a very common ploy. If your aim is to
defeat your opponent – or to make it seem as if you have defeated them
– then success is more likely if you attack a weakened form of your opponent's argument. In a context like that of a public debate, this is often a
good strategy. For what you are trying to do is to appear, in the eyes of
the audience, to get the upper hand. By representing your opponent's
position as weaker than it really is, you are more likely to appear to be
the victor. You also put your opponent on the defensive, forcing him to
scramble, saying things like 'that's not what I meant'. If your aim is
to persuade, or to appear to be the victor, then you may be well-advised

to choose the weaker version, especially if your audience is not aware that a stronger version is available.

However, *if what matters to you is whether or not the conclusion of the person's argument is true, then you should choose the best representation of the argument.*

Why? Suppose you are wondering whether some particular proposition is true. You are wondering, for example, whether increasing taxes for the wealthy would lead to a rise in unemployment. Suppose further that you honestly have no idea whether or not this is true. Now suppose that someone attempts to persuade you that this proposition is true by giving you an argument for it. But you find that this argument admits of being reconstructed in either of two ways. On one reconstruction, the argument is good, that is, it provides a good reason for accepting the proposition as true. On the other reconstruction, however, it is no good at all; you find that the reasons you have represented the person as giving in favour of this proposition do not support it at all. Suppose you decide on this latter representation of the argument, the one which represents it as bad.

Can you now conclude that the proposition is true, or that it is false? Since, reconstructed that way, the argument was no good, you certainly cannot conclude, on the basis of it, that the proposition is true. *But nor can you conclude that the proposition is false.* The fact that someone has given a bad argument for some proposition is not, in itself, a reason to reject the proposition as false. For example, someone might argue that since three is a lucky number, there will not be a third world war. That is a bad argument; it gives you no reason to believe that there will not be a third world war. But (fortunately!) its being a bad argument provides no reason to believe that there *will* be a third world war. In short, the fact that someone has given a bad argument for the proposition in question leaves you in precisely the same position as you were when you started. If you began with no evidence either for or against the proposition, then your position is unchanged – you've no reason to accept the proposition as true, and none to reject it as false.

Suppose, then, that you accept the first reconstruction of the argument. Since this constitutes a good argument, you are now in a different position; now you do have some indication as to whether or not the proposition is true. In particular, you have a reason for its being true. On this first reconstruction, then, you represent the person as having made a useful contribution to the debate. You now have reasons that you lacked before. Thus, insofar as we engage in critical thinking – insofar as our interest is in discovering the truth of things, and not just in persuading or refuting people – we are most interested to discover good arguments, not bad ones. So we should always choose the best reconstruction of a given argument. That way, we discover reasons for accepting or rejecting particular propositions, advancing the cause of knowledge. This is an application of the **principle of charity**.

There is a further reason for observing the principle of charity, which has more to do with ethics than with logic. When you give an argument, you may or may not succeed in expressing yourself clearly, but you do want your listener to try to understand you. If your listener impatiently seizes upon your words in order to refute your argument as swiftly as possible without taking the trouble to understand you, naturally you feel ill-used, that the person is not being fair to you. You think it wrong, unjust to be treated that way. If so, then we ought to try to be equally receptive to others – to try to understand them, rather than be too eager to refute them or discredit them. When people give arguments, they almost always have some reason or other for what they are saying (although, of course, sometimes people do try to persuade us of things – especially to do things like buy Coke – without actually trying to give us good reasons). People are very seldom completely illogical. But they are seldom very well-practised at expressing their reasons clearly either, and often they are not so interested in clarity as in persuasion or eloquence. Still, beneath it all, they will usually have genuine reasons of some sort in mind, so it seems only right and proper that we should try to bring them to light, to understand what the person is really trying to say. If we do not attempt this, then we are not really doing the person justice; we are not being as receptive to his or her attempts at communication, as we would surely wish others to be to ours.

The principle of charity, however, has a certain limit, beyond which the nature of what we are doing changes somewhat: If our task is to reconstruct the argument actually intended by the person, then we must not go beyond what, based upon the evidence available to us, we may reasonably expect the arguer to have had in mind. Once we go beyond what we may reasonably assume the arguer to have had in mind, then we are no longer in the business of interpreting their argument. Instead, we have become the arguer.

If our concern is with how well a particular person has argued, then we should not overstep this boundary. *However, if our concern is simply with the truth of the matter in question, then to overstep this boundary is perfectly all right.* It often happens that, in reconstructing an argument, we hit upon another, similar or related argument for the same conclusion which is better than the one we are reconstructing. *If what concerns us is simply finding the best arguments on either side of an issue, then we will want to give a representation of this better argument.*

Truth

If your aim is to give the best possible reconstruction of an argument, then you have to know something of what makes an argument good or bad. Fortunately, logic gives us some very clear answers as to what does make arguments good or bad.

The fundamental concept of logic is the concept of **truth**.[1] For one thing, the overarching concern of the critical thinker is typically with the truth (or lack of it) of the conclusions of arguments. Further, truth is the concept in terms of which the logician attempts to explain everything else. Thus, we begin our discussion of the concepts of logic by saying a little bit more about this uniquely important concept.

Many people are put off by the word 'truth'. This is usually the symptom of a philosophical worry that one cannot speak simply of 'truth'. One might worry that perhaps there is no one truth: that what is true for one person or group need not be true for another person or group. Or one may worry that truth is in some way beyond us, unapproachable by mere fallible human beings. But for our purposes, we can leave aside those sorts of abstruse philosophical worries as irrelevant. As noted in Chapter 1, the way in which the logician uses the word 'truth' is really very simple and down-to-earth. Properly understood, the word should not invite those sorts of controversies.

Consider the following proposition:

(A)   Fish live in water.

This proposition is true. What does it mean to say that this proposition is true? It means, simply, that that is the way things are. To say that the proposition is true is to say nothing more than: yes, fish *do* live in water. Thus, consider the proposition that says that (A) is true:

(B)   It is true that fish live in water.

(A) and (B) are *equivalent* in the sense that, *necessarily*, if (A) is true then so is (B), and if (B) is true then so is (A). In other words, to say that it is true that fish live in water comes to the same thing as saying that fish live in water. Used this way – which is all that is needed for logic or critical thinking – the word 'true' is no more mysterious than the words occurring in the sentence 'Fish live in water'. In this sense,

---

1   The great German logician Gottlob Frege – who is genuinely agreed to be the inventor of the modern science of logic – said that the laws of logic are really the 'laws of truth', in something like the way that the laws of physics are the laws of the physical world.

you cannot doubt that there is 'really' such a thing as truth, or that truth is knowable, any more than you can doubt that fish live in water, or that the sky is blue, or that the Earth is bigger than a grapefruit. For these are all known truths.

Discomfort with the word 'true' is sometimes due to a failure to distinguish truth from *belief*. If John says 'Fish live in water', then he does, of course, show that he believes that fish live in water (presumably he *knows* that fish live in water). Likewise, if Mary now refers to what John said, and says 'That's true', then she also shows that she believes that fish live in water. Despite their having done so by different means, both John and Mary have *asserted the proposition that fish live in water*. Mary, unlike John, has used the word 'true'. But they have asserted the same proposition; they have expressed the same belief. Yet clearly the *truth* of this proposition has nothing to do with what Mary *believes*. That depends only on how things stand as regards fish, and what fish do does not depend upon what people think. So despite the fact that Mary has used the word 'true' to assert something, the truth of what she asserts does not depend on her beliefs in any way.

Of course, what Mary *believes* depends on her, and it is possible that people could have different beliefs as regards fish. But that has no effect on fish (we will, however, return to this issue in the final chapter).

The reverse side of this is that to say that a proposition is **false** is just to deny it – in this case, for example, some misinformed person who thought that snakes are fish might say, 'That's false; not all fish live in water'. 'It is false that fish live in water' is equivalent to 'Fish do not live in water'.

Sometimes we will speak of the **truth-value** of a proposition. This just means the truth of the proposition, if it is true, or its falsity, if it is false. There are two truth-values, true and false. For example, we can say that the truth-value of 'Fish live in water' is truth, that that of 'Fish live in the sky' is falsity, and that the truth-value of 'It is now Tuesday' must always differ from that of 'It is now Friday'. To ask 'what is the truth-value of that proposition?' is the same as asking whether or not that proposition is true.

A question might have occurred to you: If to say that a proposition is true is the same asserting it, then why do we have the terms 'is true' and 'is false'? What is their purpose? Why are they not just redundant, superfluous appendages? One reason is convenience; saying 'that's true' is quick and easy, like saying 'yes', or nodding one's head. But a more important reason is that we sometimes want to *generalise* about propositions in terms of truth and falsity. That is, we sometimes wish to speak about true or false propositions in general, without specifying any propositions in particular. This is crucial in the formal study of logic, but less technical examples are no less important. For example, we have characterised critical thinking as aiming at truth. This means that we undertake it because we want to know whether capitalism is the fairest economic system, whether so-and-so committed the crime, whether the danger of war is increasing or decreasing . . . and so on, for everything we might want to know. That critical thinking aims at truth is a generalisation that sums this up.

Deductive validity

In fact, we need this sort of generalisation in order to define the important concept of **deductive validity**, to which we now turn. For brevity, we will sometimes call it simply 'validity'. In studying it, you should forget whatever the word might mean to you ordinarily. We mean *logical* validity, the concept of validity that concerns logic, the study of reasoning.

Consider the following arguments:

A   P1)   The Prime Minister's dog is infested with fleas.
         P2)   All fleas are bacteria.
         _____
         C)   The Prime Minister's dog is infested with bacteria.

B   P1)   Colette owned a dog.
         P2)   All French Bulldogs are dogs.
         _____
         C)   Colette owned a French Bulldog.

Argument **A** speaks of 'The Prime Minister's dog', but it is not made clear who that is, for we are given no indication of when, or even in what country, this argument was given. So we have no idea what dog, if any, has been referred to. Furthermore, P2 of **A** would be false under any circumstances in which the argument might have been given – fleas are insects, not bacteria. But scrutinise these arguments carefully. You can easily recognise that there is something right about **A**, and something wrong with **B**. The conclusion of **A** does follow from its premises, and the conclusion of **B** does not follow from its premises. What you are recognising is that **A** is **valid**, and that **B** is **invalid**.

Now what does this mean? What, exactly, are you seeing when you see that **A** is valid and **B** is invalid? Consider **A**. When you recognise its validity, you do not need to know whether or not P1 or C of **A** is true or even precisely which dog of which Prime Minister of which country is intended; nor do you care about the fact that P2 of **A** is positively false. For what you are seeing is that if the premises of **A** *were* true, then the conclusion would *have to be* true as well. In short, *it would be impossible for the premises to be true but the conclusion false*. The truth of the premises, in any possible or imaginable situation, would guarantee the truth of the conclusion. If fleas were bacteria, and the dog being referred to were infested with fleas, then it would, in that case, be infested with bacteria.

On the other hand, consider **B**. When you recognise that it is not a valid argument, what you are recognising is that even if the premises were true, it would still be possible for the conclusion to be false. The conclusion does not follow. Whether or not the premises are in fact true, it would be possible or conceivable for the premises to be true and the conclusion false. The truth of the premises would not guarantee the truth of the conclusion.

Now as it happens, the premises of **B** are true. The French author Colette did have a dog, and of course French Bulldogs are dogs. Indeed, the conclusion of **B** is also true; Colette's dog was a French Bulldog. But that is beside the point, so far as validity is concerned. It may be true that Colette had a French Bulldog, but this does not follow merely from the fact that she had a dog (along with the fact that French Bulldogs are dogs). A person given only the premises of the argument, and lacking any further information about Colette, would be in no position to infer that Colette had a French Bulldog. If this point seems strange, remember that you saw that the argument is invalid *before* you knew the truth-values of its premises or of its conclusion. And that is as it should be. You can tell that an argument is valid or not without knowing the truth-values of the propositions it comprises, because the validity of an argument (or lack thereof), does not depend upon the actual truth-values of those propositions.

To put it another way: the concept of validity pertains to the *connection* between the premises and conclusion of an argument, not their actual truth-values considered individually. This is indeed the crucial lesson about the concept of validity: it pertains to whole arguments (more exactly: it pertains to **inferences**; extended arguments may contain more than one inference, and each one is subject to being valid or invalid).

Thus, it should be clear that it would be nonsense, to say of a single proposition, that it is valid. That would be like saying, of a single word, that it rhymes (a rhyme requires a relation between words). By the same token, it would be nonsense to say, of an argument, that it is true. That would be like saying, of an entire jigsaw-puzzle, that it doesn't fit (this could be said of some or even of every piece, but not of the puzzle itself).

A single proposition can be true or false, but not valid or invalid; an argument can be valid or invalid, but not true or false.

These two points should be borne in mind, as it is a common mistake to confuse the notions of truth and validity, applying them to the wrong sorts of things.

Here then are two definitions of **validity**; they are equivalent (they come to the same thing), so you are free to make use of the one you find easiest to work with:

> To say that an argument is *valid* is to say: It would be impossible for all the premises of the argument to be true, but the conclusion false.[2]

And the second one:

> To say that an argument is *valid* is to say: If the premises are (or were) true, the conclusion would also have to be true.

If the condition specified by the definition does not hold, then the argument is **invalid**. A consequence of these definitions is that the following cases of valid arguments are all possible:

1   The premises are all (actually) true, and the conclusion is (actually) true.
2   The premises are all (actually) false, and the conclusion is (actually) false.
3   The premises are all (actually) false, and the conclusion is (actually) true.

---

2   This definition has the consequence that if any premise of an argument is a necessary falsehood, or if the conclusion is a necessary truth, then the argument is valid (a necessary falsehood is a proposition that could not possibly have been true; a necessary truth is a proposition that could not possibly have been false). In such cases the premises may be entirely irrelevant to the conclusion. For example, 'There is a married bachelor, therefore the moon is made of green cheese' is valid, as is 'The moon is made of green cheese, therefore there is no married bachelor'. Our definition, then, is quite useless as a guide to reasoning, where necessary truths and necessary falsehoods are concerned. We believe this a reasonable price to pay, for the alternative – a definition of validity whereby an argument is valid by virtue of its form – is too difficult, for our purposes, to apply profitably to ordinary language. Further, it is really very seldom that necessary truths or falsehoods figure as the conclusions or premises of arguments encountered ordinarily.

4   Some of the premises are (actually) true, some (actually) false and the conclusion is (actually) true.

5   Some of the premises are (actually) true, some (actually) false and the conclusion is (actually) false.

The only case in which an argument cannot be valid is the case when the premises are all (actually) true, but the conclusion is (actually) false. For if that is so, then obviously there is a possible case in which the premises hold true when the conclusion is false – the actual case.

This is easier to grasp by looking at some examples. The following are, respectively, examples of cases 1–5 given above; the 'T's and 'F's in parentheses to the right of each premise or conclusion indicates its actual truth or falsity, as the case may be:

1   P1)   Janet Baker is an opera singer.   (T)
    P2)   All opera singers are musicians.   (T)

    C)   **Janet Baker is a musician.**   **(T)**

2   P1)   Janet Baker is a baritone.   (F)
    P2)   All baritones are Italians.   (F)

    C)   **Janet Baker is an Italian.**   **(F)**

3   P1)   Janet Baker is a baritone.   (F)
    P2)   All baritones are English.   (F)

    C)   **Janet Baker is English.**   **(T)**

4   P1)   Janet Baker is a soprano.   (T)
    P2)   All sopranos are English.   (F)

    C)   **Janet Baker is English.**   **(T)**

5   P1)   Janet Baker is a soprano.   (T)
    P2)   All sopranos are Italians.   (F)

    C)   **Janet Baker is an Italian.**   **(F)**

And here are some *invalid* arguments (we will consider further common invalid argument-types in Chapter 4 in the section 'formal fallacies'):

6 P1) Janet Baker is a soprano. (T)
   P2) Janet Baker is a musician. (T)

   C) Janet Baker is an Italian. (F)

7 P1) Janet Baker is a woman. (T)
   P2) All baritones are women. (F)

   C) Janet Baker is a baritone. (F)

8 P1) Janet Baker is a singer. (T)
   P2) All sopranos are singers. (T)

   C) Janet Baker is a soprano. (T)

9 P1) Janet Baker is a baritone. (F)
   P2) All singers are baritones. (F)

   C) Janet Baker is a singer. (T) ·

How to judge validity

The way to determine whether or not an argument is valid is to *ignore* the actual truth-values of the premises and the actual truth-value of the conclusion (of course, if the conclusion is actually false, and the premises are all true, then the argument must be invalid. But normally when assessing arguments we do not know the truth-value of the conclusion, because the whole reason for considering the argument is that we want to find out the truth-value of the conclusion). The way to do it – and this is what the definition of validity should lead you to expect – is to reason as follows:

Whether or not they are actually true, suppose or pretend that the premises were all true; then in that situation – aside from how things *actually* are – could the conclusion conceivably be false? If it could not be false, then the argument is *valid*. If it could be false, then the argument is *invalid*.

The systematic study of validity is the concern of **logic**. Logicians are concerned to devise perfectly reliable procedures for detecting validity, or the lack of it, even in the case of extremely complex arguments such as those occurring in mathematical proofs. Since the validity of an argument is independent of the truth-values of its premises, logic has a unique status among the sciences; for other sciences are concerned to find out the truth-values of particular propositions about its characteristic subject-matter. Ichthyology, for example, seeks to know which propositions about fish are true, and which false. The logician has no particular concern with fish, nor with the truth as regards anything else in particular. Logic has no concern with particular truths. The logician is concerned only with relations between propositions, not with their actual truth-values. These are the sorts of relations displayed between premises and conclusion in valid arguments such as 1–5.

Further examples

The examples so far of valid arguments have all been of the same type or form. Here are some further, still quite simple, types of valid arguments. The examples are all fictional. Their being fictional helps us to realise that the actual truth-values of premises and conclusions are usually irrelevant to determining whether or not arguments are valid:

P1) No Zormons are ticklish.
P2) Trozak is a Zormon.

C)   **Trozak is not ticklish.**

P1) Either Trozak is on Mars, or he is on Venus.
P2) Trozak is not on Mars.

C)   **Trozak is on Venus.**

P1) It is not possible to visit Mars and Venus in the
      same day.

C)   **If Trozak visited Mars today, then he did not visit Venus
      today.**

P1) If Ichnik is ticklish, then Zadon is ticklish.
P2) If Trozak is ticklish, then Ichnik is ticklish.
P3) Trozak is ticklish.

C)   **Zadon is ticklish.**

P1)   If Trozak is on Mars, he will visit Ichnik.

P2)   Trozak is on Mars.

C)   **Trozak will visit Ichnik.**

P1)   If Trozak ate all the biscuits, then the biscuit tin is empty.

P2)   The biscuit tin is not empty.

C)   **Trozak did not eat all the biscuits.**

Conditional propositions

This is a good point at which to distinguish arguments from a certain kind of statement, which both logicians and grammarians call the **conditional**. Conditionals are most characteristically expressed using the 'if–then' form of declarative sentence. For example:

If it is raining, then it is cloudy.

Another example is P1 of the last example of the preceding section of this chapter. Conditionals can also be expressed in other ways, however. In fact, *all* of the following statements express the very same proposition as the example just given; they represent exactly the same connection between rain and clouds:

▶   It is raining only if it is cloudy.
▶   Either it is cloudy, or it is not raining.
▶   It is not raining unless it is cloudy.
▶   If it is not cloudy, then it is not raining.
▶   It is not raining if it is not cloudy.
▶   It is cloudy if it is raining.
▶   There is no rain without clouds.

At first, it may not be obvious that each of these is equivalent to 'If it is raining, then it is cloudy'. So let us stop to consider the ones that people most often find puzzling.

I.   'If not. . .then not. . .'. If it is raining then it is cloudy; there is no rain without clouds. Therefore, if it is *not* raining, then it is not cloudy. So if we have 'If P then Q', we also have 'If not-Q then not-P'. But we can also go the other way, from 'If not-Q then not-P' to 'If P then Q'. You can see this by thinking about the rain example, but take another.

The detective says 'If there is no mud on Smith's shoes, then Smith is not the murderer'. The detective is *not* saying that if there is mud on Smith's shoes, then Smith is the murderer. What he *is* saying is that if Smith *is* the murderer, then there is mud on his shoes. So saying 'If not-Q then not-P' is equivalent to saying 'If P then Q'.

II. 'Either–or'. Usually, when two statements are joined by 'either–or', or just by 'or', to form a compound statement, the compound is equivalent to a statement using 'if–then', and vice versa. But to pass from the version using 'or' to the version using 'if–then', or vice versa, we have to insert the word 'not'. For example, the following pairs of statements are equivalent:[3]

> Rangers will win the league or Celtic will win the league.
> If Rangers do not win the league then Celtic will win the league.

> Either Jane will practice diligently or she will fail her exam.
> If Jane does not practice diligently then she will fail her exam.

III. 'Only if'. This one is trickier. It should be clear that the following are equivalent, in the sense that they state the same relationship between rain and clouds:

▶ It is raining only if it is cloudy.
▶ If it is raining then it is cloudy.

In the first, the word 'if' precedes the bit about clouds rather than the bit about the rain. It says: 'It is raining only on condition that it is cloudy.' Thus if it *is* raining, then that condition must be fulfilled – so it must be

---

3   A complication is that the word 'or' is used in either of two ways, known as the 'inclusive' and 'exclusive' sense. In the inclusive sense, 'P or Q' means that either P is true, or Q is true, or they are both true; so the compound sentence is false only if both P and Q are false. This is the sense intended if one says something like 'Real Madrid will lose if either Beckham receives a red card or Carlos receives a red card'. In the exclusive sense, 'P or Q' means that either P is true or Q is true, but not both. This is the sense normally intended if one says something like 'Either you go to bed now or I will not read you a story' (the child would rightly feel cheated if he or she goes to bed immediately but doesn't get a story). A conditional statement 'If P then Q' is equivalent only to 'Either not-P or Q' only in the inclusive sense of 'or'. Where it is clear that the exclusive sense is intended, the reconstructed argument should contain conditionals running in both directions. A sentence such as 'Either the murder took place here or there was an accident here', intended in the exclusive sense, would be represented as 'If no accident took place here then the murder took place here' and 'If an accident took place here then the murder did not take place here'.

cloudy. Note that it would be *false* to put it the other way round; it would be false to say: 'It is cloudy only if it is raining.' For the very same reason, it would false to say: 'If it is cloudy, then it is raining.' What makes these false is that sometimes it is cloudy but not raining.

Take another, more real-life sort of example. Someone says: 'Jane is coming to the party only if Joe is.' Suppose that's true. Then *if* Jane is coming to the party, *then* Joe is coming to the party also. Note further that someone who says 'Jane is coming to the party only if Joe is' is *not* committed to 'If Joe is coming to the party then Jane is coming to the party'. Perhaps Jane won't come to the party without Joe being there, but might not come even if Joe does.

We can express this last point by saying that 'P only if Q' makes the same assertion as 'If P then Q', but does not logically commit one to 'If Q then P'. What makes this difficult to appreciate is that in some cases 'P only if Q' *implicates* 'If Q then P' in the sense explained in Chapter 1 (pp. 9–10). For example, suppose a parent says: 'You'll get ice cream only if you finish your peas.' This tells the child that if he does not finish his peas he won't get ice cream. And unless the parent is being mean, the child rightly assumes that if he eats his peas, he will get ice cream. Still, the parent's announcement does *not* actually *assert* 'If you finish your peas, you'll get ice cream'. We know this because if it did, then we would have to say that to assert 'It is raining only if it is cloudy' is also to assert 'If it is cloudy then it is raining', which it certainly is not. The reason that things seem otherwise in the ice-cream case is that the parent's announcement, though it does not assert that the child will get ice cream if he eats his peas, implicates it.

Finally, care should be taken not to confuse 'only if' with another device, 'if and only if'. To say 'P if and only if Q' is to say 'P if Q' *and* 'P only if Q'. 'P if Q' means the same as 'If Q then P'. According to what we have said about 'only if', 'P only if Q' means the same as 'If P then Q'. Therefore: 'P if and only if Q' means the same as 'If P then Q, and if Q then P'. It means 'Either both P and Q, or neither'. So, for example, 'It is raining if and only if it is cloudy' is *false*. On the other hand, if we wanted to say that Jane will not come to the party without Joe, but will definitely come if he does come, we could say 'Jane will come to the party if and only if Joe comes to the party'.

IV. 'Unless'. Begin with these, each of which, again, states the same relationship between rain and clouds:

▶ It is not raining unless it is cloudy.
▶ If it is raining then it is cloudy.

'Unless' is confusing in many of the same ways that 'only if' is confusing. For example, someone says 'That plant will grow well unless it gets whitefly'. Are they saying 'If the plant doesn't get whitefly it will grow well', or 'If the plant gets whitefly it will not grow well'? Look again at the example about rain and clouds. What it tells us is that 'not-P unless Q' is equivalent to 'If P then Q'. The transition from the 'unless' form to the 'if–then' form can be represented as follows. Begin with 'unless':

Not-P unless Q. (It is not raining unless it is cloudy.)

Replace 'unless' with 'if not':

Not-P if not-Q. (It is not raining if it is not cloudy.)

This is clearly just another way of saying:

If not-Q then not-P. (If it is not cloudy then it is not raining.)

But according to what we said above (under I), this is equivalent to:

If P then Q. (If it is raining then it is cloudy.)

In other words, the trick for dealing with 'unless' is to think of it as meaning 'if not': 'P unless Q' means 'P if not Q', which is the same as 'If not-Q then P'. Therefore, the statement 'That plant will grow well unless it gets whitefly' means 'If that plant doesn't get whitefly then it will grow well'. It does *not* mean 'If that plant gets whitefly then it will not grow well'. Similarly, 'You will fail unless you study' means 'If you don't study then you will fail', but not 'If you study, then you will not fail'. On the other hand, 'You will *not* fail unless you don't study' means 'If you do study then you will not fail'.

In general, a conditional is a compound proposition consisting of two parts, each of which is itself a proposition, where these two parts are joined by some connecting words (they are called 'logical connectives') such as 'if–then', 'either–or', 'unless', or 'only–if', or something similar. Sometimes the presence of two whole propositions is somewhat concealed, as in the last example about rain and clouds. However they are joined, what a conditional says is that the truth of one proposition ensures that of another. In formal logic this relation is represented by a single device, usually an arrow:

It is raining → It is cloudy.
P → Q.

The one *from* which the arrow points is called the **antecedent**; the one *to* which the arrow points is called the **consequent**, for obvious reasons. We will use this terminology a lot, so you should memorise it.

Now, here is a tricky and important point. In one way or another, the examples on p. 57 express the very same conditional proposition about rain and clouds. They express the same relation between rain and clouds. *Thus the antecedent and consequent in all those examples is the same –* in all of them, the logical antecedent is the proposition that it is raining, and the logical consequent is the proposition that it is cloudy. In this sense, the fact that one proposition is the antecedent and another the consequent of a conditional statement is a matter of the *logic* of the statements. It is not a matter of the grammar of the sentences. It does not matter in what order, in the whole sentence, the two smaller sentences occur; what matters is the logical relationship asserted by the sentence. You can see this from the fact that in the sentences in the box the bit about rain, sometimes occurs before and sometimes after the bit about clouds.

Our example of a conditional is a true statement. Some conditionals are false, such as 'If it is cloudy, then it is raining' (since, sometimes, it is cloudy but it is not raining). A conditional is said to be true or false, rather than valid or invalid. For a conditional is not itself an argument. A conditional is *one* proposition that comprises *two* propositions as parts, joined by 'if–then' or a similar device. An argument cannot be just one proposition. It needs at least two.

The following, however, would be an argument:

It is raining. Therefore, it is cloudy.

This is not a conditional, but an argument composed of two propositions. Moreover, this argument actually asserts that it is raining, and also that it is cloudy. A person giving it would actually be asserting those things. Not so for the corresponding conditional: to say 'If it is raining then it is cloudy' is not itself to assert that it is raining, or that it is cloudy. People sometimes make a mistake on this point; we sometimes witness conversations like this:

Mary: If Edna gets drunk, then her graduation party will be a mess.

Jane: Why do you say Edna's going to get drunk? You're always so unfair to her.

Mary: I didn't say Edna is going to get drunk, I said *if* Edna gets drunk . . .

Jane: Well, it's the same thing!

Mary: No it isn't!

Jane: Don't try to get out of it! You always think the worst of
           Edna, and you're always trying to take back what you say!

What Jane seems not to understand is that a conditional does not assert either its antecedent or its consequent. An argument asserts its premises and its conclusion, but Mary is not arguing that the party is going to be a mess; she is only saying that it will be if Edna gets drunk (presumably because she thinks Edna misbehaves when she drinks too much). Strictly speaking, she is not even saying that Edna is *likely* to get drunk. Of course, she would not have brought the whole thing up if she did not think there was some danger of Edna's getting drunk. The grain of truth in Jane's reaction is that the assertion of a conditional often *implicates* that there is some probability that the antecedent of the conditional is or will be true (on **conversational implicature** see Chapter 1, pp. 9–10). Even so, Mary might well think this probability to be less than fifty–fifty, and she did *not* say that Edna's going to get drunk.

Finally, it is important to recognise that many arguments have conditional conclusions – that is, conclusions which are themselves conditionals. For example:

P1)   If Labour does not change its platform, it will not attract new
       supporters.

P2)   If Labour does not attract new supporters, it will lose the next
       election.

**C)   If Labour does not change its platform, then it will lose
the next election.**

Here both premises as well as the conclusion are conditionals. This particular pattern is very common, and is called a 'chain' argument. A chain of conditionals is set up, like a row of dominoes. What the argument is saying is that if the antecedent of P1 comes true, then the consequent of P2 is true. Chain arguments can have any number of links. One of the 'further examples' earlier in this chapter (p. 56) involved a chain.

Deductive soundness

Normally, you assess an argument because you wonder whether or not the conclusion is true. You want to know whether the arguer has given you a reason for thinking that the conclusion is true. If you find that the argument is invalid, then you know that even if the premises are true, the conclusion could be false. Therefore, the reasons given by the arguer – the premises – do not suffice to establish the conclusion, even if they are true. But suppose you find that the argument is valid. Then there are two possibilities.

(A) *One or more of the premises are (actually) false.*
(B) *All of the premises are (actually) true.*

Now, as illustrated by examples 2 and 5 on p. 54, knowing that the argument is valid is not enough to show you that the conclusion is true. In order to determine that, you need a further step: you must determine the truth-values of the premises. You might already know them. But if you don't, then of course, logic is no help. If one of the premises is that the octopus is a fish, then unless you know already, you have to consult a book or ask an ichthyologist. Suppose now that you have done this, and what you have is a case of (A), i.e. one (or more) of the premises is false. In that case, you can draw no conclusion as to the truth-value of the conclusion (as illustrated by arguments 4 and 5 on p. 54, a valid argument with one or more false premises may have either a true or a false conclusion). But now suppose you find the argument to be a case of (B) – that is, you have found it to be a valid argument with true premises. Eureka! For according to the definition of validity, a valid argument with true premises *cannot* have a false conclusion. So the conclusion must be true. The argument has accomplished its purpose; it has demonstrated its conclusion to be true. We call this a **deductively sound** argument. Argument 1 above about Janet Baker, for example, is a deductively sound argument:

To say that an argument is *deductively sound* is to say: The argument is valid, and all its premises are (actually) true.

This reveals the importance of the concept of validity. Given the definition of validity, it follows from the definition of deductive soundness that the conclusion of a deductively sound argument must be true. There cannot be a deductively sound argument with a false conclusion.

An argument that is not deductively sound – one which has one or more false premises, or is invalid, or both – is said to be **deductively unsound**. Deductive soundness, like validity, pertains to whole arguments, and not to single propositions.

It is important to recognise what follows if you happen to know that the conclusion of an argument is *not* true. Suppose someone gives you an argument, the conclusion of which is that there are platypuses at the local zoo. And suppose you know that this is not true. You know that the local zoo has no platypuses. Therefore, you know that this argument is not deductively sound. You should make it clear to yourself why this is so; check the definitions again if this is not clear.

If you do know that there are no platypuses at the zoo, then you know it is possible to give a deductively sound argument for that conclusion. *But there cannot be deductively sound arguments on both sides of the issue.* For deductively sound arguments have true conclusions. If there were deductively sound arguments on both sides of this issue, it would follow that there are platypuses at the zoo, and also that there are not, which is impossible. This is important to recognise, because frequently we do say that there can be 'good' arguments on both sides of a given issue (especially a controversial one); we say this, perhaps, out of a wish to show respect for different opinions, or simply to express our own indecision over the issue. But in saying this, we cannot mean that there are *deductively sound* arguments on both sides of an issue. Later, we will explain in exactly what sense there can be 'good' arguments on both sides of an issue (for, to be sure, there can be).

If we know that the conclusion of an argument is false, then we know that the argument is **deductively unsound**. What follows from that? Look at the definition of deductive soundness. If the argument is deductively unsound, it follows that *either* the argument has (at least) one false premise, or the argument is invalid (or perhaps both – perhaps it is invalid *and* it has one or more false premises). Suppose then that you determine the argument to be valid. Then you know that at least one premise must be false. On the other hand, suppose that you find that the argument is invalid. What can you conclude about the truth-values of the premises? Nothing! For you know that an invalid argument with a false conclusion may have either true premises or false premises.

Similarly, if you perhaps do not *know* (for you are not certain), but you do believe, or hope, that the conclusion of a given argument is false, then you must run through the same procedure. Suppose you merely hope that there are no platypuses at the zoo, because you fear they would not be happy there (this might be reasonable; platypuses are extremely shy, so being put on display might stress them out). Then you must hope that the argument is deductively unsound, in which case you must hope that either the argument is invalid, or it has a false premise. This is the sort of thing you might do if you were a court-room barrister, hoping to refute the opposing side's arguments. You might want to show that the prosecution's argument for your client's guilt is unsound.

The connection to formal logic

Occasionally in discussing logical points we have used 'dummy' letters to stand in place of sentences. For example, we said that 'P unless Q' is equivalent to 'If not-Q, then P'. The letters 'P' and 'Q' were used to stand in place of arbitrary declarative sentences like 'It is raining' or 'The cat is on the mat'. We can do this because the point we wish to make does not depend on what particular sentences we put for 'P' and 'Q'. The point concerns only the meaning or *logical properties* of such expressions as 'unless' and 'if–then', and it would hold for *any* sentences put for 'P' and 'Q'.

Look now at the set of valid arguments about Janet Baker on p. 54. As we noted, they are all of the *same form*. We can display this form in the following way:

P1)   x is an F.
P2)   All F are G.

___

C)   x is a G.

This is one example of what is known as a *valid argument-form*, sometimes called a valid argument *schema*. This means that whatever *name* we put for 'x' – whether 'Janet Baker', 'Mt. Fuji' or 'Vienna' – and whatever *general terms* we put for 'F' and 'G' – whether 'soprano', 'volcano' or 'capital city' – the resulting argument will be valid (so long as we always put the same name or term for the same letter). The validity of the argument is independent of the particular meanings of 'Janet Baker', 'soprano', and so on. More exactly, we say that for *whatever* grammatically suitable expressions are put for 'x', 'F' and 'G', and *whatever those expressions are taken to mean*, the result will never have true premises and a false conclusion. Interestingly, you can readily see that this is so: you can easily see that whatever 'x' is, and whatever is taken for 'F' and 'G', the argument-form is valid. In advance of studying formal logic, we already have a good eye for formal validity.

Here is another valid form:

P1)   If P then Q.
P2)   P.

___

C)   Q.

An instance of this form is given on p. 56, the third example about Trozak: 'If Trozak is on Mars, then he will visit Ichnik; Trozak is on Mars;

therefore Trozak will visit Ichnik.' The difference between this and the previous example is that in this one, the letters 'P' and 'Q' are place-holders for *whole sentences*, not for names or general terms. Note that we used 'F' and 'G' for general terms, and 'P' and 'Q' for sentences (if more were needed, we would use 'H', 'I' and so on for general terms, 'R', 'S' and so on for sentences). We used lower-case letters in place of names. This is the usual practice in logic, but there is no need for a strict rule in this context.

This is typical of what is known as *formal logic*: claims about logical relationships are made most efficiently by *abstracting* from the particular subject-matter we talk about and concentrating on the logical forms of the arguments. However, logical forms are not *completely* without content or meaning. In the first example, what we are really focussing on is the meaning of the word 'All'; in the second, we are focussing on the meaning of the expression 'if–then'. We don't put in dummy letters for those. Accordingly, these words are often known as 'logical words' or 'logical particles', and formal logic may appropriately be said to concern itself with those. Other logical particles in English include 'or', 'and', 'unless', 'not', 'every', 'some', 'each', 'there is' and 'there are', 'no' (in its use as a quantifier), and 'is' (in the sense of 'is the very same thing as').

Representing the logical form of an argument by means of dummy letters can be very useful for showing that an argument is *invalid*. For an argument-form is invalid if it has what we call an 'instance' with true premises and a false conclusion. Thus consider invalid argument number 7 on p. 55:

P1) Janet Baker is a woman.   (T)
P2) All baritones are women.   (F)

C) Janet Baker is a baritone.   (F)

We can represent its logical form as the following schema:

P1) x is an F.
P2) All G are F.

C) x is a G.

Here is an instance of this schema – that is, an argument with the same logical form – that has true premises and a false conclusion, thereby proving that the logical form of the original argument is invalid, and therefore that the original argument is itself invalid. We put 'Luciano Pavarotti' for 'x', 'human' for 'F' and 'women' for 'G':

P1) Luciano Pavarotti is human.   (T)
P2) All women are human.   (T)

C) Luciano Pavarotti is a woman.   (F)

This technique is called 'refutation by counterexample'; we will return to it in Chapter 6.

There are sophisticated technical procedures for exploring formal logical relationships in a systematic, detailed way. For the most part, it is necessary to invent artificial languages for this purpose employing special symbols in place of the logical particles of English such as the '→' sign for the conditional 'if–then' we mentioned earlier. The reason is that logical relationships in a 'natural' language such as English tend to be too cumbersome and poorly defined to represent clearly and systematically (look at all the different ways of representing the conditional, when really only one way is needed!). The logical forms of arguments in English are not always as clear as they are in our examples. By contrast, the validity of arguments expressed in symbolic notation is determined by precise rules, and the forms of the arguments are always exactly determined. Courses on 'formal logic' – otherwise known as 'mathematical logic' or 'symbolic logic' – are taught in Philosophy, Mathematics, Linguistics and Computer Science. In critical thinking we are doing what you might call 'practical logic'. We want to learn to identify the reasoning in commonly encountered attempts to persuade us, and to assess it as good or bad. For this, we need the concept of validity, but we do not need artificial symbols or elaborate technical procedures for detecting validity. The reason is that the logic of the vast majority of arguments in everyday life is rarely of any great complexity. Once we know exactly what the argument is, whether or not it is valid can almost always be seen by applying the definition given above. Most of the work goes into the reconstruction. And as we have seen – and will see in more detail later – we cannot profitably reconstruct an argument without knowing what makes a good argument, hence not without grasping the concept of validity.

Nevertheless, it will sometimes be useful to use 'dummy' letters as we have already done, to draw attention to the forms of arguments and statements where appropriate.

Argument trees

An **argument tree** is a device that can be used for representing arguments in the form of a diagram. They are helpful when we are reconstructing arguments, particularly complex ones, because they provide a means of showing the ways in which the different parts of an argument are related to each other. They show how the premises support the conclusion. Constructing argument trees is a very valuable tool and you will find it helpful to use them in your own analyses of complex real-world arguments.

Note: the process of constructing an argument tree is especially useful before you have supplied missing premises, and before you have settled upon a reconstruction of the argument in standard form. In fact, it can be useful to construct an argument tree at almost any stage in the reconstruction, including when the reconstruction is complete, simply as way illustrating the structure of the argument, of making it clear to oneself and to others.

To illustrate, we stick to arguments already in standard form. Consider the following simple arguments:

A P1) Susan is a marathon runner.
    P2) Susan eats well and sleeps well.

    C) **Susan is healthy.**

B P1) Willy is in the music club.
    P2) No member of the music club plays jazz.

    C) **Willy does not play jazz.**

These arguments both infer a conclusion from two premises, but there is an important difference.

In argument **A**, each premise supports the conclusion individually. That is, P1 is cited as a reason for **C**, and P2 is cited as another reason for **C**. One could argue from P1 alone to **C**; one could also argue from P2 alone to **C**. By contrast, in argument **B**, neither premise supports **C** by itself. Neither P1 nor P2 would, by itself, be a reason to accept **C**. Rather, they work together to support **C**. This is always the case when one premise is a conditional and another is the antecedent of that same conditional.

Argument **A** is represented as in Figure 2.1 and argument **B** is represented as in Figure 2.2.

Now these examples are very simple. Argument trees are especially helpful when used to represent more complex arguments with intermediate conclusions. For example:

P1) Consumption is increasing.
P2) The Pound is weakening against other currencies.

C1) **Inflation will increase.**

P3)   Whenever inflation increases, mortgage rates rise.

C2)   Mortgage rates will rise.

P4)   Whenever mortgage rates rise, the building trade suffers.

C3)   The building trade will suffer.

The correct argument tree for this is shown in Figure 2.3 (see over). Note that the first sub-argument is not valid as it stands. P1 and P2 may be said to support C1, but only by virtue of a relation that is not explicitly stated between consumption rates, the relative strength of currencies and inflation. Thus the argument does not explicitly include what later in the book we will call its 'connecting' premise or premises. The most plausible connecting premise would be of the form, 'If P1 and P2, then C1'. We had the same sort of situation in the argument about Susan the marathon

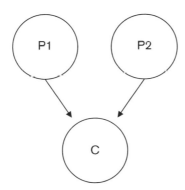

Figure 2.1 Two premises supporting a conclusion individually

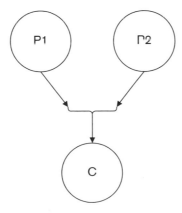

Figure 2.2 Two premises supporting a conclusion jointly

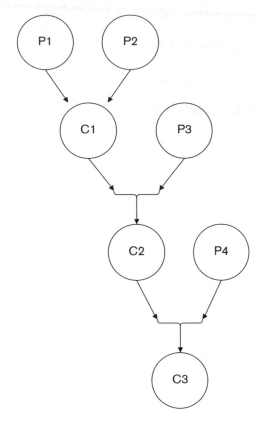

Figure 2.3 Extended argument

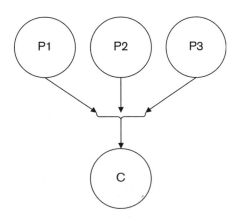

Figure 2.4 Three premises supporting an conclusion jointly

runner. The connecting premise was left implicit. A plausible connecting premise, in this case, might be something like:

P3) No marathon runner who eats and sleeps well is not healthy.

If we do it this way, then the three premises work together to support the conclusion; an instance of this generalisation would be: 'If P1 and P2, then Susan is healthy.' So the argument would be represented as shown in Figure 2.4.

CHAPTER SUMMARY

The aim of **argument-reconstruction** is to **clarify**, and make fully **explicit**, the argument intended by an arguer. We do this by putting the argument into **standard form**. If our main concern is whether or not the conclusion of the argument is **true**, then our reconstruction should be guided by the **principle of charity**: we should aim for the best possible reconstruction of the argument.

In order to do this, we need precise concepts in terms of which to assess arguments. We need, to begin with, the concepts of **truth**, **deductive validity**, and **deductive soundness**. A deductively valid argument (a **valid** argument for short) is one whose premises could not possibly be true without the conclusion being true also. A deductively sound argument is a valid argument with true premises. It follows that a deductively sound argument must have a true conclusion.

The conclusion of one argument may serve as a premise for another. We call such a conclusion an **intermediate conclusion** for an **extended argument**.

Individual propositions can be true or false, but not valid or invalid. Arguments can be valid or invalid, but not true or false. **Conditional propositions** are not arguments, but single propositions: a conditional proposition is a single proposition made up of two propositions, the **antecedent** and **consequent**. Typically the antecedent and consequent of a conditional proposition are joined by 'if–then', but many other devices can do the same job. The crucial thing is the logical relationship between them.

Arguments do stand in a certain relationship to conditional propositions. If the argument is valid, then this conditional proposition is true: *if* the argument's premises are true, *then* its conclusion is true.

It is sometimes useful to employ 'dummy' letters in place of sentences, names or general terms in order to display the **logical form** of an argument; this is the first step towards the study of formal logic. From the formal point of view, the definition of validity is: an argument is valid if (and only if) its logical form is valid. A logical form is valid if (and only if) there is no instance of that form with true premises and a false conclusion (not even if we are allowed to change the meanings of the non-logical expressions contained in an instance). For our purposes the most useful implication of this is that if a given argument has the same form as another argument with the same form, the given argument is invalid. Showing invalidity in this way is called **refutation by counterexample**.

EXERCISES

1 Study the section that describes the principle of charity. Then, without looking at the section again, and in your own words, write a short essay of about 250 words that explains the principle, and why it should be observed.

2 Suppose that someone says: 'The purpose of argument is to defeat the opponent.' Write a short essay (about 250 words) commenting on this.

3 Again, without consulting the book, and in your own words, explain the purpose of argument-reconstruction. Try to invoke some of the concepts you have learned in this chapter, such as validity.

4 Suppose that Mr Smith argues as follows:

Mr Jones argues that the unemployment rate will rise this year. However, as we have explained, Mr Jones' argument is clearly invalid. Furthermore, we have shown that the premises of the argument are false. Therefore, Mr Jones is wrong. The unemployment rate will not rise this year.

Criticise Mr Smith's argument.

5 Suppose that Bob says:

Sarah is so arrogant. She's entitled to her opinions, of course. I don't mind her *saying* that landlords have an ancient right to prevent walkers' access to their property. That's her opinion. But she has to say it's *true*. I hate that. She always thinks she's right. She always thinks *her* opinion is *the* truth.

Does Bob have a point, or is he confused? Explain your answer an essay of about 150 words.

6   For each argument, decide whether or not it is deductively valid. If it is not valid, briefly explain why. If it seems useful, describe a possible situation in which the premises are true, but the conclusion false.

Example

P1)   Every Roman emperor before Constantine was a pagan.

P2)   Julian was a Roman emperor.

C)   Julian was a pagan.

✎   Invalid. P2 says that Julian was a Roman emperor, but not that he ruled before Constantine. It would be possible for the premises to be true but the conclusion false, then, if Julian were a non-pagan Roman emperor after Constantine.

a   P1)   Either Jane is in the kitchen, or Mary is in the kitchen.

     P2)   Jane is not in the kitchen.

C)   Mary is in the kitchen.

b   P1)   Either inflation will increase, or personal debt will increase.

     P2)   If the central bank does not increase interest rates, inflation will not increase.

     P3)   The central bank will not increase interest rates.

C)   Personal debt will increase.

c   P1)   If the guerrillas have left the area, then there is traffic on the roads.

     P2)   There is no traffic on the roads.

C)   The guerrillas have not left the area.

d   P1)   No member of the Green Party voted for the tax cut.

     P2)   Mr Jacobs did not vote for the tax cut.

C)   Mr Jacobs is a member of the Green Party.

e   P1)   No member of the Green Party voted for the tax cut.

     P2)   Mr Jacobs voted for the tax cut.

C)   Mr Jacobs is not a member of the Green Party.

Logic: deductive validity

f   P1)   Every member of the Conservative Party voted for the tax cut.

       P2)   Mr Winterbottom voted for the tax cut.

       C)   **Mr Winterbottom is a member of the Conservative Party.**

g   P1)   Some members of the Liberal Party voted for the tax cut.

       P2)   Some who voted for the tax cut voted for new defence spending.

       C)   **Some members of the Liberal Party voted for new defence spending.**

h   P1)   If abortion is morally permissible, then infanticide is morally permissible.

       C)   **Abortion is not morally permissible.**

i   P1)   If abortion is not murder, then infanticide is not murder.

       P2)   If infanticide is not murder, then killing innocent children is not murder.

       P3)   Killing innocent children is murder.

       C)   **Abortion is murder.**

j   P1)   If each person has the right to determine what happens to his or her own body, then suicide should be legal.

       P2)   Suicide should not be legal.

       C)   **No person has the right to determine what happens to his or her own body.**

k   P1)   Every regime is either corrupt or inefficient.

       P2)   The Soviet regime was inefficient.

       C)   **The Soviet regime was not corrupt.**

l   P1)   If there is no blown resistor, then there is failed connection.

       P2)   There is a blown resistor.

       C)   **There is no failed connection.**

m   P1)   Constantine ruled Rome before Constantius.

       P2)   Constantius ruled Rome before Julian.

       C)   **Constantine ruled Rome before Julian.**

n P1) Only democracies are just political systems.
   P2) Rome's political system was unjust.
   _____
   C)   Rome's political system was not a democracy.

o P1) The only just political systems are democracies.
   P2) Rome's political system was unjust.
   _____
   C)   Rome's political system was not a democracy.

p P1) Unless some historians have told lies, there were miracles
        during the first century.
   P2) There were no miracles during the first century.
   _____
   C)   Some historians have told lies.

q P1) Analysis has shown that Mr Cleever's accident was caused by
        faulty brakes, not by drunk driving.
   P2) If Mr Cleever was not drunk at the time of the accident, then
        he should be acquitted of drunk driving.
   _____
   C)   Mr Cleever should be acquitted of drunk driving.

r P1) If Constantius' professed Christianity was genuine, then history
        has represented him unfairly.
   P2) There is no convincing evidence that Constantius' professed
        Christianity was *not* genuine.
   _____
   C)   History has represented Constantius unfairly.

s P1) If Germanicus had not died at the German front, he would
        have become emperor.
   P2) If Germanicus had become emperor, then Tiberius would not
        have become emperor.
   P3) If Tiberius had not become emperor, then Caligula would not
        have become emperor.
   P4) If Caligula had not become emperor, then he would not have
        been murdered.
   P5) If Caligula had not been murdered, then Claudius would not
        have become emperor.
   _____
   **C)   If Germanicus had not died at the German front, then
        Claudius would not have become emperor.**

Logic: deductive validity

t   P1) If any Roman emperor was wise, then Marcus Aurelius was wise.
    P2) Augustus was a Roman emperor.
    P3) If Augustus was wise, then Marcus Aurelius was not wise.

C) **Marcus Aurelius was wise.**

u   P1) If any Roman emperor was wise, then Marcus Aurelius was wise.
    P2) Augustus was a Roman emperor.
    P3) If Augustus was wise, then Marcus Aurelius was not wise.

C) **Augustus was not wise.**

v   P1) If John or Susan are late, then Mary will be disappointed.
    P2) John is late.
    P3) Susan is late.

C) **Mary will be disappointed.**

w   P1) If John and Susan are late, then Mary will be disappointed.
    P2) John is late.

C) **Mary will be disappointed.**

x   P1) If John and Susan are late, then Mary will be disappointed.
    P2) John is late.
    P3) Susan is not late.

C) **Mary will not be disappointed.**

y   P1) If John and Susan are married, then Mary will be disappointed.
    P2) John is married.
    P3) Susan is married.

C) **Mary will be disappointed.**

z   P1) If the Prime Minister does what the opinion polls say the people want, then he is cowardly.
    P2) If the Prime Minister does not do what the opinion polls say the people want, then he is arrogant.

C) **If the Prime Minister is not arrogant, then he is cowardly.**

7 Which of the following statements are true, and which false?

a It is impossible for all the premises of a valid argument to be false.

b It is possible for the conclusion of a valid argument to be false.

c It is possible for a deductively sound argument to have a false conclusion.

d A valid argument cannot have all true premises and a false conclusion.

e A valid argument cannot have all false premises and a true conclusion.

f It is impossible for all the premises of a valid argument to be true, if the conclusion is false.

g A valid argument must have true premises.

h If the conclusion of a valid argument is false, then all the premises must be false.

i If an argument has more than one premise, then if one of the premises is true, then the others must also be true.

j If a valid argument is sound, then one of its premises must be false.

k A sound argument cannot have a false premise.

l An argument cannot be both valid and sound.

m If an argument has true premises and a true conclusion, then it is valid.

n If an argument does not have all true premises and a false conclusion, then it is valid.

o An argument may have all true premises and a false conclusion.

p If a valid argument has a false conclusion, then all its premises must be false.

q If a valid argument has a false conclusion, the at least one of its premises must be false.

8 In Exercise 7, a–f, various scenarios are said to be possible or impossible. In cases where the thing is possible, give an example.

9 Rewrite the following sentences using 'if–then' and 'not', in order to express the same relation between propositions. Sometimes you may have to remove, rather than insert, a 'not'.

a Either Trajan was great or Hadrian was great.

b Dogs are loyal to their masters unless they are mistreated.

c   Unless there were no benevolent emperors, Marcus Aurelius was a benevolent emperor.

d   You will not pass unless you study.

e   My dog will get the ball unless your dog gets the ball.

f   You will be admitted only if you are wearing a tie.

g   You will not be admitted if you are not wearing a tie.

h   My dog barks only if your dog barks.

i   You will pass only if you do not drink every night.

j   You will pass only if you study.

k   You will only pass if you study.

l   The champion will win only if he fights aggressively.

m   Either your dog will get the ball or mine will, unless the ball goes in the water.

n   Galerius and Maximin were not both admired in Rome.

10 Can there be more than one deductively sound argument for the same conclusion? If so, give an example. If not, explain why not.

11 Consider the following two sentences:

Lee Harvey Oswald murdered John Kennedy.
Lee Harvey Oswald did not murder John Kennedy.

Suppose we have two arguments, one with the first as conclusion and the other with second as conclusion. Could both arguments be valid? Could both arguments be deductively sound? Why or why not?

12 Using the 'dummy' letters 'P', 'Q', 'R' and so on to stand in for sentences such as 'Your dog barks' and 'Trajan was great', rewrite the sentences in Exercise 9. Then rewrite your answers in the same way, writing them next to the corresponding original sentence.

   Example

   a   Either Trajan was great or Hadrian was great.

   ✎ **Either P or Q. If not-P, then Q.**

13 Using the 'dummy' letters 'P', 'Q' and 'R' and so on for whole sentences, 'F' and 'G' for general terms, and 'x' and 'y' for names, try to construct argument-forms corresponding to the following problems in Exercise 6: a, b, f–j, p–w.

Example

P1)   Only fools are drug-users.
P2)   Ross Lambeau is a drug-user.

C)   **Ross Lambeau is a fool.**

✎   P1)   Only F are G.
      P2)   x is a G.

   C)   **x is an F.**

14 Draw tree-diagrams for the 'further examples', p. 56. Consider the diagrams for arguments with two premises. What do they have in common? Can you explain why?

Chapter 3

Logic: inductive force

Inductive force

Consider this argument:

P1) Fiona lives in Inverness.

_____

C) **Fiona owns at least one item of woollen clothing.**

Is this argument valid? You might think so. Inverness is a pretty cold place. And wool is plentiful: Scotland has millions of sheep. So surely you may conclude that Fiona must have a woollen jumper or two. Nevertheless, the argument is clearly invalid: it would not be *impossible* for someone to live in Inverness, yet not have any woollen items of clothing. Indeed, there probably are people there without any (some people are allergic to wool, for example).

We could make the argument valid by adding the premise, 'Everyone in Inverness owns at least one woollen item of clothing'. Thus:

P1) Fiona lives in Inverness.
P2) Everyone in Inverness owns at least one woollen item of clothing.

___

C)   Fiona owns at least one woollen item of clothing.

But this argument, though valid, is probably not sound, since P2 is probably false. Yet the original argument is surely a good argument, in some sense. The truth of the premise would be a good reason for expecting the conclusion to be true; it would be surprising to find it was false. Certainly if you had to bet on whether or not the conclusion is true, then, given no relevant information except for P1, you would bet that it is true, not that it is false. It would be reasonable to infer the truth of C from P1, and unreasonable to infer its falsity.

However, we must notice something very important about the inference from P1 to C. A logician would not be in a position to recognise the forcefulness of this argument as we have written it so far. For in order to recognise it, one has to know certain facts about Inverness – the facts that make it different from, say, a hot place around which they grow cotton such as Cairo. Someone giving the argument is implicitly relying on a proposition that is similar to P2 in the argument given directly above, but that is much more likely to be true – namely, that the vast majority of people in Inverness own some items of woollen clothing. Almost no one owns none. That is to say, the use of the quantifier 'everyone' would be inappropriate here, but use of the weaker quantifier 'almost everyone' is appropriate. Given what we know about Inverness, we can be almost completely certain that almost everyone in Inverness owns at least one woollen item of clothing. (Recall from Chapter 1 that expressions such as 'most', 'almost all' and 'few' are called 'quantifiers'.) We can represent the argument, then, as follows:

P1) Fiona lives in Inverness.
P2) Almost everyone in Inverness owns at least one item of woollen clothing.

___

C)   Fiona owns at least one woollen item of clothing.

This argument is still not *deductively valid*, since Fiona still might conceivably be one of those few who do not have any woollen clothing. Still, these premises, just by themselves, do provide a good reason for accepting the conclusion; the logician, knowing nothing about the matter except the truth of P1 and P2, could happily accept that if the premises are true, then, probably, so is C. We recognise this by calling such an argument **inductively forceful** (the word 'inductively' is meant to contrast with 'deductively'), and inserting the word 'probably', in parentheses, before the conclusion:[1]

P1)   Fiona lives in Inverness.
P2)   Almost everyone in Inverness owns at least one item of woollen clothing.

C)   **(Probably) Fiona owns at least one woollen item of clothing.**

The word 'probably', here, is *not to be regarded as part of C*. It is not, strictly speaking, part of the argument. What it is, rather, is an indication to the reader that the argument has been judged, by the person doing the reconstruction, to be inductively forceful. If we were to remove it from the above reconstruction, the inductive force of the argument, and its status as not being deductively valid, would be unaffected.

Roughly, then, an inductively forceful argument is one that is not deductively valid – the truth of the premises would not ensure the truth of the conclusion – but whose premises provide good reason to expect the conclusion to be true rather than false. Before we characterise the concept of inductive force more accurately, however, it will be useful to look briefly at the more basic concept of **probability**.

Probability

We express the probability that a given proposition is true (or that a given event has occurred or will occur) on a numerical scale between 0 and 1, expressed either as a decimal or as a fraction. For example, the probability that a tossed coin will land heads up is 0.5 or 1/2. Perhaps surprisingly,

---

1   Inductive force is often called *inductive strength*, and sometimes *inductive cogency* or simply *cogency*. The term 'inductive validity' is used by some writers and might have been expected, but it is not usual. The reason is that if 'inductively valid' is used, then 'valid' becomes ambiguous between the inductive and deductive variety, thus spoiling the entrenched and convenient practice of using 'valid' as short for 'deductively valid'.

there are different ways in which to explain probability. We will briefly consider three: **proportion**, **frequency** and **rational expectation**.[2]

First, **proportion**. Many arguments contain a premise that says something like 'Most X are Y' or '7/8 of Xs are Ys'. Such quantifiers as 'most' and '7/8 of' indicate proportions, and are importantly related to probability. Suppose you want to know the probability that the card you have drawn from an ordinary, complete deck of playing cards is an ace. One way to do this would be to assume that this probability is equal to the proportion of aces in the deck to the total number of cards in the deck. Since this figure is 1/13 (there are four aces and fifty-two cards, and 4/52 = 1/13), you assume that probability that you'll draw an ace is 1/13 (about 0.077).

Now **frequency**. Suppose you want to know the probability that it is going to snow in December in London, when December is still several months away. One simple way to do this would be find out how frequently this has actually happened over the past, say, one hundred years. Suppose you find that, out of the past one hundred Decembers, it has snowed during fourteen of them. Then you might infer that the probability that it will snow in London this coming December is 14/100 (0.14).

These strategies are extremely important in the general theory of probability and statistics, but they are not sufficiently general for our purposes. There seem to be cases for which neither proportion nor frequency will serve as a direct indicator of probability. For example, bookmakers sometimes give odds that a given politician will become the next leader of his or her party. Suppose they say that the odds of Mr X becoming the next leader of the Labour Party are 1:1 (i.e. the probability is 1/2). Estimates such as these are often perfectly reasonable. But clearly the bookmaker, in this case, is not basing the probability on the frequency with which Mr X has become leader of the Labour Party in the past; that frequency is zero! Probability-estimates of this kind are sometimes quite reasonable, but there is no immediate and simple recipe for basing them upon frequencies or proportions.[3] In such cases, we cannot simply convert a proportion or a frequency into a probability.

---

2   Another common basis for probability-estimates is the use of models. For example, if an engineer wants to estimate the probability that a new aeroplane design will be stable at very high speeds, he or she might build a real or computer model and test it under simulated conditions; if the model is stable under the simulated conditions, then the engineer might infer that the actual aeroplane is likely to be stable under actual conditions.

3   This is not to say that such estimates cannot be based upon proportions or frequencies. In fact, they typically are: it is precisely the task of those whose profession is to estimate probabilities (in the insurance industry, for example) to base the estimates upon relevant proportions, frequencies and other data. More generally, to say that a degree of

Because of these complications, we shall take **degree of rational expectation** as our general concept of probability.[4] A person's degree of rational expectation in a given proposition is the degree to which he or she is entitled to believe it, given the evidence he or she has. Besides the fact that this concept of probability is more widely applicable than others, it has the further advantage that it corresponds to the way that the word 'probably' is typically used: when we say: 'That's probably true,' we typically mean that our total sum of evidence makes it reasonable to expect the proposition in question to be true.

This can best be appreciated by thinking again of something like cards. Suppose George has a card face down on the table before him; he doesn't know what it is, but he has been correctly informed that it is red. Since George knows that clubs are black, he can be perfectly certain – rationally completely certain – that the card is not a club. So his degree of rational expectation that the card is not a club is 1 (equivalently: his degree of rational expectation that the card is a club is 0). Provided he knows that hearts and diamonds are the only red suits, his degree of rational expectation that the card is a heart is 1/2.

Notice two things about this characterisation of probability in terms of rational expectation. First, it is clear that the basis for assigning degrees of rational expectation may consist in proportions. It is because George knows the relevant proportions that we can assign degrees of rational expectation in this case. In other cases, frequencies provide the basis for assigning degrees of rational expectation. In further cases, we may assign degrees of rational expectation without knowing either relevant proportions or relevant frequencies.

Second, notice that when assigning degrees of rational expectation, we spoke of the degree to which one is entitled to believe something *given such-and-such evidence*. Since we are taking the degree of rational expectation as our concept of probability, what this means can be expressed by saying that our key concept is the concept of **conditional probability**. That is to say, what we are interested in is the probability that a proposition is true,

---

(*Footnote 3 cont.*)   expectation is rational, it seems, is precisely to say that some such statistical facts are available in terms of which the expectation can be justified. However, such justifications often turn out to be extremely complex, and in many cases we seem to know that probability-estimates are well-founded even when we are unable to explain them adequately. Since degree of rational expectation is arguably the most inclusive or general characterisation of probability, our strategy here is to proceed without requiring that probability-claims always be justified in terms of statistics. The science of such justifications – taught in courses in Statistics and Probability Theory – is extremely interesting and of ever increasing importance.

4   There are many terms in the existing literature for this; common ones include 'epistemic probability' and 'rational credence'.

given that, or on the assumption that, some given set of propositions is true. More exactly, this is the degree to which it would be reasonable to accept a certain proposition, given no other relevant information except that contained within a certain set of propositions. In George's case, his evidence is that the card is red (along with the fact that exactly half the red cards are hearts). So the conditional probability of the proposition the card is a heart, relative to the proposition the card is red, is 1/2.

We can now say more precisely what an inductively forceful argument is:

Let [P] stand for one or more premises, and let A stand for a conclusion. Suppose we have an argument:

[P] . . .

_____

C) A

To say that such an argument is **inductively forceful** is to say that the conditional probability of A relative to the set [P] is greater than one-half, but less than 1. (The *degree of inductive force* of an argument is the conditional probability of A relative to [P].)

This is our 'official' explanation, but you may find it more helpful to think of inductive force along the lines of the following:

To say that an argument is **inductively forceful** is to say: The argument is not deductively valid, but, if the premises are true (or were true), then, given no information about the subject-matter of the argument except that contained in the premises, it would be more reasonable to expect the conclusion to be true than it would to expect it to be false.

Or we can say: relative to the information contained in the premises [P], the conclusion is more likely to be true than false. There are several further points to bear in mind as regards probability and inductive force.

1 It is true that we do not always express probabilities as conditional probabilities. For example, if we simply pick a card at random from the deck, it seems we can say outright that the chance of its being an ace is 1/13. So, it seems we do ordinarily attribute probability to a single proposition without stopping to specify any further information. Usually, however, this is only because the relevant further information upon which the probability-claim is based is left implicit; it is sufficiently well known such that we don't have to mention it explicitly. In this case, the relevant information that one would normally take for granted is that the deck is standard and complete, in which case four of its fifty-two cards are aces. Thus, given the information that the deck is standard and complete, it would be reasonable for you to conclude that the card is probably not an ace. But, so long as it is kept in mind that there must be a relevant set of information or some premises in the picture, it is perfectly harmless to attribute probability to single propositions, and we will sometimes do so.

2   Probability of the kind that we are speaking of is not an *alternative* to truth or falsity in the way that finishing in the middle of the league table is an alternative to finishing at the top or at the bottom. Nor is probability a *kind* of truth. To say that a proposition is probable, in this sense, is to say that it is most likely true. It is to express an expectation, which falls short of perfect certainty, that a proposition is correct. What one says is true, if the evidence upon which the claim is based really does make the expectation rational. The idea is not that there is some third thing between truth and falsity, namely probability. For example, if I know that Reggie has taken his driving test today, and I say 'Probably, Reggie failed his driving test', I am not saying 'It isn't true that Reggie failed his driving test, and it isn't false; it's probable that he failed it'. No: either it is true that Reggie failed his driving test or it is false. That is, there are two possible states of affairs: either he failed the test or he did not. There is no mysterious third state of affairs, i.e. that he *probably* failed it. Rather, the function of the word 'probably' is to indicate that the evidence makes it rational to believe, but does not make it certain, that the proposition is true.

3   Unlike truth, probability is a matter of degree; different propositions may have various degrees of probability (relative to a given body of information). For example, given the information we have, it is very highly probable that in the year 863 BC, someone ate a rabbit. But there is a very tiny possibility that no one did. It is somewhat less probable, but still probable, that someone will swim the English Channel during the year 2046. It is possible, but *im*probable, that someone swam the English Channel in the year 863 BC. We do sometimes specify probabilities in terms of numerical values, but often the probability of something being the case cannot be estimated with enough precision to justify assigning an exact numerical value. Sometimes the most we can do is to *rank* probabilities; for example, we can say with confidence that a certain man is more likely to eat a cucumber than he is to visit Japan during the coming year, but we cannot assign precise numerical probabilities to these propositions in the way that we can with the cards. And sometimes we cannot even rank them with confidence. Of single propositions, the most we can say in such cases is, 'that's probable', or 'that's very probable', or 'that's improbable'. (By 'probable', remember, we mean the case in which the probability is greater than 1/2; by 'improbable' mean the case in which it is less than 1/2; something can be neither probable nor improbable, if its probability is exactly 1/2.)

Because of this, inductive force, unlike deductive validity, is also a matter of degree. We cannot say that one argument is more valid than another, but we can say that one argument is more inductively forceful than another. Validity was defined in terms of impossibility, in which case the probability is zero (look at the definition of validity again). Validity is thus all-or-nothing. Indeed, one could define validity simply as the 'limiting case' of inductive force – the case in which the conditional probability of the conclusion relative to the premises is 1. Thus we can think of arguments as being arranged on a scale of conditional probability, ranging from deductively valid to a complete lack of inductive force (see Figure 3.1).

Because we defined inductive force in the way that we did, an argument may be inductively forceful but only to a very small degree. For example, if you know that fifteen of the twenty-nine children in the class are wearing white shoes, then you have an inductively forceful argument for the conclusion that the child who got the highest mark in spelling is wearing white shoes. But the probability of that conclusion, relative to the premise, is only slightly better than 1/2; so the argument is just barely inductively forceful. It is inductively forceful, but only to a low degree.

4 As ordinarily used, the term 'probably' is somewhat vague. Usually, when we say something like 'David will probably win the match', we don't just mean the probability of his winning is greater than 1/2; we mean it is substantially higher than that. But exactly how much higher must it be, if it is to be appropriate to say 'probably'? Of course, there is no exact answer. The person saying this *may* be willing to give a more precise figure, but they needn't in order to be entitled to use the word 'probably'. In fact, there is good reason to maintain that the use of "probably" *is* appropriate if, and only if, the intended probability exceeds 1/2. If you are asked 'Is David going to win?', and you think his chances are better than 50–50 but only just, it *is* appropriate to say 'probably' – but in doing so, you would normally use a hesitating tone of voice to convey that you put the probability at only just over the 50–50 threshold.

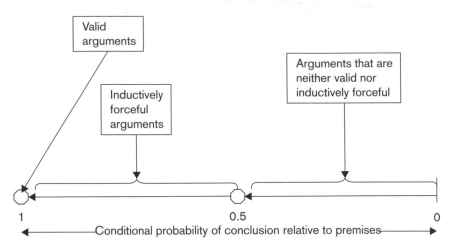

Figure 3.1 Arguments on a scale of conditional probability

What is very likely is that ordinary uses of 'probably' *mean* a probability of greater than 1/2, but typically carry a *conversational implicature* that the probability substantially exceeds that threshold (see Chapter 1, pp. 9–10 for discussion of conversational implicature). We can cancel the implicature through tone of voice.

Exactly the same point goes for the quantifier 'most'. If someone were to make an accusation by saying 'Most students cheated on the exam', they would probably intend to convey that substantially more than half of them cheated, not just a bare majority. Nevertheless, if were to turn out that 15 of the 29 students in the class cheated, the accuser might be surprised, but would not thereby be found to have spoken literally falsely. The concept of conversational implicature captures this point perfectly.

For these reasons we define inductive force as conditional probability of premises to conclusion greater than 1/2. Because of this, it is sometimes important to make sure we do not underestimate the inductive force of an argument; if an argument has a *high degree* of inductive force, we should say so, and not pronounce simply that the argument is inductively forceful. When assessing inductive arguments, it is usually important to specify, as accurately as we can, the *degree* of inductive force.

5   Whether or not an argument is deductively valid does not depend on whether anyone *thinks* it is. Likewise, probability, in our sense, is the degree to which it is *rational* or *reasonable* to expect something to be true (given a certain set of premises), irrespective of how likely we actually think it to be. When we claim that an argument is inductively forceful, we are not always correct. We may think that a set of premises (our evidence) makes it reasonable to accept a conclusion, when in fact it is not. Rational expectation concerns what is in fact reasonable, not what any particular person thinks is reasonable.

We can reinforce this point by considering a case in which everyone will agree that rational expectation depends on proportion. Suppose that Fiona is asked to pick a card at random. Her chance of getting, say, a heart, is exactly one in four. Her chance of not getting a heart, then, is three in four, or 3/4. So she will probably not get a heart. If she is perfectly rational and well-informed, she will be 3/4 certain that she won't get a heart. Suppose, however, that Fiona is not perfectly rational. She thinks that since she has recently fallen in love, she probably will choose a heart. She might express her thinking so by saying, 'I'll probably choose a heart'. Nevertheless, the probability that she will not choose a heart is greater – indeed three times as great – as the probability that she will. Fiona's actual degree of expectation is higher than the degree of rational expectation. More generally, we can observe that different people, going on the same set of premises, can have different degrees of expectation that something is or will be true; but there is only one correct answer as to how reasonable it is to infer the conclusion from the premises.

6   Like the validity or invalidity of an argument, the degree of inductive force of an argument is independent of the truth-values of the premises. This can be seen most easily in the case of a completely fictional example, in which the question of the truth-values of the premises cannot even arise:

P1)   Almost all Zormons play chess.
P2)   Trozak is a Zormon.

_____

C)   **(Probably) Trozak plays chess.**

Of course this is not even a real argument, since there are no such beings as Zormons, and no such being as Trozak. Nevertheless, if there were, then this certainly would be an inductively forceful argument: if there were a being named 'Trozak' who was a member of some class of beings called 'Zormons', and P1 were true, then it would be reasonable to infer C if P1 and P2 were all one had to go on. If you did not know whether or not these beings exist, you would still be right to say that if this did express a real argument, it would be inductively forceful. Whether or not there is such a being as Trozak or such beings as Zormons, and whether or not P1 is true, are thus irrelevant to the estimate of inductive force.

7   The same point goes for conclusions; estimates of inductive force should not be affected by information relevant to the truth-value of the conclusion, except for that given in the premises. Consider this argument:

P1)   Sweden is a Scandinavian country.
P2)   At least one Scandinavian country exports cars.

C)   **Sweden exports cars.**

Almost everyone knows that Sweden – home of Volvo and Saab – exports cars. Furthermore, both premises of this argument are true. However, it is clearly not an inductively forceful argument. If the only propositions you knew relevant to the conclusion were P1 and P2, then you would be wrong to think that C is probably true.

'All', 'most' and 'some'

To say that all rodents have tails is the same as saying: 'Every rodent has a tail', or 'Any rodent has a tail', or 'No rodent has no tail'. To say that most rodents have tails is to say that more than half of all rodents have tails, or that there are more rodents with tails than there are without them. But what about 'Some rodents have tails'? What proportion of rodents must have tails for that to be true? In fact, that is a bad question. Such a statement does not tell you what proportion of rodents have tails. Consider this argument:

P1)   Some patients who have been treated with X have developed liver disease.

C)   **If I am treated with X then I will develop liver disease.**

This argument is not inductively forceful. P1 could be true even if, say, three patients developed liver disease upon being treated with X, yet thousands were treated with X without developing liver disease.

That much should be fairly obvious. But the word 'some', as ordinarily used, can be rather tricky. Often, when we actually say something of the form 'Some A are B' (such as P1), we say it when we believe that more than one A is B, but that not all A are B. Often when using the word this way, we say, 'Only some A are B'. Other times, we say it when we believe that more than one A is B, but do not know whether or not all A are B. For example, a medical researcher who discovers a few patients that have developed liver disease after being treated with X might use the sentence P1 to announce the discovery – but this would be to leave open the possibility that perhaps all patients treated with X develop liver disease. He would not be ruling it out.

For the purpose of reconstructing arguments it is most convenient to assume the latter understanding of 'some', whereby 'some A are B' does not rule out that all A are B. It does not say 'Some, but not all, A are B'. In this sense, 'Some A are B' means 'Some, perhaps all, A are B'.

Further, when using 'some' in our argument-reconstructions, we will take it to mean 'at least one'. That is: if only one A is B, then it will be true that some A are B. On this understanding of 'some', what 'Some rodents have tails' means is simply that it is not the case that *no* rodents have tails. Similarly, 'Some rodents do not have tails' means the same as 'Not all rodents have tails'. This departs slightly from what ordinary language typically suggests, but it is much more convenient for our purposes. If, when reconstructing an argument, it is clear that by 'some' the arguer means 'at least two', then we can simply make this explicit in the reconstruction, writing 'at least two'.

Soft generalisations: a reminder

It is worth re-stressing a point introduced in Chapter 1 (pp. 34–5), namely that in reconstructing arguments with generalisations, we should always supply missing quantifiers. We often run across arguments like this:

> The Government's policy is based on the claim that violent offenders re-offend. I resent and refute this claim utterly. My nephew was imprisoned in his late teens on an armed robbery conviction but unlike a lot of these wasters he thoroughly sorted himself out; he's now been married with a steady job for many years and there is no way he's going to commit a crime again.

The arguer seems to argue that the generalisation 'violent offenders re-offend' is refuted by the existence of a violent offender who has not re-offended. And of course this argument would be valid:

P1) My nephew is violent offender who has not re-offended and will not.

C) **Not all violent offenders re-offend.**

But it's very unlikely that the Government asserted that *all* violent offenders re-offend. More likely, they asserted that *most* do, or that the frequency of violent offending among those who have already committed a violent crime is significantly higher than it is among those who have not, or some such thing. If so, then the single example of the arguer's nephew does little or nothing to undermine the Government's claim.

Inductive soundness

You can probably guess what this is, by analogy with the definition of deductive soundness:

> To say that an argument is ***inductively sound*** is to say: It is inductively forceful and its premises are (actually) true.

The important thing to note here is that an inductively sound argument, unlike a deductively sound argument, *may have a false conclusion*. That possibility is precisely what is left open by the definition of inductive force – an inductively forceful argument is the case where the truth of the premises makes the truth of the conclusion probable, but does not guarantee it. Look again at the last argument given concerning Fiona, who lives in Inverness. Suppose it is true that Fiona lives in Inverness, and that almost everyone there has some woollen garments. An argument with those two facts as premises, and that Fiona has at least one woollen garment as a conclusion, would be inductively sound – even if, as it happens, Fiona has no woollen garments.

Note that we have not said that one should always be *convinced* by inductively sound arguments. You could know that an argument is inductively sound, but also know, for independent reasons, that the conclusion is false (review the discussion of inductive soundness if this is surprising). We will return to this point in Chapter 6.

Probability in the premises

So far in this chapter we have mostly considered premises expressing proportions, such as 'Most Zormons plays chess'. Proportions are expressed using quantifiers such as 'most', '95 per cent of', and the like. But consider this case:

P1) If Napoleon is not ill then the French will attack.
P2) Probably, Napoleon is not ill.

C1) (Probably) The French will attack.

This argument is inductively forceful, but it does not contain any quantifiers. The reason that the truth of the premises would not guarantee that the French will attack, of course, is the presence of the word 'probably' in P2; it is only said to be probable that Napoleon is not ill. (We would get the same result if in place of P2 we wrote 'Napoleon is probably not ill', or 'It is unlikely that Napoleon is ill', or some other sentence synonymous with P2 as written.)

Note that words such as 'probably' can also occur in the antecedents and consequents of conditionals. For example:

P1)   If Napoleon is not ill then, probably, the French will attack.
P2)   Napoleon is not ill,

C1)   (Probably) The French will attack.

This too is an inductively forceful argument.[5]

Arguments with multiple probabilistic premises

Sometimes, probabilistic elements can occur in more than one premise. Assessing such arguments can be tricky. For example, we may have the following sort of case:

P1)   Most people in Glasgow live in council housing.
P2)   Most council housing is substandard.

C)   Most people in Glasgow live in substandard housing.

Note that the argument tree for this is as shown in Figure 3.2 (see over).

This argument is not inductively forceful. Strictly speaking, 'most' guarantees only that the statement is true for more than half of the given group. The premises could well be true, then, in the following circumstances: slightly more than half the residents of Glasgow live in council

---

5   Some readers may wonder why we enclose the word 'probably' in parentheses before the conclusion of an inductive argument, but do not enclose it in parentheses when it occurs in a premise or as the consequent of a conditional conclusion. The reason is somewhat complicated, but what it boils down to is that we want to preserve the simple and common-sense contrast between deductive and inductive arguments, according to which the inductive case is that where the premises provide good but not water-tight reasons to accept the conclusion. Thus when we write '(Probably) such-and-such' beneath the inference bar, the conclusion is 'such-and-such', not '(Probably) such-and-such'. If the probability-indicator were regarded as part of the conclusion, then the distinction between deductive and inductive arguments becomes more complicated, and less intuitive.

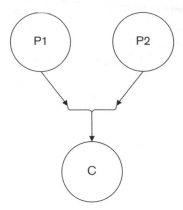

Figure 3.2

housing; slightly more than half the council housing units in Glasgow are substandard, yet no other housing in Glasgow is substandard. If that were so, then the proportion of substandard housing in Glasgow would be slightly more than half of slightly more than half the total housing units in Glasgow. Since half of a half is $1/2 \times 1/2 = 1/4$, this means that, in these circumstances, the proportion of housing units in Glasgow that are substandard would be a little bit more than $1/4$. Of course, if a much greater majority in Glasgow lived in council housing, and a sufficiently high proportion of it were substandard, then an inductively sound argument along these lines could be constructed.[6] It is important, in such cases, to determine whether or not the proportions indicated by 'most' are sufficient for the purpose of the argument.

The same sort of thing applies when a word such as 'probably' occurs more than once in the premises. Here is a somewhat more difficult case involving an explicitly conditional probability:

P1) Edna will probably come to the party.
P2) If Edna comes to the party, then probably she'll get drunk.

C) Edna will get drunk.

Is this argument inductively forceful? Not as written. All that is required for something to be probable is that its probability be greater than $1/2$. Suppose, then, that the chance of Edna coming to the party is exactly

---

6   Of course, these premises are not true.

0.6 (6 in 10) and that if she were to come to the party, then the chance of her getting drunk would be 0.6. Then the premises of the above argument would be true. But the conclusion would not thereby be probable. It might be that if she does not come to the party then she certainly will not get drunk, in which case the probability of her getting drunk will be 6/10 of 6/10, thus 36/100 or 0.36. Of course, if the probability of Edna's coming to the party were higher, or the likelihood of her getting drunk if she did were higher, or both, then the probability of her getting drunk would be higher. And as we noted earlier, someone using the word 'probably' might well have a higher probability in mind. If we were to replace both occurences of 'probably' with something like 'It is highly likely that', then it would be reasonable to interpret the argument as inductively forceful, perhaps even as very inductively forceful.

Some arguments contain a premise with a word like 'probably' and a premise with a quantifier such as 'most':

P1)　Probably, James will gain a science degree.
P2)　Most people with science degrees earn better-than-average salaries.

___

C)　James will earn a better-than-average salary.

Once again, this argument is not inductively forceful. However, if the argument were changed so as to indicate a sufficiently high probability of James' gaining a science degree, and/or to indicate a sufficiently high proportion of science degree-earners earning better-than-average salaries, then the argument would be inductively forceful. Of course the argument becomes inductively forceful if the word 'probably' is simply deleted from P1. It would also be inductively forceful if the word 'most' in P2 were changed to 'all'; but it would not be inductively sound, since P2 would be false. Not everyone with a science degree earns a better-than-average salary.

Another tricky situation that sometimes arises is illustrated by the following:

P1)　Nine out of ten Green Party members are vegetarians.
P2)　Only one in ten non-Green Party members are vegetarians.
P3)　Alastair is a vegetarian.

___

C)　Alastair is a Green Party member.

It is tempting to think that this argument is inductively forceful; you might reason: very few outside the Green Party are vegetarians, and almost all Green Party members are vegetarians; so surely if Alastair is a vegetarian, then mostly likely he's a Green Party member. But this would be a mistake (the mistake is known as the 'base rate fallacy'; see the discussion in Chapter 4, pp. 130–1). In fact, even if P1 said that *all* Green Party members are vegetarians, the inference would be mistaken. For suppose that only one out of every 101 people (in the UK, for example) is a member of the Green Party. If the remaining (non-Green) population is 10 per cent vegetarian, then, since every Green is vegetarian, eleven out of every 101 people are vegetarian. But only *one* of those eleven is a Green. Thus ten out of every 101 people are non-Green vegetarians, and the non-Green vegetarians outnumber the Green vegetarians by ten to one! So if you meet a vegetarian such as Alastair, then, unless you had other reasons to think he is a Green, the reasonable expectation would be that he is *not* a Green. Summing up, then, the premises do not give you a good reason to think that Alastair is a Green.

The problem is that the premises seem to tell us that if someone is a vegetarian, then, probably, they are a Green. But they do not. Similarly: all plumbers own pipe wrenches, and few non-plumbers own them; but these facts do not entitle us to say that if someone owns a pipe wrench, then probably, they are a plumber. As a matter of fact, many DIYers own pipe wrenches. And there are a lot more DIYers than there are plumbers. So the number of non-plumbers owning pipe wrenches may well outnumber the plumbers.

Inductive force in extended arguments

The conclusion of an inductively forceful argument may serve as a premise for a further argument, which may itself be deductively valid, inductively forceful or neither. However, if any sub-argument of an extended argument is not deductively valid, then the argument as a whole is not deductively valid. At most, it is inductively forceful. Here is a hybrid extended argument that illustrates the point:

P1)   If Napoleon is not ill then the French will attack.
P2)   Probably, Napoleon is not ill.

C1)   (Probably) The French will attack.

P3)   If the French attack, then the Prussians will be routed.

C2)   (Probably) The Prussians will be routed.

If the first argument were valid, entitling us to assert C1 categorically – that is, without the qualifier 'probably' – then since the argument from C1 and P2 to C2 is deductively valid, there would be no need to write 'probably' beneath the second inference bar. As it stands, however, C2 inherits the qualifier 'probably' from its ultimate source in P2. The simplest way to think of this is to think of C2 as a proposition inferred from three premises: P1, P2 and P3. If the word 'probably' were deleted from P2, then that argument would be deductively valid. As it stands, however, that argument is only inductively forceful.

Note that in carrying out the inference from C1 and P3 to C2, we think of that sub-argument just as if it were presented like this:

C1) Probably, the French will attack.

P3)   If the French attack, then the Prussians will be routed.

C2) (Probably) The Prussians will be routed.

That is, we think of it just as if there were no parentheses around the word 'probably' in C1. When the conclusion of an inductively forceful argument is regarded as a premise in a further argument, the parentheses should be ignored.

Conditional probability in the conclusion

Consider the following argument:

> If you start a new internet company, then probably it will fold, or get bought by another company within three years. Most new internet companies do.

The conclusion of this argument is not 'Probably, your new internet company will fold or be bought by another company within three years'. It is, rather, '*If* you start a new internet company, then, probably, it will fold or get bought by another company within three years'. Its conclusion, then, states a conditional probability. We can reconstruct it like this:

P1)   Most new internet companies either fold, or get bought by another company, within three years.

C)   If you start a new internet company, then, probably, it will either fold, or be bought by another company, within three years.

You can see that the inference is correct. But is this argument deductively valid, or only inductively forceful? The presence of the word 'probably' might make it seem that the argument is only inductively forceful, but strictly speaking the argument is deductively valid. The conclusion, it seems, can be asserted on the basis of P1 with perfect confidence; there is no need to insert a 'probably' before the conditional conclusion *as well as* before its consequent.[7] Note, however, that once the new internet company gets started, it would be appropriate to construct an inductively forceful argument from P1 to '(Probably) Your new internet company will fold or be bought by another company within three years'.

Evidence

Arguments presented as being inductively forceful may have several premises. Consider the following:

> The case against Dr X can be summed up as follows. Dr X, a medical doctor, has the knowledge, and had the opportunity, to carry out the type of gradual programme of strychnine poisoning that killed the victim. He had a strong motive for the murder. And finally, Miss Y, a reliable witness, has testified that Dr X expressed to her his wish that the victim were dead.

Let us grant that the case against Dr X is compelling. Here are four facts that seem jointly to condemn Dr X as the murderer. The case does not take the form of a deductively valid argument; it would not be impossible for these facts to be as the arguer says, yet Dr X be innocent. But it is crucial to recognise that the case should not be reconstructed as four separate arguments, each presented as inductively forceful in its own right. The prosecutor's case is based on four premises:

---

7   Note that a conclusion of the form 'If P, then, probably, Q' is quite different from something of the form 'Probably, if P then Q'. In fact in ordinary speech, the latter form is quite unusual, and we never use it in this book. Even when we *say*, for example, 'Probably if Ronaldo plays, he'll score' what we *mean* is 'If Ronaldo plays, then, probably, he will score'. It depends on exactly what the English 'if–then' is taken to mean, but at least on one orthodox reading of it, the probability that a conditional 'If P then Q' is true is much higher than the conditional probability of Q relative to P. Thus 'Probably (If P then Q)' can be true when 'If P, then, probably, Q' is false. For example, if the initial probability of P and Q are both very low, then the former can be true even though P and Q are completely independent, so the conditional probability is low (in which case the latter statement is false).

P1) Dr X has the knowledge to carry out the type of gradual
     programme of strychnine poisoning that killed the victim.
P2) Dr X had the opportunity to carry out the murder.
P3) Dr X had a strong motive for the murder.
P4) Miss Y, a reliable witness, has testified that Dr X expressed to
     her his wish that the victim were dead.

These constitute the evidence against Dr X. But an argument for the conclusion that Dr X murdered the victim based on P1 alone, would not be
inductively forceful. If it were, then the argument would point with equal
force to the guilt of a great many other people with the requisite knowledge of strychnine. Nor would an argument similarly based only upon
P2, P3 or P4. If the prosecutor were to advance any of these four separate arguments by itself, then the jury could only conclude that the
prosecutor lacks a compelling case: none of the arguments would be inductively forceful. It is essential to the prosecutor's case that these four items
of evidence point jointly to the defendant's guilt. We do not have four
arguments like this:

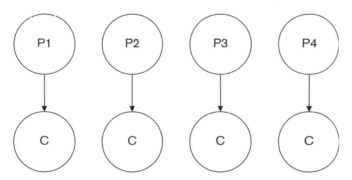

Figure 3.3

But a single argument like this:

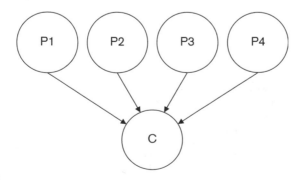

Figure 3.4

The argument, then, should be constructed like this:

P1) Dr X has the knowledge to carry out the type of gradual programme of strychnine poisoning that killed the victim.
P2) Dr X had the opportunity to commit the murder.
P3) Dr X had a strong motive for the murder.
P4) Miss Y, a reliable witness, has testified that Dr X expressed to her his wish that the victim were dead.

C)   (It is highly probable that) Dr X murdered the victim.

This is how it is with items of evidence: if both B and C are evidence for A, the conjunction of B and C is (typically) stronger evidence than B or C alone.[8] Put in terms of arguments, the argument with B and C as

---

8   This holds so long as B and C are *independent*: whether or not B occurs has no bearing on whether or not C occurs, and vice versa. Otherwise the situation is more complicated. The exact meaning of the independence of two events is: B and C are independent if and only if the conditional probability of B given C is equal to the probability of B. When B and C are independent, then some simple, useful relationships hold. First, the probability that event A does *not* happen is always $1 - A$. Then the probability of the *conjunction* of B and C (i.e. both happen) is simply the probability of B multiplied by the probability of C. In symbols: $\Pr(B \text{ and } C) = \Pr(B) \times \Pr(C)$. Then since 'B or C' means the same as 'Not both: not-B and not-C', it follows that the probability of the *disjunction* (B or C) is 1 minus the probability of neither B nor C. In symbols: $\Pr(B \text{ or } C) = 1 - [\Pr(\text{not-B and not-C})]$. The *conditional probability* of B given C is normally written $\Pr(B/C)$, and is defined as the probability of the conjunction (B and C) divided by the probability of C. In symbols:

$$\Pr(B/C) = \frac{\Pr(B \text{ and } C)}{\Pr(C)}$$

A familiar example of a set of possible outcomes that are independent is the case of rolling a die; if the possible outcomes are specified as the six possibilities of rolling a one, a two and so on, then each outcome has no bearing, either logically or causally, on any other. So if you roll it *n* times, you have *n* independent outcomes. A familiar example of a set of possible outcomes that are not independent is the case of drawing cards. What are the chances that the first card you draw from a complete deck is a heart? One in four cards in the deck is a heart, so the chance 0.25. What is the chance that your next card is a heart? It depends, and it is *not* 0.25! If the first card you drew was a heart, then 12 of the remaining 51 cards are hearts, so the probability is about 0.235. If the first card was not a heart, then 13 of the remaining 51 are hearts, so the probability is about 0.255. The outcome of the second draw is not independent of the outcome of the first, and this shows up in the difference between the conditional probability of drawing a heart given that you first drew a heart, and that of drawing a heart given that you first drew a non-heart. This is only scratching the surface of the vast subject of probability and statistics. However, you can learn enough from the most basic textbooks on probability or statistics to equip you to be far more savvy and critical than most people in interpreting and evaluating the sorts of statistical claims made in the media and elsewhere. For example, when the results of polls and surveys are reported, what exactly does 'margin of error' mean, and how can they know what the margin of error is?

premises is more forceful than either the argument with B as a premise or that with C as a premise.

Note also that in this example we have a case where the estimate of inductive force does not appeal to a proportion or a frequency, and does not depend on the presence of a probabilistic premise. The basis for the inference from premises to conclusion is left inexplicit. This does not mean that we could not at least to some degree make it more explicit. For example, we might include the premise that very few people have the kind of knowledge described in P1. But it is not always appropriate to try to do so; for example, the exact ways in which P2–P4 contribute to the argument cannot easily, and probably not very usefully, be spelled out.

Inductive inferences

Consider the following argument:

> So far, every goldfish I've had has died when I fed it cat food.
> Therefore, if I feed my new goldfish cat food, it will die.

This inference seems reasonable, but how do we reconstruct the argument? We might try:

P1   (a) All goldfish die if fed cat food.

C)   **My new goldfish will die if I feed it cat food.**

Or:

P1   (b) Most goldfish die if fed cat food.

C)   **(Probably) My new goldfish will die if I food it cat food.**

The first argument is valid and the second inductively forceful, and perhaps both are sound. But there is a logical problem. The arguer has not asserted either version of P1. What he has asserted is that all the goldfish *to which he has fed cat food* have died. The sample of goldfish with which the arguer has had this experience is only a tiny fraction of the total number of goldfish in the universe. So the arguer has not said anything about all, or most, goldfish. Presumably the arguer does believe either P1(a) or P1(b), but if so, he does so on the basis of his previous experience with goldfish and cat food. Somehow, the arguer must get from the proposition 'Every goldfish I've had has died when I fed it cat food' to 'My new goldfish will die if fed cat food', or even 'Most (or all) goldfish die when fed cat food'. So far, in our discussions of arguments, we have said nothing to help us with this sort of inference.[9]

However, this kind of inference is very common, both in science and in ordinary life. We call it an **inductive inference**. This is our name for the case when you *extrapolate* from a sample of a total population of things either to something outside the sample, or to a generalisation about the population as a whole (so far, we have always gone the other way, either from a generalisation about a whole population to a claim about some smaller sample, or from the whole population to a claim about a single member of it). In the above case, the arguer needs to extrapolate directly from the sample of goldfish they have experimented with to a proposition about the new goldfish:

P1)   Every observed goldfish has died when fed cat food.

C1)   **My new goldfish will die if I feed it cat food.**

If we judge this inference to be inductively forceful – let as assume that it is – then, just as with any inductively forceful argument, we write 'probably', in parentheses, before the conclusion:

P1)   Every observed goldfish has died when fed cat food.

C1)   **(Probably) My new goldfish will die if I feed it cat food.**

Alternatively, the arguer could have obtained this conclusion by a slightly longer route. The arguer might have reached the conclusion by means of an extended argument, comprising an inductive inference to a generalisation about all goldfish, together with a second, deductively valid inference

---

9   As we pointed out, many probabilities can be based upon proportion. One of the tasks of statistical analysis is to show how this is so, even in cases that might initially seem to resist this strategy. Inductive inferences represent a class of cases where proportion certainly cannot be applied straightforwardly. If we know that, say, 74 per cent of the past 956 cases of A have been cases of B, we cannot without further ado assume that the probability that the next case of A will be a case of B is 74 per cent. The next case of A is not among the set of cases for which that proportion is known to have held. So it is not like the case of a card face down on the table, which is drawn from set of cards for which the relevant proportion is known. In the inductive case we have to make the further assumption that probabilities taken from proportions of known cases can be transferred to unknown cases. Of course such inferences do often seem to be rationally justified; the question of why this is so – the 'Problem of Induction' – was first raised by David Hume in his *Treatise of Human Nature* (1739), and remains an open problem.

from that generalisation to the conclusion concerning the arguer's new goldfish:

P1)   Every observed goldfish has died when fed cat food.
_____

C1)   **All goldfish die if fed cat food.**
_____

C2)   **My new goldfish will die if I feed it cat food.**

However, assuming the truth of P1, one could not assert the conclusion here with quite as much confidence as in the first case. We may assert C2 with as much, but no more, confidence than that with which we may assert C1. But since C1 is a generalisation about all goldfish, it stands a greater chance of being false than C1 of the first goldfish-argument – a statement about a single goldfish. The reason is that the second argument depends upon a more ambitious extrapolation than the first, one that is not needed for the desired conclusion. Yet, the inferences to C1 in either case are fundamentally of the same type. They are both extrapolations from observed cases to unobserved cases. Each can be thought of as an extrapolation from a sample to a larger population of which the sample is a part. In the first case we can think of the larger population referred to as comprising the sample (the observed goldfish) plus this one new goldfish. In the second case, obviously, the larger population is simply the total population of goldfish. Some inductive inferences are concerned to make a broad generalisation (all goldfish), others are concerned only to extend to a few new cases, or to a single new case (the new goldfish). But they are fundamentally the same type of inference. Thus we define:

> To say that an inference is an ***inductive inference*** is to say: (a) it is not deductively valid; (b) its premises include a generalisation about a sample of a given population, and (c) its conclusion either extrapolates the generalisation to the total population from which the sample is drawn, or extrapolates it to a single case outside the sample but within the total population.

Requirement (a) is to avoid counting the following sort of inference as inductive: 'Some black cats have no tails; therefore not all cats have tails.'

Inductive inferences frequently extrapolate from past to future. For example, if we infer, from Ireland's never having won the football World Cup, that probably it never will, our sample is all the World Cups that have so far been contested, and the total population is the set of all World Cups – past, present and future.

Often the conclusion of an inductive inference is a statistical gener-alisation such as '37 per cent'. For example, when a pollster finds that 37 per cent of a sample of the adult British population supports a given political party, the pollster might conclude that 37 per cent of the adult British population supports that party. In such a case, the sample is the sample polled, and the total population is the entire adult population of Great Britain. Instead of extrapolating 100 per cent ('all') from sample to total population, we extrapolate the figure 37. How probable this conclu-sion is, however, will depend on how **representative** the sample is. In other words, in order to guess how far the proportion of the total is likely to stray from the figure 37 per cent, we need to know the degree to which the sample typifies the attitudes of the total population. This point requires further attention.

How representative is the sample?

Suppose you live near the North Pole, and every bear you've ever seen is white. So you argue:

P1)   Every observed bear is white.

C)   **All bears are white.**

Formally, this argument is just like the one about the goldfish. But, whereas the goldfish-inference seemed to be correct, this one seems not to be. Only a minority of bears are white (polar bears, and perhaps some albinos of other species). The difference is that, whereas the goldfish-arguer can reasonably assume that the sample of observed goldfish was **representative** of the total population of goldfish, the bear-arguer cannot. That is, the goldfish-arguer can reasonably assume that the sample of goldfish was **relevantly similar** to the total population, but the bear-arguer cannot. Polar bears are only one of many species of bears, and if you know anything about zoology and adaptation, you know that a trait like colour, though somewhat likely to be similar across a single species, is not nearly so likely to be similar across different species, even within the same genus. Further, you can reasonably assume that mammals living in non-snowy regions are much less likely to be white than ones living in perpetual snow (it is advantageous to carnivores to blend visually into the background, so in snowy regions white bears will have a greater chance of survival and procreation, in which case the gene for white fur is more likely to get passed on). Being a different species, which lives in a completely different climate, is certainly a relevant difference when drawing inductive inferences about colour with respect to classes of mammals, even if the species is a closely related one.

How do you know whether a sample is representative of the total population, i.e. relevantly similar to it? There is no simple rule for this, our estimate of relevant similarity must be based upon our knowledge of the subject-matter in question. For example, we drew upon some basic evolutionary biology in criticising the bear-inference. Where such statistical inference as the one mentioned above are concerned, the question is much more complicated, calling for more specialised expertise. A pollster sampling the population for voting preferences must study the many ways in which voting behaviour correlates with factors such as income, geographical location, profession and so on, and then ensure the that polled sample reflects the distribution of these factors in the population as a whole.

Nevertheless, in general, the larger and more representative the sample used for a given generalisation, the more inductively forceful, or the **stronger** the inductive inference. An inductive inference that is not forceful – one whose premise does not really support its conclusion – is a **weak** one. For example, suppose someone argues: 'My brother is a fool. Therefore, probably, all boys are fools.' That is a very weak inductive inference; it is totally unwarranted. The bear-arguer's inference is not quite as bad as that, but it is also very weak. Also, from a given sample, an inference to a generalisation about *most* of the totality is a stronger one than an inference to a generalisation about *all* of the totality, since obviously the latter is less certain.

A programme for assessment

We are now in a position to outline a basic procedure for the assessment of arguments represented in standard form. We first consider arguments that have only one inference (that is, ones that are not extended arguments). When you represent an argument in standard form, do not include the word 'probably', or any similar word, in the conclusion – not yet. Put such words in the premises only. Once you have reconstructed the argument in this way, you should proceed as follows (and you should, looking back at the definitions given in this chapter, stop to see why the chart is arranged as it is):

1   Is the argument deductively valid?
     If not, proceed to 2.
     If yes, are all the premises true?
     If yes, the argument is deductively sound. Stop.
     If not, the argument is valid but unsound. Stop.

2 Is the argument inductively forceful?

If not, the argument is neither valid nor inductively forceful. Stop.

If yes, how forceful is it? Write 'probably', or suitable variant, in the appropriate place in the conclusion. Are the premises true? If yes, the argument is inductively sound. Stop.

If not, the argument is neither deductively nor inductively sound. Stop.

In the case of extended arguments, this procedure is to be carried out first with respect to the sub-arguments whose conclusions are premises of the extended argument. For example, suppose we have an extended argument whose form is like this:

P1) ...
P2) ...

C1) ...

P3) ...

C2) ...

In this case the argument whose conclusion is C1 is a sub-argument for an extended argument whose conclusion is C2. You would first assess the argument from P1 and P2 to C1; you would then assess the argument from C1 and P3 to C2. Finally, you would use these results to assess the total argument from P1, P2 and P3 to C2.

Assessment is to be distinguished from **reconstruction**, which is discussed in more detail in the next chapter. Broadly speaking, assessment may be said to fall into two categories. The first we may call **logical assessment**, which is that whereby we make judgements of deductive validity and inductive force. The second we may call **factual assessment**; here is where we ask after the truth-values of premises, in determining the soundness of arguments already found to be deductively valid or inductively forceful. However, as noted, the evaluation of inductive inferences is not purely independent of matters of fact in the way that judgements of validity are. For example, the evaluation of inductive inferences depends on judgements about how representative a sample is, which requires knowledge of matters of fact.

It is important to realise that if your verdict is that the argument, as you have reconstructed it, is not *de*ductively sound, you might be able to reconstruct it so as to make it *inductively* sound. Look again at the example involving Fiona and wool. An early attempt at reconstructing it used the premise 'Everyone in Inverness owns at least one article of woollen clothing'. So rendered, the argument was valid, but not sound. We then weakened the premise to 'Almost everyone in Inverness owns at least one article of woollen clothing'. The result was not deductively valid, but it was inductively forceful. In general, it is best to sacrifice validity to soundness when reconstructing; an inductively sound argument is more useful than a valid but unsound argument.

Later, we will learn some techniques that aid logical assessment. There is, you will appreciate, no readily definable procedure for factual assessment; for this is simply the task of determining whether particular propositions are true – e.g. whether there are whales in the Black Sea, whether inflation rose in 1993, and so on. For that we must look outside logic books!

CHAPTER SUMMARY

The **conditional probability** of a proposition relative to a set of a premises is the degree to which it would be rational to expect it to be true, given no information relevant to the conclusion except that given in the premises. Estimates of **rational expectation** are often based upon other measures of probability such as **proportion** and **frequency**, but need not be.

A deductively valid argument enables us to be certain of the truth of its conclusion, if we are certain of the truth of its premises. An **inductively forceful** argument does not allow this, but it does allow us, in the absence of other information relevant to the truth-value of the conclusion, to think its conclusion more likely to be true than not: an inductively forceful argument is one for which the conditional probability of the conclusion relative to the premises is greater than 0.5.

Like deductive validity, both probability and inductive force are objective: the conditional probability of a conclusion relative to a given set of premises is independent of people's actual estimates of conditional probability. But unlike deductive validity, both probability and inductive force are a matter of degree. An argument may be inductively forceful but only just barely. It is important to estimate the degree of an argument's inductive force as accurately as the case allows.

> **Inductively sound** arguments are inductively forceful arguments with true premises. Unlike deductively sound arguments, they may have false conclusions.
>
> Some arguments contain **inductive inferences**. An inductive inference is a deductively invalid inference whose premise is a generalisation about some **sample** of a given population, and whose conclusion is a generalisation about the population as a whole, or about a member of the population outside the sample. In general, the force of an inductive inference depends on the degree to which the sample is **representative** of the population.

EXERCISES

1 Each argument below contains at least one premise with a missing quantifier. (A) Reconstruct the argument, adding appropriate quantifiers. Use the strongest quantifiers you can, so long as the resulting premises are what someone giving the argument would have intended (that is, don't use 'most', if it seems that the arguer would have intended *all* or *almost all*, or some such). (B) If the resulting argument is deductively valid, say so. If the argument is inductively forceful, say so, and insert 'probably' before the conclusion.

a   Sex crimes are committed by people who have themselves been victims of child abuse. The defendant has committed a sex crime. Therefore, the defendant was a victim of child abuse.

b   Children love the Harry Potter books. Therefore your child will love the Harry Potter books.

c   If doctors in this country are overworked, then the general health of the population will decline. Doctors in this country are overworked. Therefore, the general health of the population will decline.

d   Old people have poor eyesight. People with poor eyesight should not be allowed to drive. Therefore, old people should not be allowed to drive.

e   In countries colonised by Spain, there are many people of Spanish descent. There are very few people of Spanish descent in Laos. Therefore Laos was not colonised by Spain.

2   Consider the following pair of arguments:

P1)   Most AIDS patients in California are homosexual.
P2)   Mr X is a California AIDS patient.

C)   Mr X is a homosexual.

P1)   Most residents of Orange County, California, are not
        homosexual.
P2)   Mr X is a resident of Orange County, California.

C)   Mr X is not homosexual.

Assume that this is the same Mr X referred to in each argument. (A) Are
these arguments inductively forceful? (B) Could both arguments be inductively sound? If not, explain why not. Otherwise, describe a scenario in
which they would both be sound. (C) If we knew the premises of both
arguments to be true, would we have reason to believe, or not to believe,
that Mr X is homosexual?

3   Statements are incompatible if it is impossible for both of them to be
true (if they are incompatible, it may or may not be possible for both to
be false). Which of the following pairs of statements are incompatible?

a   Some hamsters are black. All hamsters are white.

b   Some hamsters are black. Some hamsters are white.

c   Some hamsters are black. Most hamsters are not black.

d   Some hamsters are black. All hamsters are black.

e   Many hamsters are black. Many hamsters are white.

f   Every hamster is black. This hamster is white.

g   This hamster is black. Some hamsters are white.

h   No hamster is black. No hamster is not black.

i   No hamster is black. No hamster is white.

j   Few hamsters are black. Many black hamsters are small.

k   Most hamsters are black. Many hamsters are white.

l   Most hamsters are black. All my hamsters are white.

m   Most hamsters are black. Every English hamster is white.

4 Reconstruct the following as either three separate arguments or as one, depending on which strategy would amount to a more forceful case. Also draw a tree-diagram for it.

Lewis is probably not going to win another gold medal in the 100 metres. He is now older than any previous winner of the event. His form has been poor this year, and he has a hamstring injury.

5 (A) Reconstruct the following arguments. (B) Say whether or not they are valid or inductively forceful. (C) If the argument is neither valid nor inductively forceful, change or add one premise, or change the conclusion, so that it becomes valid or inductively forceful. There may be more than one reasonable answer. (D) Add any further remarks that seem appropriate to evaluating the argument.

a   If alcohol advertising is banned, then, probably, drinking would decline. If drinking declines, then domestic violence would decline. Therefore, if alcohol advertising is banned, then, probably, domestic violence would decline.

b   If alcohol advertising is banned, then, probably, drinking would decline. If drinking declines, then, probably, domestic violence would decline. Therefore, if alcohol advertising is banned, then, probably, domestic violence would decline.

c   Most children who go without breakfast have trouble concentrating at school in the morning. Johnny concentrates well at school in the morning. Therefore, probably, he does not go without breakfast.

d   If this meat was grown in Scotland, then it is extremely unlikely that it is infected with BSE. And even if it is infected, then it is very unlikely that eating it will make you ill. Therefore, if this meat was grown is Scotland, eating this meat will not make you ill.

e   Brazil is more likely to win the World Cup than Argentina. Therefore, probably, Brazil will win the World Cup.

f   Scotland has never won the World Cup. Therefore, probably, Scotland will never win the World Cup.

g   Probably, English football fans will make trouble at the next World Cup. If English football fans do make trouble at the next World Cup, then England may be expelled from the European Cup. Therefore, it is likely that England will be expelled from the European Cup.

h   If the murderer passed through here, then, probably, there would be hairs from the victim on the rug. But there are no hairs from the victim on the rug. Therefore, the murderer did not pass through here.

i   Very few habitual cannabis users are violent. The murderer is clearly very violent. Mr X is a habitual cannabis user. Therefore, probably, Mr X is not the murderer.

j   UN intervention in local conflicts usually leads to a more stable political situation. A more stable political situation usually leads to economic growth. Therefore, probably, UN intervention in this local conflict will lead to economic growth.

k   Almost all successful athletes have trained long and hard to become successful. Therefore, if you train long and hard, you will become a successful athlete.

l   Many teachers at Lenman secondary school are known to smoke cannabis. Mr X is a teacher at Lenman secondary school. Therefore, probably, Mr X smokes cannabis.

m   Most vegetarians eat eggs. A great many people in Berkeley are vegetarians. Roger is from Berkeley. Therefore, probably, Roger eats eggs.

n   If Hansen is leaving early tomorrow, then, probably, he isn't in the bar. Hansen isn't in the bar. So he is probably leaving early tomorrow.

6   The following passages contain inductive inferences. (A) Rewrite them as arguments in standard form. (You may have to supply a missing quantifier.) (B) Can you think of any reasons why the sample might not be representative? If so, list them.

a   The elimination of sweets and other junk food from school lunch menus has resulted in improved student performance in schools all over the country, and in every case in which it has been tried. If we do this at our school, then, we can look forward to improved performance.

b   No communist system can succeed. Since communist regimes began early in the twentieth century, every one has either collapsed, or is near collapse.

c   Surprisingly, musicians have a higher average IQ than either doctors or lawyers. A study of seventeen conductors of major orchestras found their average IQ to be 17 points higher than that of UK doctors, and 18 points higher than that of UK lawyers.

d   Most teenagers who take illicit drugs have serious family problems. I know, because as a counsellor for teenagers I have found that most of those who have come to me and confessed to taking illicit drugs do have serious family problems.

e Manchester United are an English team that have won the treble once, but they're not going to win it again. No English team has won it twice.

f Studies have shown that people who regularly take vitamins live longer than average. Jenna takes vitamins regularly, so probably she'll live longer than average.

Chapter 4

Rhetorical ploys and fallacies

Sometimes we are moved to accept or reject claims when we have been
given no good grounds for doing so. Often this is because speakers or writers attempt to persuade us in ways that appear to provide good reasons but

that do not really. We'll call these persuasive devices **sham-reasons** and the process of employing them **sham-reasoning**. As critical thinkers we should be alert to the possibility of sham-reasoning, take care to avoid being convinced by arguments that rely upon it, and avoid using sham-reasons in our own attempts to persuade others. We are interested in two types of sham-reasoning: **rhetorical ploys** and **fallacies**. This chapter aims to equip you to distinguish between rhetorical ploys and fallacies, to familiarise you with various common types of sham-reasoning and to develop strategies of reconstruction and evaluation that will enable you to deal with them when analysing, assessing and constructing attempts to persuade.

Neither rhetorical ploys nor fallacies provide us with good reasons to accept the claim they are intended to support. **Fallacies** are **argumentative sham-reasoning**. That is, they are still arguments in the sense that fits our definition of a set of propositions, some of which are premises, one of which is a conclusion, the latter intended to follow from the former. But in one way or another, they are bad arguments. **Rhetorical ploys**, on the other hand, are **non-argumentative sham-reasoning**: some of these persuasive devices may pretend to provide reasons for accepting a claim, but their real persuasive capacity depends on something non-argumentative. Recall our earlier definition of rhetoric as:

Rhetoric
Any verbal or written attempt to persuade someone to believe, desire or do something that does not attempt to give good reasons for the belief, desire or action, but attempts to motivate that belief, desire or action solely through the power of the words used.

The difference between fallacies and rhetorical ploys is understood most easily as a difference in the **function** of the language being employed. As we saw in Chapter 1, politicians, advertisers and newspaper columnists tend to be experts when it comes to using rhetorical ploys. Rhetorical ploys typically make a more or less direct appeal to feeling and emotion rather than to reason, which is the domain of argument. Fallacies, on the other hand, are simply defective attempts at argument (they may be defective in any of various different ways, as explained below). They may fool us into thinking they are not defective, but they are still presented as attempts at argument. Of course, many writers and speakers will use a mixture of rhetorical ploys, fallacies and genuine arguments when attempting to persuade us of the truth of their claim. In fact, it is possible for a given form of words, as advanced by a would-be persuader, to constitute a fallacy, yet, at the same time, function as a rhetorical ploy. For example, the following sort of advertisement is ubiquitous:

More mothers use Namby-pambies for their babies than any other disposable nappy. Shouldn't you?

As we will explain in more detail below, this is an example of the fallacy of **majority belief**; the advertisement wants mothers to accept the argument: X is used by more people than any other product of its kind, therefore X is the best such product. That argument is fallacious because its implicit premise – that the most popular thing is the best, or most popular belief is true – is unjustified. But the advertisement also exemplifies the rhetorical ploy of **appeal to popularity**: the mere fact that something is popular often *causes* us to desire it (possibly by awakening a fear of being left out). The point can be put this way: the detection of fallacies is an exercise in logical and factual assessment; it involves the assessment of reasons. The detection of rhetorical ploys, on the other hand, is an exercise of psychology: we consider ways in which our desires, fears, beliefs and actions could be non-rationally influenced by uses of language which are intended to persuade us to hold beliefs and perform actions.

As critical thinkers, we aim to become adept at distinguishing and identifying these different types of sham-reasoning. We want to understand how they work, and how to avoid being taken in by them. In the next section, we consider specific types of rhetorical ploy and examples thereof. Later we turn to a comprehensive consideration of fallacies.

Rhetorical ploys

Appeals to specific feelings

There is a range of rhetorical ploys that attempt to tap into specific feelings in order to influence our behaviour and opinions (especially our consumer behaviour). Here we discuss a number of the most common. Some of them are not strictly or specifically linguistic ploys, but this will not affect the points we need to make.

Appeal to novelty

Here someone attempts to persuade us to try or buy something because the item is new and, by implication, different from and better than existing related items. Often this ploy appeals to our desire not to miss out on a new trend, or arouses our fear of appearing outdated in our tastes. Sometimes it appeals to our (vain) sense of our selves as flexible and willing to try out new experiences. It may also persuade us that because the product is new, it must be an improved version of the existing product. Familiar examples of the appeal to novelty include the re-naming of the Labour Party as the New Labour Party; advertising that attempts to persuade us to upgrade to frequently newly released, but little-changed or improved computer software packages; and attempts to persuade us to switch to allegedly new and improved washing detergents. The appeal to novelty may also be employed to persuade us to adopt new ideas or beliefs. Again, this appeals to our desire not to appear inflexible or stick-in-the-mud. Thus we might be enjoined to give up a belief in the value of trade union participation on the grounds that trade unionism is 'old-fashioned' and 'has no place in the workplace of the twenty-first century'. Notice that we have been given no reason to reject trade unionism, we are just told that it is 'old-fashioned' and thus, by implication, something undesirable that we wouldn't want to be involved with.

Appeal to popularity

Like the appeal to novelty, this ploy appeals to our desire to run with the crowd, not to appear different from the norm and not to miss out on what others have. Again, it is commonly used to persuade us to buy things, but also occurs frequently as a means to persuade us to adopt a belief or to follow a certain course of action. Consider the following attempt to persuade students to buy a computer software package:

> Get Hotstuff! – the best-selling comprehensive software package among today's students – and turn your assignments into hot stuff.

Such an advertisement can work in various ways. It makes a straightforward appeal to our desire to have what others have and not to miss out on the benefits enjoyed by those who already use the package in question. But, in addition, it tends to lead us to make some unjustified assumptions about why the product is the most popular ('best-selling'). If we take insufficient care, we are inclined to think that the most popular product must be the most effective, but its popularity might stem purely from its competitive price or the success of the marketing campaign. The fact that the software package is the best-selling does not give us a compelling reason either to buy the product or to conclude that it must be the most suitable software package for student-use.

Like many rhetorical ploys, the appeal to popularity can sometimes be construed as presenting an argument – in this case, as presenting a reason to buy something. As we can see from the following reconstruction, the reason given is not typically a good one (so the argument is fallacious):

P1)   The software package that sells best among students must be the best software package for students.

P2)   The software package that sells best among students is Hotstuff.

C1)   Hotstuff is the best software package for students.

This argument would be valid but almost certainly not sound because the assumption made explicit in P1 is not plausible; it is not the case in general that the best-selling product of a given kind is the best of that kind (see the discussion of the fallacy of majority belief, below). Certainly if you were a student intending to invest in an expensive software package, you would want much stronger evidence that Hotstuff is the best (and further-more, you might well think that since different students have different needs, the claim that a given software package is the best for students in general must be pretty vague, and without any direct implication for you, with your particular needs; we will discuss this kind of vagueness in more on pp. 122–3).

Appeal to compassion, pity or guilt

This common rhetorical ploy operates by attempting to move us to do something purely by evoking a feeling of compassion towards the recipients of the suggested act or belief, or a feeling of guilt about their plight. The feeling alone does not provide a good reason for us to perform the act in question. Examples of this ploy are myriad. Charity appeals and advertising provide plenty of instances. Pictures of hungry children, suffering animals and so forth, accompanied by simple slogans are designed to tweak our feelings of compassion, pity and guilt about the situation of the people or animals featured. Remember that the primary purpose of our examination of rhetorical ploys is a critical one; that is, we encourage critical thinkers not to be persuaded by rhetoric and to avoid rhetoric in their own attempts rationally to persuade others.

As we pointed out in Chapter 1, however, rhetoric can play a useful role when put to good ends. In the case of the appeal to compassion, it serves a positive role by pricking our conscience and opening us up to rational argument regarding how we should act in the given situation. Feelings of compassion can prompt us to look for arguments that do provide good reasons for the course of action recommended by the rhetorical ploy. Suppose, for example, you read a charity advertisement that appeals to your sense of compassion toward hungry children. You may go on to reason that if one can do something to alleviate hardship, one should; and if you are in a position to do so then you should make a donation to the charity. Such an argument might look thus when recon-structed and rendered in standard form:

P1)   A donation to the Worldwide Fund for Children would probably help to alleviate the suffering of children from extreme hunger.

P2)   I should try to alleviate extreme suffering where it's possible for me to do so.

P3)   It is possible for me to make a donation to the WWFC.

C)   **(Probably) I should make a donation to the WWFC.**

Notice that the argument is inductively forceful, its premises make it probable that I should act in the way prescribed. It is certainly not implausible to say that this argument is sound. Suppose then that you were moved to donate to the WWFC by a message simply stating that many children throughout the world suffer from extreme hunger, along with instructions on how to donate to the WWFC. The message certainly does not present the above argument, nor any other. But it might have moved you to act by causing you to think of the argument yourself.

Appeal to cuteness

This rhetorical technique supplements its words with images of children, animals or animated characters to deliver a message. The product that we are urged to buy or the action we are urged to take is made to seem attractive by its association with the cute character that urges us to buy it or take it. The appeal can also work by helping us to remember a product (what advertisers would call making us brand-aware) via its association with the cute figure delivering the sales pitch.

Appeal to sexiness

This is similar to the appeal to cuteness, except that it uses a different type of image. It also has a further dimension. To those who would desire the sexy person depicted in the advertisement, the product is made to seem desirable by its association with the sexy person. But it is also made to seem desirable to those who would like to think of themselves as sexy in the way that the sexy person is. The ad seeks to flatter us. It may even invite us to reason, fallaciously: all sexy people buy or do this; therefore if I buy or do this, I'm sexy. This would be the fallacy of affirming the consequent, discussed below.

Appeals to wealth, status, power, hipness, coolness, etc.

You can easily work out what these are by analogy with the appeals to cuteness and sexiness.

Appeal to fear (also known as scare tactics)

This is the tactic of trying to elicit a fear in one's readers or listeners in order to influence their behaviour or attitudes. A frequent example of the appeal to fear occurs in discussions about immigration into countries such as the UK. Many politicians and other opinion-formers such as journalists use the tactic of eliciting citizens' fears of economic destitution and cultural demise by constructing deliberately exaggerated images of 'waves of immigrants'[1] entering a country illegally and generally living a life better than that they deserve; taking jobs, education, health care and state benefits to which they have no rightful entitlement and thereby making Mr and Ms Average Citizen worse off. This familiar scare tactic (that almost certainly also makes appeal to some people's racist attitudes) is often used by politicians to persuade people to support draconian immigration policies and infringements of people's civil rights, and to demonstrate that support by voting for them at election time. But no reason has been given for the belief that disaster would result if such extreme policies were not enacted. Instead, it is hoped that describing these disastrous scenarios will alarm people so severely as to disturb their reason, prompting the confused supposition that the disastrousness of the worst possible scenario should be matched by the severity of the preventive measures taken.

The appeal to fear should be distinguished from genuine warnings. In instances of the former, there is no warranted connection between the fear elicited and taking the suggested course of action or accepting the claim. Whereas in the case of a warning, we are given a good reason to act. This is usually because the circumstances of the warning are themselves such as to warrant the belief that the warning is well-founded. For example, the warning 'Don't touch the dog, it may look cute and friendly but it bites!' would normally be given only by someone who knows that the dog bites; _____ ___ _____ _____ e very seldom given insincerely or _____ _____ such a warning has been given is _____ nce, needless to say, would be much _____ sing or political discourse.

_____ nces of rhetorical ploys intended to _____ eby to influence our attitudes and

'waves of immigrants', connoting as it does

behaviour, but there are others that occur frequently. Try to think of some and find some examples of your own.

The direct attack and hard sell

The direct attack is the simplest of all rhetorical ploys. It occurs most frequently in advertising, though it also appears in political campaigning. It often takes the form of a very simple slogan. For instance, 'Say no to tuition fees!', 'Drink cola!' Notice that we are given no reason to say 'no' or to drink cola. The belief of those who employ the direct attack is that the more we hear or read these commands and internalise them, the more likely we are to do as they advocate, despite having been given no reason to do so. We often talk about 'giving someone the hard sell'. The hard sell is simply the direct attack repeated persistently. Children are notably effective with it. The persuader just keeps it up until the subject of their attack gives in and does as they want, the persuader thereby having influenced their target by verbal means without giving reasons for doing as they command.

Buzzwords

This is the technique of using fashionable or otherwise currently 'hot' words or phrases that are loaded with rhetorical power due to their rich secondary connotation. (If you don't feel familiar with the concept of secondary connotation, have another look at the relevant section of Chapter 1.) Buzzwords can be enormously provocative and therefore hard to tame, and this makes them especially problematic for the critical thinker. If we want to make an objective analysis of a passage or speech act, we should rephrase what is said or written in such a way as to eliminate the buzzwords, and then embark on the analysis. Here is an example of a passage containing several buzzwords:

> The Prime Minister's solid stance against European Union bureaucrats' latest attempts to create yet more employment rights for European workers and yet more financial burdens for European employers sent a message to business that his Government would continue to stand tall in its commitment to the free market and to wealth creation.

The writer uses the terms 'bureaucrats', 'business', 'free market' and 'wealth creation' as buzzwords to manipulate readers' sympathies towards the Prime Minister's anti-European stance. In combination with the rhetorical import of some of the other words used in the passage, these buzzwords have the effect of showing the Prime Minister to be protecting these (allegedly) uncontroversially good things in the face of an unwarranted attack on them by the European Union, which the writer casts in a bad light by their use of the negative connotations of the buzzword 'bureaucrats'.

Scare quotes

This tactic is a means of influencing opinion against a view that one opposes. The speaker/writer takes key words in terms of which their opponent expresses their views and attempts to discredit those views by making them appear ridiculous or suspicious through the use of scare quotes. No reason is given for rejecting the view, we are simply manipulated into rejecting it because it has been made to appear ridiculous or suspicious. Suppose someone makes the following claim about people trying to settle in the UK for reasons of political asylum:

> Almost all asylum seekers are economic migrants.

Now consider the effect of using scare quotes around the term 'asylum seekers' so that the claim becomes:

> Almost all 'asylum seekers' are economic migrants.

As you can see, the addition of scare quotes has the same rhetorical effect as putting the phrase 'so-called' before the crucial term or phrase. The claim becomes much more explicitly negative in respect of its questioning of the legitimacy of people's claims for asylum. Indeed, it has virtually the same effect as the rhetorically explosive phrase 'bogus asylum seekers'.

This tactic can also be used more subtly but to similar effect. In such cases an opponent's opinion is made to seem dubious by placing scare quotes around words used to describe what would be perfectly normal, acceptable facts about them. This can turn a perfectly innocuous statement into one that casts doubt on someone's credibility. Compare:

> My opponent does of course have his reasons for what he believes
> to be right.

with the scare-quoted:

> My opponent does of course have his 'reasons' for what he believes
> to be right.

While the first sentence suggests disagreement with the opponent's view, the use of scare quotes in the second lends it increased rhetorical power, not only expressing disagreement with the opinion in question, but also casting doubt on the legitimacy of the justification provided for those views.

Care should be taken not to confuse the rhetorical ploy of scare quoting with the legitimate use of quotation marks to demarcate a direct citation of what someone has said or written. Sometimes we use quotation marks in this way even if the view we are quoting is one with which we disagree. For instance, in responding to a letter one has read in a newspaper, one might write:

> Ms Long is simply mistaken when she claims that 'men are better critical thinkers than women'.

Here the writer is simply using quotation marks to show that she is using the original writer's words verbatim. Sometimes we do use citations of what people actually say or write to rhetorical effect and we use quotation marks to demarcate their actual words, but this is not the same as the tactic of scare quoting. A good example of this latter technique is the use of someone else's words taken out of context in order to give rhetorical support to one's own opinions.

Trading on an equivocation

This ploy deliberately exploits the **ambiguity**, and in some cases the **vagueness**, of a word or phrase in the given context. Although nothing false is claimed, the speaker or writer manages to influence our actions or beliefs by misleading us. It is generally used when someone is attempting to persuade us of the benefits and virtues of their product or policy; hence it is common in advertising, particularly when an advertisement uses a superlative such as 'best', 'biggest', 'most successful' and so on. So imagine we come across the following advertisement:

> Britburgers: Britain's favourite hamburger restaurant!

To equivocate is misleadingly to use the same word in more than one sense; the ploy is to get us to interpret a message in a way that favours the product or view being advanced, when it is only under another interpretation that the message is true or well-founded. In this case, the word 'favourite' is ambiguous, having at least two possible meanings: it could mean (i) that Britburgers is the hamburger restaurant that most

British people prefer or like best, or (ii) that Britburgers is the hamburger restaurant with the most customers in Britain (or possibly that it's the one that sells the most hamburgers in Britain, or that has the most franchise outlets in Britain). Obviously the advertisers hope that we'll understand the message according to (i): this is much more favourable to the restaurant than merely having the most customers, since its market domination might be due to some factor other than actual customer preference.

Now we might realise that Britburgers would risk prosecution if they made this claim knowing it wasn't true, and thus conclude that Britburgers really is actively preferred by more British hamburger-eaters. But there's the rub with equivocation: the slogan could be true without the proposition it expresses giving us a good reason to expect Britburgers' burgers to be any good, for the truth expressed by the slogan might not be the one we take it to be. The slogan might be true only under interpretation (ii), and not under interpretation (i). In that case the advertisers could not rightly be convicted of having said something false; they can always claim that (ii) is all that was intended.

Another common instance of equivocation occurs when the ambiguity and vagueness of the phrase 'links to' is used rhetorically to imply that someone is involved in some kind of illegal or immoral activity (and is therefore a bad person). Suppose you read a newspaper article which reports that:

> Mr Smith, who is believed to have links to terrorist organisations, was seen boarding a flight at Heathrow Airport.

you may well be inclined to think that Mr Smith is a terrorist. But all that you have been told is that someone believes he has 'links to' terrorist organisations. These 'links' could amount to nothing more than his having visited premises belonging to such organisations, or he may have attended a meeting, or bought propaganda material, or done business with members of such an organisation, or simply have a relation who is involved in such an organisation. The ploy is also commonly employed using the phrase 'associated with', as in 'Mr Smith is believed to be associated with El Bayda'.[2]

---

2   Notice that the word 'terrorism' is itself vague in that the boundaries of what counts as terrorism are fluid and the meaning of the term remains contested. Public discourse about terrorism often involves trading on equivocation about the meaning of 'terrorism'. As the cliché goes, one person's terrorist is another's freedom fighter.

The ploy of equivocation also occurs when someone attempts to mislead with statistics by saying something that is true, but which they expect their audience to understand according to an interpretation that is false. The following example of attempting to mislead with statistics, which comes from a speech by George W. Bush, also includes an equivocation on the meaning of 'average':

> These tax reductions will bring real and immediate benefits to middle-income Americans. Ninety-two million Americans will keep an average of $1,083 more of their own money.

This claim sounds like the average American will get a little over $1,000. But hang on. Ninety-two million is the number of Americans who pay income tax. One might understand Bush, as his speechwriters intend one to, as saying that the tax bill of the average American will reduce by $1,083. But if 'average American' means 'American with average income', then Bush's claim is false. What is true is that $1,083 is the average tax reduction under the new plan. But that's because the highest earners save hundreds of thousands (similarly, if Bill Gates is in the room along with ten call-centre workers, then the average net worth is still in the billions). The American with average income still only gets a few hundred dollars relief.

Trading on implicature

This is the tactic of using a statement's implicature to mislead the audience (if you are not clear on what implicature is, revisit the discussion in Chapter 1, pp. 9–10). Since the proposition implicated is not actually stated by the speaker, the speaker can hope to avoid responsibility for having misled the audience. This is common in political discussion. For instance, suppose an opposition politician says:

> If the Government increases the income tax, it will be a further burden on working families.

Suppose the politician knows that the Government is not actually considering the tax increase. Still, the audience is led to believe that the Government is considering it – for why else would the politician think it relevant to specify the negative consequence of a tax increase? In using implicature in his way, the speaker or writer intends their audience to interpret their words in this misleading way and to be emotionally moved as a result. Yet if accused of having misled the audience, the politician can say that he did not actually *say* anything false, since he did not *assert* that the Government is considering a tax increase.

Smokescreen (changing the subject)

This is the tactic of avoiding discussion of an issue or acknowledgement of a point through diverting or distracting one's opponent from the issue at hand by addressing a different (possibly related) issue. The issue irrelevant to the discussion thereby acts like a smokescreen by obscuring our view of the real issue. The more subtle the smokescreen, the more effective at distracting the listener or reader it tends to be. Consider, for instance, a Government minister trying to defend her Government's proposed changes to immigration legislation. The proposals have come to light because a civil servant has leaked some classified documents. In defending the proposals, the minister responds to questions by launching into a speech about how the leak constitutes a dreadful dereliction of duty and breach of trust. Instead of addressing the issue at hand – whether or not the proposed legislative changes are good ones – the minister is attempting to distract attention from it by obscuring it in the rhetoric of her speech about duty, responsibility and trust, a speech that is rhetorically powerful because duty, responsibility and trust are the sorts of things that right-minded people are supposed to uphold and admire.

The smokescreen tactic is very similar to the **red herring** fallacy, discussed in more detail below (p. 155). The crucial difference is that while the smokescreen works via its rhetorical power, the red herring is still an attempt to persuade by argument: it gives **reasons** for accepting a claim, just not good reasons. When we are trying to distinguish the smokescreen ploy from the red herring fallacy, we must first work out whether or not the writer or speaker is attempting to persuade by argument.

Fallacies

Strictly speaking, a fallacy is a mistake in reasoning. One commits a fallacy when the reasons advanced or accepted in support of a claim fail to justify its acceptance. A fallacy can be committed either when one is deciding whether to accept a claim on the basis of a fallacious argument with which one has been presented, or when one is presenting the fallacious argument oneself.

A fallacious argument or inference is one in which there is an **inappropriate connection** between premises and conclusion. Almost all fallacies fall under one of the following two types:

- **Formal fallacies.** Sometimes the inappropriate connections are failures of **logical connection**, for example, in the case of the fallacy (below) of affirming the consequent; here the argument or inference is neither deductively valid nor inductively forceful, even where all implicit premises have been made explicit. It is simply a logical mistake.

- **Substantive fallacies.** Sometimes the inappropriate connections involve reliance on some very general unjustified assumptions or inferences. We need only make these **premises** explicit in order to see that they are false and unjustified. What distinguishes a fallacious argument of this kind from an ordinary unsound argument is that the implicit, false or dubious premise will be of a very general nature, having nothing specifically to do with the subject-matter of the argument. What this means will become apparent when we turn to examples.

The vast majority of fallacies that we encounter in everyday texts and speech are substantive fallacies, but some are formal fallacies, and a few are neither formal nor substantive. Arguments embodying formal or substantive fallacies are necessarily unsound, but not all fallacious arguments are actually unsound. Since fallacies are many and various in this way, it would be tedious and distracting to formulate a precise definition. We will simply take fallacies to be mistakes in reasoning that arise because of inappropriate connections between premises and conclusions; we will identify the most commonly encountered fallacies, and we will demonstrate different strategies for dealing with them.

It is important at the outset to note the general point, however, that a fallacious argument can have true or false premises: *simply having false premises does not make an argument fallacious.* Nor does having *true* premises guarantee that an argument is *not* fallacious.

Furthermore, a proposition accepted on the basis of a fallacious argument may turn out to be true as a matter of actual fact. Suppose that someone reasons as follows:

> There is blood on the candelabra. And if Colonel Mustard killed the victim with the candelabra, then there would be. So Colonel Mustard must be the murderer.

Laid out in standard form the argument is thus:

P1) If Colonel Mustard killed the victim with the candelabra, then there is blood on the candelabra.

P2) There is blood on the candelabra.

C) **Colonel Mustard killed the victim.**

Now suppose that, in fact, the conclusion is true: Colonel Mustard is the murderer. Still, the reasoning that takes us to that conclusion is fallacious (the fallacy is the fallacy of **affirming the consequent**). It is not legitimate to infer on the basis of P1 and P2 that Colonel Mustard is the murderer. Even if both premises were true, it would be possible for the conclusion to be false: for example, someone else could have killed the victim with the candelabra. Knowledge of the truth of those premises, just by themselves, would not be sufficient to infer the conclusion, even if that conclusion were actually true. If you were to be fooled by such an argument, you would end up with a true belief, but for mistaken reasons.

Like linguistic phenomena and rhetorical ploys, the best way to become acquainted with the different types of fallacies considered in this chapter is to practise identifying and analysing them. As they are attempts to persuade by argument, you need to reconstruct them in standard form and then use techniques of argument analysis and assessment to demonstrate the ways in which they are fallacious.

And one last thing to bear in mind before we work through specific types of fallacies: as we have already mentioned, many types of fallacious argument **are effective as rhetorical ploys**. Someone might be aware that their argument commits a fallacy, but will use it to try to persuade us because they are aware of its rhetorical power: they are aware, that is, that it does tend to persuade people. Fallacies tend to be effective as attempts to persuade because the psychological effect of their rhetorical power means that we often find them persuasive even though we ought not to. Common examples include uses of *ad hominem*, majority belief and slippery slope fallacies to rhetorical effect.

Formal fallacies

The first group of fallacies we want to discuss here are strictly formal fallacies; these are patterns of argument whose reasoning makes purely **logical** mistakes. Each type of fallacy constitutes an **invalid argument** and once you are familiar with the patterns, the fallacies will be recognised by the presence of the particular invalid pattern.

Affirming the consequent of a conditional

Or 'affirming the consequent' for short. This occurs when we argue from the conditional premise that if P (the antecedent), then Q (the consequent) together with the premise that Q to the conclusion that P, as in the following example:

If mortgage rates go up, then house prices fall. House prices have fallen. Therefore, mortgage rates have gone up.

Reconstruction of the argument reveals its invalidity:

P1)   If mortgage rates go up (P), then house prices fall (Q).

P2)   House prices have fallen (Q).

C)   **Mortgage rates have gone up (P).**

If the premises were true, the conclusion would *not* have to be true. There are a variety of circumstances other than a rise in mortgage rates under which house prices might fall. So the fact that they have fallen would be insufficient for us to draw the conclusion that mortgage rates had gone up. That the inference is fallacious is obvious if we consider a true conditional such as 'If it is raining, then there are clouds'; it certainly does not follow, from this and the premise 'there are clouds', that it is raining.

Notice that affirming the **antecedent** of a conditional premise does not make for an invalid argument:

P1)   If mortgage rates go up (P), house prices will fall (Q).

P2)   Mortgage rates have gone up (P).

C)   **House prices will fall (Q).**

This is of course valid because the conditional gives one condition under which house prices will fall and P2 asserts that the condition is met; so it is legitimate to conclude that house prices will fall.

Denying the antecedent of a conditional

Or 'denying the antecedent' for short. This is the fallacy that occurs when we argue from a conditional premise (if P then Q) together with the negation of its antecedent (not-P) for the conclusion that the consequent is also negated (not-Q). The invalidity of this pattern can be seen clearly using a version of the example above:

P1)   If mortgage rates go up (P), house prices will fall (Q).

P2)   Mortgage rates have not gone up (not P).

C)   **House prices will not fall (not Q).**

The invalidity here has similar grounds to that of the fallacy of affirming the consequent. There are conditions other than mortgage rates going up that could precipitate a fall in house prices, so the fact that mortgage rates have stayed the same (or decreased) does not give us sufficient grounds for concluding that house prices will not fall; other factors may lead to their falling. Or again: from 'If it is raining then there are clouds' and 'it is not raining', it does not follow that there are no clouds.

Fallacy of deriving 'ought' from 'is'

The Scottish philosopher, David Hume, famously argued that an 'ought' cannot be derived from an 'is'. The claim can be understood in two ways: first, as a claim about *motivations* to act or refrain from acting. The fact that something is thus-and-so, argued Hume, is insufficient as a reason for thinking that one ought to act in such-and-such a way. The fact that torturing animals causes them suffering is not, according to this argument, sufficient reason to refrain from torturing animals. An additional motivating force – a desire to avoid harm to animals – must also play a role in our motivation to act in such cases. Although an interesting and controversial thesis, this way of interpreting Hume's claim is not the one that interests us here.[3] Rather, we are interested in Hume's claim understood as the claim that a prescriptive conclusion cannot be validly derived from purely descriptive premises, such an inference is fallacious. Thus the fallacy of deriving an 'ought' from an 'is' occurs when a **prescriptive conclusion** – a conclusion making a claim about something that *should* or *ought* to be done or avoided or believed or not believed – is deduced solely on the basis of **descriptive**, fact-stating, premises. Inferences from descriptive to prescriptive propositions are considered fallacious because the fact that something *happens to be the case*, or *happens not to be the case*, is insufficient grounds for concluding that it *ought* or *ought not to be the case*. If we want to make a valid argument for a prescriptive conclusion, we must always do so from premises at least one of which is prescriptive. Thus the following commits the fallacy of deriving 'ought' from 'is':

> How can anyone claim that the monarchy should be abolished? The monarchy as we know it has been central to British life for nearly a thousand years, arguably longer.

Although it is not expressed as such, the conclusion of this argument is really a prescriptive one – that the British monarchy *should* be retained – but the conclusion is arrived at purely on the basis of the premise that it exists, and has done so for a long time. As such, the argument is plainly invalid:

---

3   For a detailed discussion of this debate see J.L. Mackie, *Ethics: Inventing Right and Wrong* (Harmondsworth: Penguin, 1977).

P1)   The British monarchy has existed for nearly a thousand years.

C)   **The British monarchy should be retained.**

In this particular case we can make the argument valid by adding a prescriptive premise as follows:

P1)   The British monarchy has existed for nearly a thousand years.
P2)   Anything that has existed for nearly a thousand years should be retained.

C)   **The British monarchy should be retained.**

But the argument is clearly deductively unsound: poverty has existed for at least a thousand years, but it is surely false to claim that it should be retained. Note that P2 does not become more plausible if we make it into a soft generalisation. Thus the argument cannot be saved by attempting to make it inductively forceful and inductively sound.

The base rate fallacy

This fallacy has already been mentioned in Chapter 3 (see pp. 95–6). It is committed when an argument takes the following form: the proportion of one group that has a certain feature is higher than the proportion of another group that has that feature. Therefore, some X that has that feature is more likely to be from the first group than the second. Suppose someone reasons, for example: Rex is either a rat or a cat, 75 per cent of cats are black whereas only 45 per cent of rats are black, Rex is black, therefore Rex is probably a cat. The inference is mistaken because the number of black rats may still be larger than the number of black cats. In fact it surely is: the overall number of rats in the world is far greater than the number of cats, so even if blackness is more common among cats than rats, the number of black rats can still be much higher than the number of black cats.

The fallacy commonly occurs when arguers resort to gender or racial stereotypes to make a point. Suppose that Ringons are a minority group outnumbered by non-Ringons by ten to one and someone argues:

P1)   Most Ringons have a criminal record.
P2)   Few non-Ringons have a criminal record.
P3)   Apex has a criminal record.

C)   **(Probably) Apex is a Ringon.**

Even though there is a high incidence of criminality among Ringons, there are so many more non-Ringons than Ringons that someone with a criminal record is still more likely to be a non-Ringon than they are to be a Ringon. Since the argument tells you nothing about the total number of Ringons as compared with non-Ringons, the argument is not inductively forceful: P1–P3 do not give you a reason to infer the conclusion. In fact, if you did know that non-Ringons outnumber Ringons ten to one, then, given P1–P3 and asked to guess whether Apex is a Ringon or a non-Ringon, 'non-Ringon' would be the better guess.

Substantive fallacies

The first two substantive fallacies that we consider involve an illegitimate inference from the prevalence of a belief or an action to its acceptability. Like many, but not all, of the fallacies we'll discuss, we can expose the fallacy by making explicit the hidden assumption that generates the illegitimate inference.

The fallacy of majority belief

This is the fallacy of concluding, on the basis of the fact that the majority believe a certain proposition, that the proposition is true. The following reasoning commits it:

> *Of course the Government must crack down on drug trafficking, after all that's what most reasonable, law-abiding people believe.*

The only reason the arguer gives for a government crack-down is that most people think such a crack-down would be a good thing. We can see this more clearly by laying out the argument in standard form:

P1) Most reasonable, law-abiding people believe that the Government should crack down on drug trafficking.

C) The Government should crack down on drug trafficking.

So rendered, the argument is invalid. But we can make the cause of the faulty reasoning clearer by making the hidden assumption explicit thus:

P1) Most reasonable, law-abiding people believe that the Government should crack down on drug trafficking.

P2) Any belief shared by most reasonable, law-abiding people is
     true.

___

C) **The Government should crack down on drug trafficking.**

Once we add the implicit premise, the argument becomes valid; but
we can now see that the assumption underlying the argument, expressed
by the hard generalisation P2, is false and that the argument is therefore
unsound. Even if a majority of people do believe a proposition and even
if they are of sound character, etc. their believing it is not sufficient to
make it true. Imagine, for example, if most reasonable, law-abiding people
believed that the Earth was flat, that would not establish that it is! More
controversially, if a majority of reasonable, law-abiding people believe
that capital punishment should be restored as a sentence for murder, the
fact that it is a majority belief is not sufficient to make it true.[4] This is
the principal strategy for dealing with substantive fallacies; by exposing
the hidden assumption generating the fallacy, we reveal that the same (or
a very similar) false proposition, usually a generalisation, figures in all
instances of a particular fallacy.

The fallacy of majority belief often places us in an apparent dilemma
when we have to take decisions on behalf of others. Suppose you are a
member of the jury in an important and high-profile trial that has received
a great deal of pre-courtroom publicity. On that basis you know that
most people believe that the defendant was the victim of a conspiracy on
the part of the investigating police officers; nevertheless, the evidence
presented in court gives you good reasons to believe that he is guilty.
Thus you might be tempted into reasoning as follows:

P1) Most people believe that the defendant was set up and is not
     guilty of the crime he is alleged to have committed.

___

C) **The defendant is innocent.**

Such reasoning would commit the fallacy of majority belief and should
be avoided as a basis for a juror's decision. Again we can make the faulty
reasoning clear by exposing the hidden false assumption, which will be a
very similar generalisation to that which figured in the previous example,
thus:

P1) Most people believe that the defendant was set up and is not
     guilty.

___

4   We consider the relationship between truth and belief in more detail in Chapter 7.

P2)   Any belief held by the majority is true.

C)   The defendant is innocent.

So the argument is valid but not sound.

The fallacy of majority belief is similar to the rhetorical ploy of appeal to popularity, because both use the fact of something's popularity or commonality to attempt to persuade us to do or believe it. Sometimes, the very act of presenting an argument that commits the fallacy of majority belief is at the same time an example of the rhetorical ploy of appealing to popularity. Still these are distinct concepts: again, to call it a (substantive) fallacy is to say that the argument presented implicitly embodies a certain sort of unjustified assumption; to call it a rhetorical ploy is to say that it attempts causally to induce us to accept a certain belief by activating our social instincts, desires and fears. Some cases exemplify the fallacy without exemplifying the rhetorical ploy: someone might, for example, be quite sincere in thinking that if something is believed by the majority it must be true, and accept a conclusion on that basis. On the other hand, some cases exemplify the rhetorical ploy without exemplifying the fallacy: an advertisement, for example, that shows someone being humiliated because they are the only person not drinking a certain brand of cola is clearly trying to influence us by way of our social instincts and feelings, not by presenting an argument.

Common practice

This is the tactic of attempting to persuade someone to do something they shouldn't do by giving them the justification that 'everyone does it'. The implication of this sham-reasoning is if everyone does X, X must be acceptable. We often use this tactic to provide justification to ourselves for doing things we ought not to do. For example: 'It won't hurt to call in sick today, everyone does it once or twice a year.' Like the fallacy of majority belief, the common practice fallacy is driven by a false assumption concerning the connection between what is commonly believed or done and what it is morally, socially or rationally acceptable to believe or do. The following reasoning is an instance of the common practice fallacy:

> Of course it's OK to fiddle your expenses once in a while, everyone does.

This standard form rendition of the argument shows it to be invalid because there is no appropriate connection between the premise and the conclusion:

P1)   Everyone fiddles their expenses occasionally.

C)   It is acceptable to fiddle one's expenses occasionally.

Once again, exposing the false assumption produces the following argument, the unsoundness of which rests on the actual falsity of both P1 and P2:

P1)   Everyone fiddles their expenses occasionally.
P2)   Any act that everyone occasionally performs is acceptable.

C)   Fiddling one's expenses is acceptable.

Surely there are some people who have never cheated when making a claim for expenses from their employer; and we can think of actions – meting out violence to an innocent stranger, for example – which, if performed occasionally by everyone would still be unacceptable. Even if the quantifier in P1 and P2 were qualified by 'almost', then although P1 might be true, it becomes even less plausible that P2 is true.

The next group of fallacies involve using alleged facts about the person(s) putting forward an argument as the basis for inferring a conclusion that their argument should not be accepted. In each case the fact about the person is irrelevant to the issue of whether or not we should accept their argument. As critical thinkers we are only interested in the argument, not in the person giving it. It is also helpful to remember this if we feel uncomfortable criticising arguments put forward by people we like, respect, fear or want to impress. If the argument is a good one, it makes no difference by whom it was given, likewise if it is a bad one.

Ad hominem

This fallacy (from the Latin, meaning 'to the man') can be committed in two ways: either by responding to someone's argument by making an attack upon the person, rather than addressing the argument itself, or by rejecting a claim because of disapproval of or dislike for the person who makes it. The following reasoning commits the *ad hominem* fallacy by citing a claim about a minister's speaking style as a reason for rejecting the legislation they propose:

> I don't see why we should accept the new Criminal Justice Bill when the minister presented it to us in such an imperious way.

An initial reconstruction displays the argument as invalid:

P1) The minister presented the Criminal Justice Bill in an imperious way.

C) **The Bill should be rejected.**

Our strategy of exposing the crucial underlying assumption results in the following argument, which is unsound because P2 is false:

P1) The minister presented the Criminal Justice Bill in an imperious way.

P2) Any legislation presented by a person with an imperious manner should be rejected.

C) **The Bill should be rejected.**

All instances of the *ad hominem* fallacy will depend upon similar underlying general assumptions referring to certain characteristics or beliefs of arguers.

Ad hominem *circumstantial*

This is a sub-species of the *ad hominem* fallacy and occurs when someone's argument in favour of doing or believing something is discounted on the grounds that they would allegedly benefit from our doing or believing it. Someone would be committing the *ad hominem* circumstantial fallacy if they were to argue:

> Of course academics argue in favour of the proposed expansion of university education: the more aspiring graduates there are, the more job opportunities there are for people like them.

Notice that the conclusion of this argument is left implicit, but given the arguer's tone, it is reasonable to conclude that they do not agree with the expansion proposal. When reconstructing we need to add the conclusion for ourselves:

P1) Academics argue in favour of the proposed expansion of university education.

P2) They would benefit from such an expansion.

C) **We should reject academics' arguments in favour of the proposal to expand university education.**

The result, however, is an argument that is neither valid nor inductively forceful. Once again, we can see the true shape of the reasoning that constitutes this fallacy by exposing the hidden assumption thus:

P1) Academics argue in favour of the proposed expansion of university education.
P2) They would benefit from such an expansion.
P3) Whenever someone would benefit from something, we should reject their arguments in favour of it.

C) **We should reject academics' arguments in favour of the proposal to expand university education.**

Note that P3 is really quite ludicrous: if it were true, then one could never hope to argue successfully for what one wants! Normally, that is exactly what we do, and there is nothing intrinsically illegitimate about it. So it is unreasonable to reject an argument because the arguer desires or would benefit from the truth of the conclusion. What matters is the strength of the reasons given for the claim, irrespective of the arguer's motives for making the claim. Reason places no strictures on arguing in favour of things from which one would benefit.

However, this is not to say that the issue of a speaker's or a writer's character is entirely irrelevant in matters of argument analysis and evaluation. A person's character and actions are certainly relevant to their **credibility**: the degree to which someone's having said something constitutes a reason to think it true. We should, for example, be on our guard against believing the claims of people whom we know to be dishonest. Even those who are not habitually dishonest are more likely to attempt deception if they are arguing for something that is strongly in their own interest. There is certainly a higher probability that someone who is not disinterested will deliberately resort to techniques of sham-reasoning in their attempts to persuade us of the truth of their claims; for they have more to lose if their arguments are not accepted. This probability increases with the degree to which the person is unscrupulous. In such cases we should check the reasoning carefully, and we should not take their having advanced a premise as a reason, in itself, to think it true. This is not, however, to say that we should positively assume their reasoning to be faulty or their premises false. That would be committing the *ad hominem* fallacy. We should never lose sight of the need to assess the argument on its own account. If the argument is found to be valid or inductively forceful, or the premises true, the character of the arguer is irrelevant.

There is one final observation to make concerning the relationship between people's characters and reputations and the strength of their arguments. This point does not directly concern a type of fallacious reasoning, but is relevant to considerations about the credibility of arguers and their arguments: sometimes we are tempted to ignore or reject criticism of a person's arguments because of the way in which they have been labelled or treated by the media. The sorts of cases we have in mind are those in which someone has received racist, sexist or homophobic treatment in the media and this has been given as a reason for avoiding criticism of or for accepting their views. An example was provided by arguments that it was acceptable to allow the convicted rapist and former heavyweight boxing champion Mike Tyson into the UK on the grounds that much of the media coverage of the case was racist. It may well be the case that a good deal of what was written and said about Mr Tyson was racist and also that there were good reasons to grant him entry. It is crucial to recognise, however, that the existence of the racist discourse was irrelevant to the strength or weakness of arguments that he should or shouldn't have been granted leave to enter the UK.

Tu quoque

In common with *ad hominem* fallacies, the *tu quoque* ('you too') fallacy occurs when we make unwarranted connections between a person's alleged lack of credibility and the strength of their argument. Here the alleged lack of credibility ensues specifically from their being hypocritical: an inconsistency between the arguer's actions and their claims. The fallacy is committed when we: reject a person's claim that a behaviour or proposal should be refrained from or discarded on the grounds that they themselves practise that behaviour; or when we reject a person's claim that a behaviour or proposal should be adopted on the grounds that they fail to follow it themselves. Consider the following argument:

> My Dad's always telling me not to talk on my mobile phone while I'm driving, but why should I take any notice of him? He's always taking calls when he's driving.

An initial reconstruction yields an invalid argument:

P1) My Dad says one shouldn't talk on the mobile phone while driving.

P2) My Dad talks on his mobile phone while he's driving.

C) **It is OK to talk on the mobile phone while driving.**

Exposing the hidden false assumption demonstrates that the argument is unsound:

P1)   My Dad says one shouldn't talk on the mobile phone while driving.

P2)   My Dad talks on his mobile phone while he's driving.

P3)   Whenever someone's behaviour is inconsistent with their advice, that advice is false.

C)   It is OK to talk on the mobile phone while driving.

The *tu quoque* fallacy occurs frequently in discussions of the gaps between politicians' policy and private decisions.

Suppose someone were to argue the following:

The Government's transport policy is a joke, how can we take them seriously when they tell us to leave the car at home and use public transport when Government ministers go everywhere in chauffeur-driven limousines?

An initial reconstruction yields an invalid argument:

P1)   The Government tells the public to use public transport.

P2)   Government ministers use cars not public transport.

C)   We should not take the Government's transport policy seriously.

Exposing the hidden false assumption demonstrates that the argument is unsound:

P1)   The Government tells the public to use public transport.

P2)   Government ministers use cars not public transport.

P3)   Whenever someone's behaviour is inconsistent with their policies, we should not take those policies seriously.

C)   We should not take Labour's transport policy seriously.

The arguer has spotted the inconsistency between what the Government does and what it says, but that inconsistency does not render false the Government's views about public transport and it does not provide a reason to reject the policies in question. Whether it would be a good idea for more people to use public transport instead of private cars does not depend on whether or not the members of the Government use public transport themselves. When we commit this fallacy we are going against the old adage: 'Don't do as I do, do as I say.' We might well think that people ought to follow their own advice and principles, in fact in most cases it is irrational for them not to do so, but it is equally irrational of us to discount their arguments solely on the grounds that they themselves don't heed the conclusions of those arguments. Of course, the fact that someone in the public arena behaves inconsistently or hypocritically does undermine their credibility and may lead us to withdraw our trust and respect, but it is not in itself a reason to reject their arguments. What seems to happen in such cases is that someone gives advice or expounds a policy that they believe applies to their audience, but apparently not to themselves. We suspect they delude themselves into thinking that they represent an exception to the prescriptive claim that they are making. For instance, in the first case above, Dad might delude himself into thinking that he's such an experienced and safe driver that when *he* talks on his mobile phone while driving, he is not a danger to himself and to others and so need not desist from doing it.

Appeal to authority

This fallacy also involves mistaken assumptions about the people mentioned by an argument. It is committed when an argument makes an unjustified appeal to an alleged authority. This can occur either because the authority appealed to is not in fact authoritative on the matter in hand or because there is good reason to doubt that the claimed authority is adequately informed of the facts of the matter. For example, the fallacy is committed when someone in power such as the Prime Minister or another political leader is unjustifiably invoked as an expert. For instance:

> It is always better to drink white wine with fish. Tony Blair says so, he must know what he's talking about, he's the Prime Minister.

An initial reconstruction shows the argument to be valid:

P1) Tony Blair says that it is always better to drink white wine with fish.
P2) Tony Blair is Prime Minister.
P3) If someone is Prime Minster, then they must always be knowledgeable about all the subjects they talk about.

C) **It is always better to drink white wine with fish.**

It is unsound, however, because of the falsity of the conditional P3. Someone's being Prime Minister is not sufficient reason to think that they are knowledgeable about everything about which they express an opinion. That does not mean, of course, that all appeals to authority are fallacious; only those which are mistaken about someone's claim to be authoritative about the matter in hand. Prime ministers *can* claim authority on those matters on which they are best qualified to speak. If Tony Blair were to say that the best way to win an election is to make realistic promises, then one might accept that claim on the basis of his evident expertise in such matters.

The appeal to authority can also function as a rhetorical ploy; the pull of the alleged authority being used to lure us into accepting the proposition argued for. A common example of this use of the appeal to authority is the use of celebrity endorsement to sell things. Although one might take Tiger Woods' endorsement of a brand of golf clubs as a good reason for buying that brand, one ought to be more wary about taking him to be an authority on makes of car, for example, whereas, Tommy Hakinnen's endorsement of a car would be authoritative but his recommendation of a particular brand of golf clubs would not.

The perfectionist fallacy

This fallacy occurs when we place excessive demands on an idea or a proposal and then reject it purely on the grounds that it will not **completely** solve a problem. Someone would commit the perfectionist fallacy if they were to argue or to accept the argument that:

> The Government should give up its plans to spend ten billion pounds on extra surgery in order to reduce hospital waiting lists. It's just not possible to get rid of waiting lists in that way.

An initial reconstruction shows that the argument is invalid:

P1) The Government's plan to spend ten billion pounds to reduce hospital waiting lists will not get rid of waiting lists completely.

C) **The Government's plan should be abandoned.**

The assumption driving this instance of the perfectionist fallacy is that governments should only pursue plans that completely solve the problems they are intended to solve; more generally, the perfectionist assumption is that no measure aimed at solving or reducing a problem is justified unless it solves or reduces it completely. This is really quite silly if you think about it. It is obvious that many measures are intended to reduce a problem, not completely eradicate it, and are justified if they do reduce the problem sufficiently. For example, fences are put around cow pastures to keep the cows in; once in a while a cow escapes, but no one would say that the occasional escape shows that the fences are unjustified.

When we include the perfectionist premise in the argument, in this case expressed as a conditional, we see that it is deductively unsound because the perfectionist premise is false:

P1) The Government's plan to spend ten billion pounds to reduce hospital waiting lists will not get rid of waiting lists completely.

P2) If a government proposal will not completely solve the problem it is intended to solve, it should be abandoned.

C) **The Government's plan should be abandoned.**

Conflation of morality with legality

This is the mistake of assuming that anything legal must be moral, or conversely, that anything illegal must be immoral. For something to be legal within the boundaries of a given political entity (nation, city, district, the United Nations) is to say that there is no law in the statutes of that entity that prohibits it. However, the fact that something is legal does not automatically make it morally acceptable. For example, it is not illegal to cheat on your lover, or to be rude to a shy person at a party just out of cruelty, but these things are immoral. More gravely, in some countries, slavery, though obviously immoral, was legal until the nineteenth century. In other countries, even today, people may legally be denied human and civil rights because of their race, ethnicity, gender or religious belief.

In some cases the laws ought to be changed in order to reflect what is morally right. Indeed, it is tempting to argue that what is legal should include only what is moral. But to try to outlaw everything immoral would be unworkable, and indeed it would overstep what are generally considered to be the proper bounds of governmental authority. Some aspects of behaviour that we find morally unacceptable are not necessarily appropriate subjects for legislation – conduct in personal relationships, for example: we would not want it to be against the law to tell a lie, break a promise, make fun of someone or fail to show up for a date. Conversely, the fact that something is illegal does not automatically make it immoral. In some countries, Australia for example, it is illegal not to cast a vote in elections, but it is not obvious that there is a moral issue at stake here. Similarly, you are breaking the law when you park on a double yellow line, but it is arguable whether or not you are doing anything immoral. And sometimes laws that are meant to legislate against immorality are mistaken; throughout the ages there have been laws against all manner of things, thought by the authorities of the time to be immoral, that in retrospect we think are not immoral, and that never were – the worship or non-worship of certain gods, the education of women, the wearing of certain clothes. Indeed, to think that everything legal is moral is to nullify the possibility of criticising existing laws on moral grounds.

Consider this example:

> I don't see why people are so hard on Donald Mirving. After all he's done nothing wrong, in this country there's no law against denying the Holocaust.

The 'there's no law against it, so it's acceptable' argument is an extremely common instance of the fallacy of conflating legality and morality. The first reconstruction shows that the argument is invalid without the conflating assumption; the second shows that it is valid but unsound with it:

P1) Donald Mirving has denied the extent and facts of the Holocaust.
P2) It is not illegal to do this in the UK.

___

C)   Donald Mirving's denial of the Holocaust was not morally wrong.

P1) Donald Mirving has denied the extent and facts of the Holocaust.
P2) It is not illegal to do this in the UK.
P3) Anything legal is moral.

___

C)   Donald Mirving's denial of the Holocaust was not morally wrong.

So, pointing out that the act in question is not against the law does not show that it is not wrong. Of course, many of the questions surrounding whether or not an issue is a moral one are controversial (the examples given above are by no means clear cut); they may require reflection and argument in their own right.

Weak analogy

Analogies are often interesting and may be **illustrative** of points one wishes to make, but arguing on the basis of analogy is often unsuccessful and often turns out to be fallacious either because the analogy is too weak to sustain the argument or because the analogy itself has not been argued for. (This makes the argument **question-begging**. We discuss the fallacy of begging the question later in this chapter.) In the case of the fallacy of weak analogy, it will be helpful first to see the **form** that instances usually take, and then to consider an example. The fallacy of weak analogy usually argues on the basis of a proposition that because one thing is similar to another in one respect, that it is, therefore, similar in a further respect. This mistaken inference is based on the false assumption that if something is similar to another thing in one respect, it is similar in all respects. Hence we construct an argument of the following valid but unsound form:

P1)   An object X is similar to an object Y in respect of characteristic A.

P2)   Whenever an object X is similar to an object Y in one respect, it is similar in all respects.

P3)   Y has characteristic B.

C)   **X has characteristic B.**

An instance of this fallacy occurs frequently in debates about legislation to control the ownership and use of firearms. So let's take such an instance as our example:

I don't see what all the fuss is about guns. Of course gun ownership shouldn't be prohibited, you can kill someone with a cricket bat, but no one proposes to ban ownership of cricket bats.

A reconstruction demonstrates that this argument takes the form characteristic of the fallacy of weak analogy except that to render the arguer's thinking fully, we have to add a further premise to the effect that things that are the same should always be treated the same:

P1)   Guns are like cricket bats in that both can be used to kill people.

P2)   Whenever an object X is similar to an object Y in one respect, it is similar in all respects.

P3)   Objects that are similar to each other in all respects should be treated identically.

P4)   We would not ban ownership of cricket bats.

C)   **We should not ban ownership of guns.**

The argument is unsound because it is obviously false to assume that similarity in one respect implies similarity in all respects. While it is of course true that cricket bats and guns have some shared similarities, those similarities are not sufficient for the analogy to hold. The dissimilarities – cricket bats have a different primary purpose; it is difficult to commit mass murder with a cricket bat, and so on – outweigh the similarities (indeed, one can kill a person with just about any solid, heavy object, such as a television; no one would argue that since we don't ban those potential murder weapons, we shouldn't ban firearms!).

The fact that arguments from analogy frequently turn out to be fallacious does not mean that they are universally unsuccessful. For an analogy to be effective in giving us a reason to accept a conclusion, an arguer must first present an argument for the claim that the objects that are allegedly analogous (cricket bats and guns in the case under consideration) are sufficiently similar in the relevant respect. Once established, this conclusion would become the first premise of a subsequent argument for the claim that gun ownership should not be banned.

Causal fallacies

These fallacies are committed when we make mistaken inferences about the cause(s) of something. Three types can be distinguished:

* *Post hoc ergo propter hoc* (from the Latin meaning 'after that, this, therefore this because of that);
* fallacy of mistaking correlation for cause; and
* inversion of cause and effect.

Post hoc ergo propter hoc

This fallacy occurs when we mistakenly infer that an event X caused an event Y merely on the basis that Y occurred after X. In the following example, the fallacy is committed twice. We can tell that the argument includes a causal claim because the proposition expressed by the conclusion states that one event – making a will – *makes* another event happen – living longer:

> Making a will makes you live longer. That's the conclusion reached by legacy specialists Live and Let Live, who compared the mortality figures of those who had made a will with those who hadn't. The average age of death for people who hadn't made a will was 72 years, 6 months. However, bequeath your personal

possessions on paper and life expectancy shoots up to 80 years, 5 months. Want to live even longer? Leave some cash to charity; generous donors lasted until the ripe old age of 83 years.

As with previous cases, we can first represent causal fallacies as neither invalid nor inductively forceful arguments, then, to demonstrate that they are driven by a false assumption, make the argument valid or inductively forceful but unsound:

P1)   Generally, people who make a will live longer than those who don't.

C)   **(Probably) Making a will causes people to live longer.**

Adding the implicit general assumption and making explicit a further implicit premise, needed to make the argument inductively forceful, gives the following, which is inductively forceful but unsound due to the falsity of P2:

P1)   Generally people who make a will live longer than those who don't.
P2)   Whenever one event (Y) occurs after another event (X), Y is caused by X.
P3)   Living longer (not dying) occurs after making a will.

C)   **(Probably) Making a will causes people to live longer.**

The *post hoc ergo propter hoc* fallacy is frequently committed in public discourse when arguers are attempting to persuade people of the merits of a policy or piece of legislation. Thus, tougher sentencing policies might be fallaciously inferred to be the cause of a drop in the crime rate, or a teachers' pay increase to be the cause of better examination marks in schools. Where the second event is alleged to be causally linked to the first, solely on the basis that it occurred after the first, the argument is almost definitely fallacious. This is not to say that tougher sentencing couldn't be a cause of a drop in the crime rate, it's just that we need to be given stronger reasons to accept the causal claim than simply the fact that one event occurred before the other.

Fallacy of mistaking correlation for cause

Whereas the fallacy of *post hoc ergo propter hoc* occurs because the temporal priority of one event over another is taken as sufficient to establish a causal relationship between those events, this fallacy is committed when the fact that one type of event or state of affairs is always or usually found in conjunction with another type is mistakenly taken to be sufficient to establish that events or states of affairs of the one type cause the other. In a word, the fallacy is committed when a statistical correlation is assumed, without any further justification, to establish a causal relation. So, for instance, someone who argues:

> You only have to look at the statistics to see that poverty is the obvious cause of educational under-achievement. Eighty per cent of those who leave school with no qualifications come from homes whose income is at least 50 per cent below the average.

commits the fallacy of mistaking correlation for cause. Our point here is not that it is completely mistaken to think that there is a link between poverty and under-achievement in school. Indeed, there is plenty of respectable research establishing a relationship between them. And certainly a statistical correlation is necessary for a causal relation: if there is no statistical correlation, then there cannot be a causal relation. What is crucial, though, is that we resist making the mistaken inferential leap from the fact of their statistical correlation to the alleged fact of a causal relationship between them. There may well be such a relationship, but correlation alone is not sufficient to conclude that the relationship is causal, as we see when we reconstruct the argument in standard form:

P1) There is a statistical correlation between students' under-achievement at school and poverty at home.

C) **Poverty at home causes students' under-achievement at school.**

Making explicit the hidden assumption, we derive the following valid but unsound argument:

P1) There is a statistical correlation between students' under-achievement at school and poverty at home.
P2) Whenever two phenomena X and Y are correlated, X is the cause of Y.

C) **Poverty at home causes students' under-achievement at school.**

That P2 is false can be made obvious by considering certain counter-examples. Creatures that wear clothes, for example, tend to be more intelligent than those that do not. These things are correlated. But wearing clothes does not cause intelligence. In cases where there is correlation between two or more events or phenomena and they are in fact causally related it is often difficult to distinguish which is cause and which is effect. Poverty and ill health tend to go together, but which causes which? It is probable that in many cases they are mutually causally efficacious. We discuss the relation between correlation and cause in more detail in Chapter 5.

Inversion of cause and effect

Here one mistakenly infers that if X causes Y, an absence of X will prevent Y:

> Research carried out by a team of researchers shows that vitamin E may be the key to the secret of everlasting youth. The team believe that the vitamin may be at work normally in humans to prevent ageing. Experiments carried out on laboratory rats have enabled the scientists to discover that animals deprived of vitamin E seem to age faster and even become senile. Their spokesperson, Dr Young, said that although the ageing process remains mysterious, these experiments have demonstrated an 'interesting causal relationship' between vitamin E and the ageing process.

Even if we grant that it is generally warranted to make inferences about human physiology from that of rats, it is *not* warranted to infer from the fact that vitamin E deficiency seems to hasten ageing to the claim that vitamin E is the secret of everlasting youth. The proposition that a lack of something (vitamin E) causes X (hastened ageing) does not entail the proposition that the presence of that thing (vitamin E) causes the opposite of X (slowed ageing). We can use a reconstruction to expose the mistaken causal assumption driving this fallacy:

P1) Vitamin E deprivation causes hastened ageing.
P2) If a lack of something X is the cause of a phenomenon Y, the presence of X will cause of the opposite of Y.

C) **Vitamin E causes the ageing process to slow.**

One sometimes encounters the inversion fallacy and the fallacy of mistaking correlation for cause committed simultaneously. The following reasoning fallaciously infers a causal relation between eating certain foods and eating disorders from a correlation between those things (in this case the correlation is anecdotal rather than statistical), but *also* commits the inversion fallacy by mistakenly inverting that causal relationship:

> Contrary to what the healthy eating lobby dictates, traditional British cooking is good for you. Remember the good old days when we ate bacon, eggs, sausages, fried tomatoes, potatoes, toast and marmalade? And that was just for breakfast. Well in those days, people didn't succumb to anorexia or bulimia and the incidence of obesity was much lower. Seems the 'experts' have got it wrong again.

This argument seems to conclude not only that eating traditional British cooking protects people from anorexia, bulimia and obesity, but that not eating it causes those things. To expose the fallacies, we can reconstruct the entire argument as an extended argument:

P1)   When we ate traditional foods (X) there was a significantly lower incidence of anorexia, bulimia and obesity (lack of Y).

P2)   Whenever two phenomena (X) and (Y) are correlated, X is the cause of Y.

_____

C1)   Eating traditional foods (X) causes a low incidence of anorexia, etc. (lack of Y).

P3)   Now we don't eat those foods (lack of X) and the incidence of anorexia, etc. is much higher (Y).

P4)   Whenever X causes a lack of Y, a lack of X causes Y.

_____

C2)   Not eating traditional foods (lack of X) causes a higher incidence of anorexia, bulimia and obesity (Y).

The fallacy of mistaking correlation for cause is signalled by P2. The mistaken inversion is signalled by P4, which is false. Some causal relationships can be inverted, but it is certainly not true of causal relationships in general that they can be. For example, drinking milk causes us not to be thirsty. But it is not true that not drinking milk causes us to be thirsty!

The next two fallacies that we consider are committed when we make unwarranted inferences from what is known, believed or proven.

Epistemic fallacies

Appeal to ignorance

This is the fallacy of concluding either that because a claim has not been proven it must be false (the negative form), or that because it has not been disproved it must be true (the positive form). It is often used when defending a belief in something that remains unproven such as astrology or the existence of a deity. The following commits the **negative form** of the fallacy:

> As no one has proven that UFOs exist, it's reasonable to assume that they don't.

whereas this equally fallacious argument commits the **positive form**:

> No one has managed to prove that UFO's don't exist, so we can reasonably conclude that they do.

As we see when we reconstruct the arguments, each fallacious and unsound argument is driven either by the false assumption that absence of proof means a proposition is false or that absence of disproof means a proposition is true. Notice that in reconstructing this argument, we omit the indicator phrase 'it is reasonable to conclude that':

P1)   No one has proven that UFOs exist.
P2)   All unproven propositions are false.

C)   UFOs do not exist.

P1)   No one has proven that UFOs don't exist.
P2)   All propositions that have not been disproved are true.

C)   UFOs do exist.

Of course, in cases where efforts to prove something have been sufficiently strenuous, it may be reasonable to infer the falsity of the proposition. For example, repeated efforts have been made, using sophisticated scientific equipment, to find the Loch Ness monster (to prove the proposition that Nessie exists); but to no avail. It is reasonable on that basis to conclude, alas, that Nessie doesn't exist. But that is because we know that if Nessie did exist, then she probably would have been detected by those efforts. The mere fact that a proposition hasn't been proven, just by itself, is no reason to think it false. Likewise, the mere fact that a proposition hasn't been disproved, just by itself, is no reason to think it true.

'Proof' connotes certainty, and part of what is going on with this fallacy is that people sometimes think that if a claim is not certain, then it can reasonably be denied. But that is not how things are, as should be reasonably clear from Chapter 3. Where we know we have an inductively very forceful argument with true premises, then despite not having perfect certainty, it would be unreasonable to deny the conclusion (with certain exceptions, as explained in Chapter 6). Some claims and theories provide the most probable explanations of the phenomena they concern even though they remain neither proven nor disproved. The theory of natural selection is one such example. The arguments in favour of it have a great deal of inductive force, but as yet no one has managed to prove it.[5] Reasons why it should be considered the most plausible explanation of the evolution of species ought to be incorporated into relevant arguments; whether or not it is proven is not essential to the question of whether we ought to believe it.

Epistemic fallacy

This fallacy (from the Greek *episteme*, meaning knowledge) arises because of the tricky nature of knowledge and belief, and the difficulty of discerning from the third-personal point of view what someone believes or knows. It is committed when we make a fallacious inference from the fact that someone believes that P that they must also believe that Q on the grounds that P and Q are about the same thing or person, even though the way in which they refer to that thing or person is different. The following provides a simple instance of the epistemic fallacy:

> Chris believes that Tony Blair enjoys skydiving. Tony Blair is the Prime Minister, so Chris believes that the Prime Minister likes skydiving.

A reconstruction gives us:

P1)   Chris believes that Tony Blair enjoys skydiving.
P2)   Tony Blair is the Prime Minister.

C)   Chris believes that the Prime Minister enjoys skydiving.

The inference is incorrect and the argument invalid because the arguer has assumed that, in addition to having beliefs about Tony Blair's pre-

---

5   We should note that although a theory may be *in principle* provable it may remain neither proven nor unproven indefinitely because there is insufficient evidence to prove or disprove it conclusively.

ferred leisure pursuits, Chris also knows that Tony Blair is the Prime Minister. But the arguer has given no grounds for this assumption. Chris may only have a belief about Tony Blair but not know that Tony Blair is the Prime Minister. If so, then C might be false. Another way of putting this is to say that Chris may not know that 'the Prime Minister' and 'Tony Blair' refer to the same person. Thus, if Chris is indeed ignorant of Tony Blair's being Prime Minister, the following argument, though valid, would be unsound due to the falsity of P3 and of C:

P1) Chris believes that Tony Blair enjoys skydiving.
P2) Tony Blair is the Prime Minister.
P3) Chris knows that Tony Blair is the Prime Minister.

C) **Chris believes that the Prime Minister enjoys skydiving.**

It is important to note that similar inferences made in different contexts are warranted and the arguments containing them valid. Consider the following:

P1) The Prime Minister is a world champion darts player.
P2) Tony Blair is Prime Minister.

C) **Tony Blair is a world champion darts player.**

Inferences such as this are sanctioned by an apparently indubitable logical principle known as **Leibniz's Law** (after the seventeenth century German philosopher and mathematician, Gottfried Leibniz). This law holds that if one thing is the same identical thing as another, then what is true of one must be true of the other. For example, if Superman has blond hair and Superman and Clark Kent are the same person, then Clark Kent must have blond hair. Sentences about people's beliefs or knowledge, such as our example about Tony Blair and skydiving, are exceptions to Leibniz's Law. If Chris believes that X is thus-and-so, even if X and Y are the same thing, it does not follow that Chris believes Y to be thus-and-so because we do not know whether or not Chris knows that X and Y are the same thing. The inference would only be warranted if the arguer knew that Chris knew this. How to make sense of these sorts of cases is a famous philosophical puzzle, but we need not let that worry us here.[6]

---

6   The most famous discussion is 'On sense and reference', by Gottlob Frege, reprinted in *Meaning and Reference*, edited by A.W. Moore (Oxford: Oxford University Press, 1993).

The epistemic fallacy is often used knowingly to discredit someone's opinion. For example:

> Mr Smith believes that the cultivation and use of cannabis should remain a criminal offence in this country. But cannabis is the most effective anti-nausea drug for chemotherapy patients. So Mr Smith believes that it should remain a criminal offence to produce or use the most effective anti-nausea drug for chemotherapy patients.

An initial reconstruction of the argument gives us the following valid argument:

P1)   Mr Smith believes that it should be a criminal offence to produce or to use cannabis.

P2)   Cannabis is the most effective anti-nausea drug for chemotherapy patients.

C)   **Mr Smith believes that it should be a criminal offence to produce or to use the most effective anti-nausea drug for chemotherapy patients.**

If we add a hidden premise of the same form as P3 in the previous example, we see that we cannot conclude that the argument is sound unless we have some grounds for saying that P3 (and hence C) are true:

P1)   Mr Smith believes that it should be a criminal offence to produce or to use cannabis.

P2)   Cannabis is the most effective anti-nausea drug for chemotherapy patients.

P3)   Mr Smith knows that the most effective anti-nausea drug for chemotherapy patients is cannabis.

C)   **Mr Smith believes that it should be a criminal offence to produce or to use the most effective anti-nausea drug for chemotherapy patients.**

We are unjustified in making this knowledge attribution if we don't know that Mr Smith is aware of the anti-nausea properties of cannabis. It is possible that Smith is unaware that cannabis is the best anti-nausea drug for chemotherapy patients. Indeed, it might well be that Smith believes that the best remedy for nausea ought to be made available to chemotherapy patients and so long as he is genuinely ignorant that cannabis *is* the best such remedy, he would not be inconsistent in making this claim. The danger of epistemic fallacies, then, is that they may attribute beliefs to persons that they do not really hold.

Notice that the familiar *if you're not with us you're against us* type of argument is an instance of the epistemic fallacy. By claiming that a non-supporter takes an opposing position, the arguer makes an unwarranted assumption about the non-supporter's beliefs when, in fact, the non-supporter may hold a view that does not amount to an opposing one, or she may simply not have a view on the issue in question.[7] Here's an example:

> The President has made it perfectly clear: we know who the terrorists are, and we are going to hunt them down. Now Senator Routman wants to set limits on the pursuit of these killers, by opposing covert overseas invasions by Special Forces. So he thinks we should simply let them go?

Notice that these examples turn on verbs such as 'knows', 'believes' and 'wants'. Philosophers and linguists call verbs such as these **propositional attitude verbs**. If we reflect upon how these verbs are used, we see that we say someone *believes that . . .*, where the blank is filled by the expression of some proposition or other. A propositional attitude, then, expresses the fact that someone holds some attitude towards a specific proposition. Smith *believes* that such-and-such is the case; Jones *wants* such-and-such to happen; Brown *knows* that such-and-such is the case. Other examples are 'desires', 'hopes', 'prays' and 'wishes'.

Further fallacies

We said early in our discussion of fallacies that almost all are either formal or substantive fallacies. All such fallacies make for unsound arguments; they are either irremediably invalid, or depend on some very general, but false, implicit assumption. We turn now, however, to a different group of fallacies. These are labelled as fallacies, but not every instance of them will be invalid, or inductively unforceful, or even unsound. However, they are all **poor techniques at argument**; they should be criticised when we analyse arguments, and avoided in our own attempts to persuade by argument. Many of them, however, are useful for non-rational persuasion: they are frequently used to avoid engagement with an opponent, or to

---

7   The *if you're not with us, you're against us* argument can also be an instance of the false dilemma fallacy. The arguer implies that there are only two positions available on the issue in question – their own and one that is in direct opposition to it.

trump an opponent in the knowledge that their premises do not actually give good reason to accept their conclusions. In many cases they do have persuasive power.

Although reconstruction will be helpful in analysing instances of these fallacies, they cannot be exposed by making explicit a false assumption that drives *all* instances of the fallacy in question. This is because there is no single false assumption (expressed as a generalisation or a conditional) that underlies *all* instances of each of these fallacies. So while we should, in order to expose their fallacious reasoning, continue the practice of reconstructing arguments that we suspect of committing these fallacies, it is not so easy to give a straightforward method for detecting these fallacies.

Equivocation

The rhetorical ploy of trading on an equivocation is the ploy whereby we deliberately use a word or form of words with the intention to confuse the audience; one hopes that the audience will conflate the two or more possible interpretations. A single unsupported claim, rather than an argument, may be the instrument of the ploy. To fall prey to the fallacy of equivocation, by contrast, is to fail to notice an ambiguity, *thereby accepting the conclusion of an argument*, when one should not have. Silly but clear examples are easy to come by; for example: 'In the Philosophy department, someone broke one of the chair's legs; therefore one of the Philosophy department's professors has a broken leg' (equivocation on the word 'chair'). Such a case is simple and amusing but no one would actually be taken in by it. In the more interesting cases, explaining the fallacy can be a subtle conceptual task. For example:

> Some conservatives claim moral universal truths; they claim that throughout history, in all times and places, people fundamentally have the same rights. This displays a lamentable ignorance of history, and – characteristically of conservatives – of other cultures. It is a plain fact that at other times in history, and in other parts of the world today, human beings do not have the same rights. In some countries, for example, a man has the right forcibly to confine his wife to the home if he sees fit; not so in our culture. The conservative claim of universal rights is plainly false.

The arguer wishes to conclude that, contrary to certain conservatives who believe in universal moral truths, whether or not a human being possesses a given right depends on what culture they are in. Thus ignoring some irrelevant material, we may reconstruct it as a very simple argument:

P1)   In some countries, men have the right to confine their wives forcibly; in other countries they do not.

C1)   It is not the case that human beings have the same rights in all places and at all times.

C2)   The conservative claim – that throughout history, in all times and places, people fundamentally have the same rights – is false.

The argument equivocates on the word 'right', however. Both senses are established items in our language, but they are close together in meaning. In one sense of the word, to possess a 'right' is be allowed, by the culture or other social environment one is in (often, but not always, this a system of laws), to perform a certain action. Call this the 'conventional' sense of the word. In the other sense, to possess a 'right' is to be such that one ought, whatever culture or other social environment one is in, to be allowed to perform a certain action – even if one is not in fact allowed to. Call this the 'philosophical' sense of the word. Thus one may possess rights in the philosophical sense that are not rights in the conventional sense. The trouble with the argument is that it uses both senses: if we keep to the conventional sense of the word, P1 is true, C1 is true, and the inference from P1 to C1 is valid. The inference to C2 would be valid if the conservative claim were intended in the conventional sense. But the conservative claim, no doubt, was that rights are invariant in the philosophical sense of the word. In that case C2 cannot be inferred from C1; the inference would be no better than the silly one about the broken chair.

Red herring

So-named after the practice of dragging a smelly, salt-cured (and therefore reddish) herring across the trail of an animal tracked by dogs. The red herring fallacy is used as a technique to throw someone off the scent of one's argument by distracting them with an irrelevance. The rhetorical ploy of the smokescreen constitutes a similar tactic. However, where an irrelevant premise(s) is given as a *reason* for accepting the conclusion being advanced, the red herring fallacy is committed. For example:

> The judge should rule against the charge of false accounting
> against the President. The President is very popular, and presides
> over an extremely healthy economy.

The arguer seems to advance the president's political success as a reason to rule against the charge of financial corruption. If we make the reasonable assumption that the judge should rule strictly on the basis of the president's guilt or innocence, then the president's political success is utterly irrelevant. Reconstructed, the argument looks like this:

P1)   The President is very popular, and presides over an extremely healthy economy.

P2)   If the president is very popular, and presides over an extremely healthy economy, then the judge should rule against the charge of false accounting.

C)   **The court should rule against the plaintiff's charge of false accounting.**

In general, the red herring fallacy is that of inferring a conclusion from a premise that is strictly irrelevant to it, but in a way that has the potential to fool the audience into accepting the inference. Normally this is accomplished by a premise that tends to instil some sort of positive attitude towards the conclusion. In this case, the premise is intended to make the audience feel supportive towards the President, thus unreceptive to the idea that he should be convicted of misconduct.

Note that, although red herring arguments can easily be represented as valid, red herring is not a substantive fallacy. P2 is obviously false, but our ability to recognise this depends on our knowledge of what is and what is not relevant to the establishment of guilt in a court of law. More generally, what is and what is not relevant to a conclusion will depend on the conclusion's particular subject-matter. So there is not going to be one characteristic premise that red herring fallacies assume, in the way that there is, for example, in the case of inverting cause and effect. So red herring, according to our categories, is not a substantive fallacy.

It is worth re-emphasising, finally, that to say that someone has been taken in by a red herring fallacy is to say that they have been fooled. Unlike most other fallacies, the ability to recognise red herring varies depending on our knowledge of the subject-matter of the argument. But if X honestly believes, for example, that cancer is always caused by thinking morally bad thoughts, then, although having developed cancer is irrelevant to the question of the moral character of their thoughts, X does not commit red herring if X infers, from the fact Y has cancer, that Y must have been thinking bad thoughts. X is just badly informed. The point of distinguishing red herring as a fallacy of irrelevance is to single out the cases where one is fooled by an irrelevance, where one ought to have known better. Every minimally educated person knows, for example, that guilt or innocence in a court of law is properly established only by the preponderance of evidence; because of this, one who advances or accepts the argument given above has been fooled by an irrelevance, and has thus committed red herring.

Slippery slope

This fallacy occurs when an arguer wrongly assumes that to permit or forbid a course of action will inevitably lead to the occurrence of further related and undesirable events, without providing *good reasons* to suppose that the further events will indeed inevitably follow; and thus to allow the first is to tread on a slippery slope down which we will slide to the other events. Since its rhetorical power is derived from fear or dislike of the undesirable events, it is from a rhetorical point of view closely related to the appeal to fear. Slippery slope arguments are sometimes used to justify particularly harsh laws or penal sentences and occur frequently in debates about the liberalisation or toughening of laws or constraints on behaviour, as in the following example about the decriminalisation of cannabis use:

> The decriminalisation of cannabis would be just the start. It would lead to a downward spiral into widespread abuse of harder drugs like heroin and cocaine.

The implicit conclusion is that cannabis should not be decriminalised. The only explicit premise is that if cannabis were decriminalised then the use of hard drugs would increase. So an initial reconstruction represents the argument as invalid:

P1)   If cannabis were to be decriminalised, the use of hard drugs would increase.

___

C)   **Cannabis should not be decriminalised.**

Notice that as it stands the argument also commits the fallacy of deriving 'ought' from 'is'. To correct this, we need to add a premise to make good the connection between the non-prescriptive premise and the prescriptive conclusion, thus ending up with the following argument:

P1)   If cannabis use were decriminalised, the use of hard drugs would increase.
P2)   Anything that leads to increased use of harder drugs should be avoided.

___

C)   **Cannabis should not be decriminalised.**

The immediate problem is that we have not been given a reason to think that P1 is true; that is, no reason to think that decriminalisation of cannabis will unavoidably be the beginning of a slippery slope to an increase the use of hard drugs. Of course, some slopes really are slippery; even in this case, it might be possible to give such reasons and they might form part of an extended argument for the same conclusion. But as it stands the argument remains fallacious, because the arguer has not given a *reason* for supposing that it is inevitable that allowing the first event will precipitate a slide into even worse events. (This form of argument is sometimes called **floodgates** – the arguer alleges without evidence that allowing X will inevitably open the floodgates to Y and Z.)

Straw man

This is the fallacy that occurs when an arguer ignores their opponent's real position on an issue and sets up a weaker version of that position by misrepresentation, exaggeration, distortion or simplification. This makes it easier to defeat; thereby creating the impression that the real argument has been refuted. The straw man argument, like the straw man himself, is easier to knock down than the real thing. Suppose that Jones is an advocate of the legalisation of voluntary euthanasia; that is Jones believes that terminally ill patients should have the legal right to choose to have their life ended if their suffering has greatly diminished their quality of life, and doctors agree that the patient's mental state is sufficiently sound to make the decision rationally. Smith, Jones' opponent, responds as follows:

> How can you support giving doctors the right to end a person's life just because they decide that the person's life is no longer worth living; no one should have that power over another person's life, and doctors should not kill patients.

According to Smith, Jones advocates that doctors should unilaterally have the power to end a patient's life, if they think that the patient's life is not worth living. That would be a very controversial position. But it is not Jones' position. Jones' position is that patients should have the choice of euthanasia, so long as that choice is approved by doctors. Of course the doctor administers the lethal drug, but only at the behest of the patient, as Jones envisages things. Smith thus fails to engage with Jones' *actual* position and instead misrepresents it as a more extreme and therefore weaker position that (as far as we know) Jones does not advocate.

Begging the question

An argument commits the fallacy of begging the question when the truth of its conclusion is assumed by one or more of its premises, and the truth of the premises depend for their justification on the truth of the conclusion. Thus the premises ask the audience to grant the conclusion even before the argument is given. Contrary to the way in which the phrase is sometimes used in ordinary discourse, 'begging the question' does not mean raising the question without offering an argument. By way of example, imagine the following scenario:

> Three thieves pull off a successful heist and steal four diamonds, but they can't decide how to divide their haul. Eventually the first thief says: 'I should get two diamonds, and you two should get one each, because I'm the leader.' The second thief says: 'Wait a minute, who says you're the leader?' The first thief replies: 'I must be the leader, I'm getting the largest share of the haul.'

A reconstruction enables us to see clearly the way in which the first thief's reasoning begs the question. Initially thief number one appears to argue from the proposition that he's the leader together with the implicit premise that leaders should always get the biggest haul to the conclusion that he should get the biggest share:

P1)   I'm the leader of the gang.
P2)   Gang leaders should always get the biggest share of their
      gang's haul.
_____

C)   I should get the biggest share of the haul.

But when requested by thief number two to justify P1 he argues as follows:

P1)   I'm getting the biggest share of the haul.
P2)   Whoever gets the biggest share of the haul is the leader.
_____

C1)   I must be the leader of the gang.

Once we put the two steps of the argument together to form a complex argument, we see that it begs the question of who should get the biggest share:

P1)   I'm getting the biggest share of the haul.
P2)   Whomever receives the biggest share of the haul is the leader.
_____

C1)   I must be the leader of the gang.

P3)   Gang leaders always receive the biggest share of their gang's haul.

C2)   I'm getting the biggest share of the haul.

Thief number one is guilty of begging the question (in addition to armed robbery) because P1, which he uses to reach C2, expresses the same proposition as that expressed by C2. So the conclusion – that thief number one gets the biggest share – is already assumed by the premises. Notice that each inference stage passes our test for validity, if the premises were true, the conclusion would have to be true, but the argument is a clear instance of the fallacy of begging the question of who should get the biggest share of the proceeds of the robbery.

An argument's premise(s) and conclusion need not express a proposition in precisely the same way (as they do in the previous example) in order for it to count as an instance of begging the question. It is sufficient that the premise be a version of, or rely upon, the claim made by the conclusion. If someone were to argue from the premise that newspaper editors claim that their publications are better than any other medium for finding out about events overseas, to the conclusion that newspapers are the best source of international news, their argument would commit the fallacy of begging the question. For obvious reasons, the fallacy of begging the question is often referred to as 'circular reasoning'.

False dilemma

This is the fallacy of limiting consideration of positions on an issue to fewer alternatives than there are that should be considered. Typically, the arguer pretends that there are only two options, when in fact there are more: the arguer sets up a dilemma where none really exists by misrepresenting the possible positions on an issue, so that there appears to be a straight choice between their own and its opposite. The fallacy is committed by a politician who argues as follows:

> There is a tough choice facing the Government and the nation:
> either we cut taxes and increase everyone's spending power,
> thereby providing much needed stimulation to the economy, or we
> increase spending on health and education. It is impossible to do
> both; and without a tax cut the economy will remain weak. So
> increased spending on health and education will have to wait.

As a reconstruction shows, the argument is valid, but the fallacy is driven by the false assumption that cutting taxes and increasing public spending on health and education preclude each other.

P1)   We should stimulate the economy.

P2)   The only way to stimulate the economy is by cutting taxes.

C1)   We should cut taxes

P3)   We cannot both cut taxes and increase public spending on health and education.

C2)   We should not increase public spending on health and education.

The assumption in P3 is not true because (a) if a tax cut does improve the economy, then even if the Government takes a smaller proportion of the Gross National Product it might take more in absolute terms (because the GNP will be larger); (b) expenditure on health and education might be increased by diverting Government funds from other areas such as defence; (c) the Government might be able to sustain a period of decreased tax revenues and increased overall expenditure by increasing its debt (or decreasing its surplus, as the case may be).

The fallacy of false dilemma is often used to make the false assumption that if someone does not agree with X, they must be anti-X, whereas they may hold some intermediate position or be undecided. For example, suppose someone asks you if you are in favour of positive discrimination towards under-represented groups in the award of promotion to higher grades of a profession (affirmative action). You reply that you are not and, employing a fallacious inference, they accuse you of being against affirmative action, when in fact you may just be undecided, neither for nor against it. Or, worse, perhaps they retort that you support discrimination against under-represented groups, and therefore are racist, ageist and misogynist (among other things).

CHAPTER SUMMARY

Rhetorical ploys and **fallacies** are both instances of **sham-reasoning**. While rhetorical ploys seek to persuade by non-argumentative means, fallacies are argumentative attempts to persuade that embody some characteristic type of confusion or mistaken assumption. Many fallacious arguments may function at the very same time as an effective rhetorical ploy, thus causing the audience not to notice the fallacy. Insofar as we aim to be rational, and to appeal to the rationality of others, we should avoid using rhetorical ploys and fallacies in our own attempts to persuade and should take care not to be persuaded by others' rhetorical or fallacious attempts to persuade us to do and believe things. The best way of doing so is to familiarise ourselves with various common rhetorical ploys and fallacious forms of argument.

Many rhetorical ploys are *appeals to specific feelings or desires*; these include the appeals to **novelty**, **popularity**, **compassion**, **pity**, **guilt**, **fear**, **cuteness**, **sexiness**, **hipness**, **coolness**, **wealth**, **power** and many others. Typically a position or consumer item is represented in association with some object of the specific feeling or desire, in order that the feeling or desire should be directed upon the position or consumer item. The **direct attack** involves the bold assertion of a position or command; the **hard sell** is the direct attack repeated. The use of **buzzwords** is the use of words with high emotive or otherwise rhetorical charge to manipulate the passions of an audience. **Scare quotes** are used mockingly to make an opponent's position or other phenomenon look ridiculous or dubious. **Trading on an equivocation** occurs when someone knowingly makes an ambiguous statement that may be true when interpreted in a certain way, but when interpreted in another way, may be false, but also more favourable to the position being advanced or to the product being advertised. **Smokescreen** occurs when one talks about some highly controversial, compelling or otherwise arresting issue or object, in an effort to divert the audience momentarily from the issue under discussion. A successful smokescreen causes the audience to overlook the fact that the issue has not been addressed.

Fallacies can be grouped together according to certain shared features. **Formal** fallacies are simply mistaken inferences – inferences of certain characteristic kinds that are often mistakenly thought to be valid or inductively forceful. These include: the fallacies of **affirming the consequent** (of a conditional proposition) and **denying the antecedent** (of a conditional proposition); the **fallacy of deriving 'ought' from 'is'**, which is committed by any argument that attempts to move from solely descriptive premises to a prescriptive conclusion; and the **base rate fallacy**.

Substantive fallacies are committed by arguments that tacitly assume some very general principle of a characteristic kind that it may be tempting to rely upon, but which is false, and which can easily be seen to be false the moment it is brought to light. The fallacies of **majority belief** and **common practice** make illegitimate inferences from the commonality of a belief or an action to its acceptability. The **ad hominem** fallacy and the **tu quoque** fallacy use facts about the person(s) putting forward a position as grounds for rejecting it. The **appeal to authority** makes a mistaken appeal to the opinion of someone who is not qualified (or under-qualified) on the matter in hand. The **perfectionist fallacy** is committed when excessive demands are placed on an idea or proposal; the fallacy of **conflating morality with legality** occurs when we mistakenly assume that anything that is legal must also be moral or that anything that is illegal must be immoral. The fallacy of **weak analogy** arises when an argument employs an unsustainable or an unjustified analogy. **Causal fallacies** are committed when we make mistaken inferences about the cause of a phenomenon or an event. There are **three types** of causal fallacy: *post hoc ergo propter hoc* – the fallacy of assuming that the temporal priority of X over Y makes X the cause of Y; **fallacy of mistaking correlation for cause** – falsely assuming that the simultaneous occurrence of X and Y makes one the cause of the other; and the **fallacy of causal inversion** – the mistaken inference that if X causes Y, an absence of X will prevent Y. **Epistemic fallacies** and the fallacy of **appeal to ignorance** occur because of unwarranted inferences from what is known, believed or proven to additional knowledge, beliefs or proof of which the arguer has no independent evidence.

Substantive fallacies can be exposed by careful argument-reconstruction. An initial reconstruction will demonstrate that the argument, as stated, is either invalid or inductively unforceful. A second reconstruction can be used to reveal the false assumption that drives the fallacious reasoning, thereby demonstrating that the (amended) argument is unsound. For each substantive fallacy, all instances of the fallacy will be driven by the same or a very similar assumption.

Some fallacies are neither formal nor substantive. Not all instances of the fallacies considered in the final grouping of this chapter are invalid, non-inductively forceful or unsound even when carefully reconstructed. A deductively sound, hence valid argument may beg the question, for example. While the method of exposing hidden assumptions will prove helpful for some instances, there is no single false assumption that underlies all instances of each of these types of fallacies.

The **red herring** fallacy occurs when irrelevant premises are given as a reason for accepting a conclusion. A **slippery slope** fallacy is committed when an arguer assumes without justification that to permit or forbid a course of action will inevitably cause a chain of undesirable events. The **straw man** is deliberately set up as a target that will be easier to defeat than an opponent's real argument. An argument commits the fallacy of **begging the question** when the truth of its conclusion is assumed by its premise(s). The fallacy of **false dilemma** is committed when an argument limits consideration of positions on an issue to two mutually exclusive ones, thereby setting up an apparent dilemma, when there are other positions that could be considered.

EXERCISES

1 Name the following rhetorical ploys:

Example

If we allow the development of genetically engineered foodstuffs, we are leaving our children and our children's children open to the threat of genetic mutation and environmental disaster.

✎ **Appeal to fear/scare tactics.**

a The 'relationships' of homosexuals cannot be compared to that of marriage: marriage is something that involves a man and a woman united through the word of God.

b Take a look at the latest hatchback from Fraud: the new *Ergo*.

c Successfully applied knowledge management is now impacting on organisations in terms of both direct competitive advantage, and in building a learning culture that identifies itself through a shared vision and common purpose.

d More pet owners feed their puppies First Choice puppy food than any other. If you want to give the little fella a head start, shouldn't you, too?

e These people say we have a moral duty to honour our United Nations commitments and provide refugees with a safe haven. I say to you: look at all these people arriving here and then claiming state benefits, they are sucking this country dry.

f Fatbusters – the most successful diet programme on the market today!

g Imagine yourself, or worse, your daughter, alone beside your broken down car on a remote country road in the middle of the night. Few people pass by and no one stops to help. Don't get caught like that – don't get caught without a Phonecom mobile phone.

h   By scheduling the broadcast at 1 a.m., the TV company is committing an act of censorship.

i   Hair unmanageable and dull? Try Goldie Glow from Bella. The latest in hair management technology.

j   Opposition MP: The proposed secrecy legislation is a threat to democracy and should be strenuously opposed. Government minister: It is scandalous that these matters have been put in the public arena via yet another document leaked by a civil servant. Such leaks are a breach of trust, a dereliction of duty.

2   Without looking back at the relevant section, name the two types of sham-reasoning and write a paragraph explaining the difference between them giving an example of each to illustrate that difference.

3   Name the fallacy committed by the following arguments. If no fallacy is committed, write 'N/F'.

   Example

   No one has ever been able to prove the existence of extrasensory perception. We must therefore conclude that extrasensory perception is a myth.

   ✎ **Appeal to ignorance.**

a   Our employees have asked us to provide lounge areas where they can spend their breaks. This request will have to be refused. If we give them lounge areas, next they'll be asking for a swimming pool and sauna. Then it will be tennis courts, football pitches, fitness centres . . .

b   A few minutes after the minister made his speech to the City of London, a devastating explosion occurred. For the safety of the people who live and work in the city, it is imperative that the minister makes no more speeches here.

c   Publishing these vile criminals' names and addresses in our paper was definitely the right thing to do. We have been inundated with calls and faxes from readers who support our stance.

d   If she doesn't finish her assignment on time, she will fail the course. She has failed the course so obviously she didn't finish her assignment on time.

e   We have a simple choice between developing genetically manipulated crops or continuing to stand by while thousands of people in the developing world die of starvation and malnutrition.

f As my client has pointed out, tax avoidance is not illegal, so she has done nothing immoral.

g The Japanese diet is low in dairy products and certain cancers have a very low incidence in Japan. So if you want to avoid cancer, give up drinking milk and eating milk products.

h Teachers say that their job is becoming harder and harder and that they deserve more pay. But the Government should ignore them, they're just a bunch of whingeing liberals.

i It's all very well for the caring middle classes to say that we should provide more aid to the developing world, but remember that most of them are preaching at us from around their well-stocked dining tables.

j Given the evidence that so many students are cheating in examinations, examinations should be abolished in favour of assessment by coursework.

4 (i) Name the fallacy committed by each of the following arguments and (ii) reconstruct the argument to demonstrate its fallaciousness.

Example

Democracy is the best system of government. Most people in the world believe in the superiority of democratic systems.

✎ (i) **Fallacy of majority belief.**

   (ii) P1) Most people believe in democratic systems.
        P2) Any belief held by the majority is true.

   _____

   C) **Democracy is the best system of government.**

a Our lecturers are always extolling the virtues of critical thinking, but they would say that wouldn't they? They only keep their jobs if they've got students to teach.

b It's not illegal for me to exaggerate skills on my curriculum vitae, so it can't be immoral either.

c My doctor says that wearing high heels is bad for your knees, but she wears high heels, so I don't think they really are.

d Smoking causes lung cancer so people who do not smoke will not suffer lung cancer.

e Jo believes that Chancellor of the Exchequer is doing a poor job. Thus Jo believes that Gordon Brown is doing a poor job.

f   Whenever the cherry trees blossom, the weather begins to get warmer. So cherry blossoms cause the weather to get warmer.

g   David Beckham is the best midfielder ever to play for England and he says that Britburgers are his favourite. They must be the best burgers.

h   We shouldn't allow children to watch *Pokemon*, because pretty soon they will be collecting farm animals and staging contests to see who has the strongest pig. It's only a short step from there to complete disrespect for animal life.

i   There's nothing wrong with getting drunk once in a while, everyone I know is partial to a few beers now and again.

j   There is no point in implementing harsh penalties for drunk drivers because there will always be some people who are going to drive drunk no matter what penalties are put in place.

k   If a car breaks down on the road, no one thinks that a passing mechanic is obligated to render emergency road service. So why expect doctors to render emergency medical assistance to all and sundry?

5   Provide an example of each of the following fallacies. Try to make your example appreciably different from those already provided for you.

Example

Denying the antecedent

✎ **If he took all of his medication, he should be feeling better by now. He flushed half of his medication down the lavatory so he can't be feeling any better.**

a   Begging the question

b   Red herring

c   Straw man

d   Mistaking correlation for cause

e   Perfectionist fallacy

f   *Ad hominem*

g   Deriving 'ought' from 'is'

h   Weak analogy

i   Base rate fallacy

j   *Tu quoque*

Chapter 5

The practice of argument-reconstruction

The goal of argument-reconstruction is to produce a clear and completely explicit statement of the argument that the arguer had in mind. The desired clarity and explicitness is achieved by putting all of the argument, and nothing but the argument, into standard form: this displays the argument's premises, intermediate conclusions and conclusion, and indicates the inferences between them. The strength of the argument is understood in terms of the concepts discussed in Chapters 2 and 3 – validity, inductive force, deductive and inductive soundness. In this chapter, we begin to see, in more detail, how the practice of reconstruction goes; in particular, we learn some ways of coping with commonly encountered difficulties.

Extraneous material

The first step in analysing and reconstructing an argument is to identify its conclusion, then its premises. But much of what people say or write, when advancing an argument, plays no argumentative role. Much is there for emphasis, or is rhetorical, or plays some other role than that of expressing the propositions that properly constitute the argument. When reconstructing arguments, then, we have to hive off this extraneous material. Here's an example; we've given each sentence a number in order to facilitate a detailed discussion of it:

> (1) Once again the problem of young people drinking in city centres and generally creating chaos rears its ugly head. (2) The recent trouble in York was some of the worst. (3) It happens over and over, so much that people just seem to shrug their shoulders, accepting it as a fact of life, or a law of nature. (4) So are we simply resigned to it? (5) Do we simply accept that our young people are going to waste the best years of their lives acting like hooligans? (or rather, being hooligans?) (6) Do we stand idly by? (7) I don't think so. (8) Not I, at any rate. (9) And there's a ready solution. (10) Let us turn to an old solution for a new problem: compulsory military service. (11) Because they would learn habits of discipline, and something about community spirit, it's pretty obvious that young people would be a lot less likely to cause trouble when finished.

The arguer's conclusion here seems to be that Britain should introduce compulsory military service for its youth. The most important premise is the conditional statement that if compulsory military service were introduced, then the problem of drunkenness and hooliganism among British youth would be curtailed. Sentence 11 seems to be provided as a premise in a sub-argument for that claim. But there is a lot of other material:

- The first two sentences function as stage-setting: they alert the reader to the problem being discussed, and perhaps serve to emphasise the immediacy and severity of the problem. Sentences 1–8, as a group, are intended to persuade the reader that the problem is serious enough that something ought to be done about it. That much is surely a premise of the main argument; but it should be evident that they do not provide an argument for that claim. They merely assert the claim in a rhetorically charged way.

- The function of sentence 9 is simply to announce that the author is now going to turn from stressing the gravity of the problem to suggesting a solution – in other words, that the author is now going to give the argument.
- Sentence 10 asserts the conclusion. But it does not do so in the most economical or straightforward way. The bit about the 'old solution for a new problem' is a rhetorical flourish that should be omitted from the reconstruction. Also, it seems clear that the arguer is saying that compulsory military service *should* be introduced, not just that it would solve the problem. The conclusion, then, should be rewritten as 'Compulsory military service should be introduced' (there will be more on this type of 'practical' conclusion later in the chapter).
- Sentence 11 includes the words 'it's pretty obvious that . . .'. Phrases of that kind – phrases that merely serve to emphasise the claim being made – should always be eliminated from reconstructed arguments.
- Sentence 11 exemplifies a use of the word 'because' that should always be eliminated from reconstructed arguments. Often we use 'because' when speaking of cause and effect, as in 'The cake is dry because it was baked too long'. In sentence 11, however, the word does something else: it indicates a relation between premise and conclusion of a sub-argument to the main argument. In particular, the arguer is giving the following sub-argument:

P1)   If British youth were to acquire habits of discipline and community spirit, then the problem of drunkenness and hooliganism among them would be reduced.

P2)   If made to perform military service, British youth would acquire habits of discipline and community service.

C1)   If British youth were made to perform military service, the problem of drunkenness and hooliganism among them would be reduced.

C1 serves as an intermediate conclusion in the arguer's overall argument. The word 'because', in this usage, is equivalent to the word 'since', which functions in the following way. If we say 'If there are no clouds, it isn't raining', then we have not asserted either that it isn't raining, nor that there aren't any clouds (review the section in Chapter 2 on conditionals if this is not clear). If we say, however, '*Since* there are no clouds, it isn't raining', then we've asserted both. So what the word '*since*' does is to transform a conditional statement into a statement that asserts both the conditional and the antecedent of that conditional, and thereby asserts its consequent. It provides a compact way of expressing simple arguments of the form: 'If P, then Q; P, therefore Q.' 'Because', in the usage we are discussing, does exactly the same thing. And since our aim in recon structing arguments is to lay out the arguments explicitly and clearly, we should eliminate such uses of 'because' and 'since', and unpack the arguments they serve to indicate. (The *causal* use of 'because' is another matter, however; it will be discussed later in this chapter; see also the discussion of 'because' in Chapter 1, pp. 18–20.)

Bearing in mind that the above argument laid out in standard form is a sub-argument for C1, a reconstruction of the remainder of the argument might go like this:

C1) If British youth were made to perform military service, the problem of drunkenness and hooliganism among them would be reduced.

P3) Something should be done to reduce the problem of drunkenness and hooliganism among British youth.

C2) Britain should introduce compulsory military service for its youth.

We will be in a better position later in the chapter to say whether or not such an argument is valid. The main lesson here is that the first step in reconstructing an argument is to make a **list** of the argument's premises and conclusion that leaves out extraneous material, and that expresses the premises and conclusion as concisely and clearly as possible. Note however, that making such a list is only the first step towards a complete reconstruction. A complete reconstruction also includes premises and conclusions that are only implicit in the original argument (and which therefore do not appear on the initial list). A complete reconstruction also displays the structure of an extended argument by displaying inter- mediate conclusions. It should be clear that the correct argument tree is as shown in Figure 5.1 (see over).

Defusing the rhetoric

Much of the task of reconstruction is the task of clarification. In Chapter 1, we discussed several linguistic phenomena that frequently impede clarity,

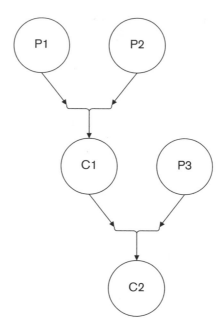

Figure 5.1

including ambiguity, vagueness, the differing roles of primary and secondary connotation and conversational implicature, rhetorical questions, figures of speech, irony and implicit relativity. We will deal with the specific problems of ambiguity and vagueness later in this chapter. At this point we deal with some other impediments to clear reconstruction. Suppose Kemp has been caught stealing money from the company, and someone says:

> That damned Kemp's been caught with his hand in the cookie jar again. He's history.

The arguer is reasoning is follows:

P1) If Kemp has been caught stealing money from the company, then he is going to be fired.
P2) Kemp has been caught stealing money from the company.

C) Kemp is going to be fired.

As you can see, in giving the reconstruction, we have eliminated the metaphor 'caught with his hand in the cookie jar', the **expressive epithet** 'that damned Kemp', and the slang 'he's history'. Not as colourful, but much more amenable to logical analysis. When reconstructing, eliminate metaphors, expressive epithets and slang.

What exactly are **expressive epithets**? These are terms used to refer to some person, group or other entity – just like a proper name such as 'Gary Kemp' or 'Paris' – but that characterise the entity referred to for rhetorical purposes (non-logically persuasive purposes, or non-persuasive purposes such as humour). Let us look at a well-known real example that demonstrates how complex their use can be. In 2003, US and British forces along with smaller forces from some other countries invaded Iraq, for the purpose of removing the Government and military capabilities of its president Sadaam Hussein. His military capabilities, it was claimed, included the so-called 'Weapons of Mass Destruction' (note that this itself might be regarded as an expressive epithet). American Secretary of State Colin Powell had in March of that year announced a list of thirty countries that had agreed to be named as supporting the invasion, including, of course, those that would actually be contributing troops or other military assistance. He announced it as 'The Coalition of the Willing'. In the weeks before the invasion, however, leaders of France, Germany and Belgium had voiced vociferous opposition to the invasion, arguing that UN inspection teams should be given more time to verify whether or not Iraq possessed illegal weapons, which constituted the primary reason for the invasion. Here is a comment from a public debate held at the time:

> You think our coalition of the willing needs the Gang of Three?
> They can sit on the fence; let 'em.

In the context, it was clear that the first sentence was a **rhetorical question**: the speaker's intention was to assert that the answer is no, the coalition of the willing does not need the Gang of Three. Rhetorical questions should always be rewritten as declarative sentences. Now as for the epithets. What the terms stand for, literally, are simply two groups of countries: one supporting the invasion, and one opposed. 'Coalition of the willing' has a rather positive 'spin' to it (for the others are made to sound 'unwilling', hence complacent or perhaps cowardly), but 'Gang of Three' sounds distinctly negative, owing to the connotation of 'Gang of Four', which signified a notorious group within the Chinese communist government in the 1970's who were partly responsible for the disastrous 'cultural revolution' of Mao Tse-Tung's later years. But shorn of all this spin and rhetoric, these emotive associations, the factual content of the sentence is merely something like this:

> In order to undertake the invasion successfully, the invading
> countries and their supporters do not require approval or support
> from France, Germany and Belgium.

The phrase 'sit on the fence' is, in this context, another pejorative phrase; the sentence containing it seems to mean that approval and support from those countries is not needed. The intended argument, then, was probably this:

P1) In order to undertake the invasion successfully, the invading countries and their supporters do not require approval or support from France, Germany and Belgium.

P2) If, in order to undertake the invasion successfully, the invading countries and their supporters do not require approval or support from France, Germany and Belgium, then they should undertake the invasion without it.

C) **The invading countries should undertake the invasion without approval or support from France, Germany and Belgium.**

Logical streamlining

In Chapter 2 we devoted a good deal of attention to certain expressions whose logical nature is comparatively easy to grasp. These include 'if–then', 'not', 'every', 'all' and 'or'. For example, one exercise asked you to translate sentences containing the comparatively difficult expressions 'only if' and 'unless' into easier forms using 'if–then' and, where needed, 'not'. So we learned that 'A unless B' means the same as 'If not-B, then A'. In general, when reconstructing arguments we should strive to display the logical relationships in an argument in the simplest, clearest and most familiar ways possible. An example will illustrate this:

> We read over and over that when all is said and done, what is best for the child is the family. But what would the elimination of the marriage tax-credit mean? Less incentive to marry. And what would that mean? Fewer couples getting married. And what would that mean? A reduction in the proportion of children living in families.

It should be clear that after the first sentence that the arguer is expressing some *conditionals*: if the marriage tax-credit is eliminated, then there will be less incentive to get married. If there is less incentive to get married, then fewer couples will get married. If fewer couples get married then the proportion of children living in families will be reduced. But this, according to the arguer's first sentence, should be avoided. Thus the argument might be reconstructed like this:

P1) If the marriage tax-credit is eliminated, then there will be less incentive to get married.

P2) If there is less incentive to get married, then fewer couples will get married.

P3) If fewer couples get married, then the proportion of children living in families will be reduced.

P4) The proportion of children living in families should not be reduced.

C)   The marriage tax-credit should not be eliminated.

This reconstruction, however, leaves two intermediate conclusions implicit. A completely explicit reconstruction represents it as an extended argument:

P1) If the marriage tax-credit is eliminated, then there will be less incentive to get married.

P2) If there is less incentive to get married, then fewer couples will get married.

C1)   If the marriage tax-credit is eliminated, then fewer couples will get married.

P3) If fewer couples get married, then the proportion of children living in families will be reduced.

C2)   If the marriage tax-credit is eliminated, then the proportion of children living in families will be reduced.

P4) The proportion of children living in families should not be reduced.

C3)   The marriage tax-credit should not be eliminated.

The point we want to stress here is that we have replaced the language used by the arguer to express these conditional propositions with explicit if–then sentences. The language used by the arguer is not especially unclear, but it is awkward to deal with because it does not even take the form of proper sentences. Rewriting the material in terms of if–then sentences makes the argument easier to handle and its logic more obvious.

This is just one example of what we mean by logical streamlining. There are many, many ways in which ordinary language can be awkward to reconstruct, and in which logical relationships can be concealed; so we cannot give anything like an exhaustive list of exact rules for logical streamlining. But here are some 'rules of thumb' that you should apply whenever you can do so in a way that remains faithful to the arguer's apparent meaning:

1   Where appropriate, rewrite sentences as either *conditional* or *disjunctive sentences* of one of the following forms:

If A then B.	If not-A then not-B.
If not-A then B.	If A then not-B.
A or B.	A or not-B.
Not-A or B.	Not-A or not-B.

2   Rewrite generalisations in one of the following forms, where the blank '__' is filled by a quantifier such as 'all', 'some', 'most', 'no', 'almost all', etc.:

__ F are G.
__ are not-G.

We will not stick to this religiously, as it is not always possible, and doing it will sometimes distract from other points we are trying to make. What we will do, rather, is continue to practise it on many occasions throughout the book. For example, in the section on rewriting for rhetorical neutrality we employed simple if–then sentences. If you pay attention, you should gradually develop a feel for logical streamlining.

Implicit and explicit

Not only do actual statements of arguments typically include a lot of material that is inessential to the argument, they often *exclude* some of what is essential to the argument: some essential propositions are left **implicit**. Our task in reconstruction is to make the argument fully **explicit**. To say that a proposition is **implicit** in an argument is to say that it is part of the argument intended by the arguer – either as a premise or as the conclusion – but that it has not actually been stated by the arguer. To **make the proposition explicit** is simply to state it – in particular, to include it in our reconstruction of the argument. So a large part of argument-reconstruction is to make explicit what was merely implicit in the original statement of the argument.

Consider a very simple case:

Is Mr Jenkins well-educated? Well of course. Didn't you know that he's a successful politician?

The arguer might be presumed to be arguing as follows:

P1)   Mr Jenkins is a successful politician.

C)   Mr Jenkins is well-educated.

So rendered, the argument is invalid. Nor is it inductively forceful, since in order to know whether or not the premise makes the conclusion probable, you have to know something the argument's premise does not tell us – namely whether or not successful politicians, at least usually, are well-educated. But it is clear that, in drawing this inference, the arguer is making the assumption that successful politicians are well-educated. We have to make this assumption explicit:

P1)   Mr Jenkins is a successful politician.
P2)   All successful politicians are well-educated.

C)   Mr Jenkins is well-educated.

Or perhaps we should write 'almost all' rather than 'all'.

Let us now consider a real and more complicated example. The moa was a very large, flightless bird, which was native to New Zealand but which is now believed to be extinct. The yeti is a large, white-furred ape, which is probably only mythical, but which some people believe actually inhabits the Himalayas. Here is the argument:

> The moa is thought to have been extinct for at least 100 years. So naturally a great deal of scepticism is met by Paddy Freaney's claim to have seen a moa in 1993. But as Freaney himself has pointed out, Freaney has climbed Mount Everest twice, and has not claimed to have seen a yeti. So we ought to believe Mr Freaney's claim.[1]

The first task of argument-reconstruction should be to identify, and if necessary, to restate, the conclusion of the argument. Now in this case it might seem obvious that the conclusion of this argument is stated explicitly in the last sentence: 'we ought to believe Mr Freaney's claim.' But this is not the most straightforward and informative way to put it. Ask yourself: exactly what proposition is the ultimate concern of the arguer here? The arguer attempts to persuade us to accept a certain claim of Paddy Freaney's; but this does not really tell us the ultimate concern of

---

1   Sunday *Star-Times*, Auckland, New Zealand, 10 December 1995, p. C5.

the arguer until we specify what claim that is. Freaney's claim, the one that ultimately concerns the arguer, is the claim that he saw a moa. So what the arguer is really trying to persuade us of is that Paddy Freaney did see a moa. Here then is a case in which the conclusion is at least partly implicit; none of the sentences directly says that Paddy Freaney saw a moa. Indeed, it might plausibly be suggested that the conclusion ultimately at issue here is one that is inferred from the proposition that Freaney saw a moa, namely, that the moa is not extinct. In that case it would be even more obvious that the conclusion of the argument is only implicit in the original statement of the argument. But let us not push the matter quite as far as that. For simplicity we shall take the conclusion to be that Paddy Freaney saw a moa.

Once we have identified the conclusion, we must identify the argument's premises. It is clear that the first two sentences in the example function as stage-setting, informing the reader of some of the relevant concerns surrounding the issue, and are not premises of the argument. The arguer is arguing that Paddy Freaney saw a moa; this proposition is certainly not supported by the fact that the moa is thought to be extinct, nor by the fact that many people doubt Freaney's claim to have seen one. If anything, those facts make it *less* credible that Freaney saw a moa. So, by the **principle of charity**, we should not take the arguer to be citing those facts in support of the conclusion that Freaney saw a moa. Rather, the function of these propositions is to acknowledge that there is reasonable resistance to Freaney's claim. This sort of thing is very common: very frequently, an arguer will begin by explaining why there is opposition to his or her conclusion.

The only premise explicitly given is that Freaney has twice climbed Mount Everest, and has not claimed to see a yeti. So our first shot at a reconstruction might look like this:

P1)   Paddy Freaney climbed Mount Everest twice, and did not claim to see a yeti.

C)   **Paddy Freaney saw a moa.**

Now this is a start, but clearly it does not do justice to the arguer's intentions. As it stands, the argument is neither deductively valid nor inductively forceful. To see this, suppose the only information you are given is that a certain person climbed Mount Everest twice, and that that person did not claim that he saw a yeti. Does that give you any reason to infer that that person saw a moa? Obviously not. P1 does not support the conclusion by itself.

Yet the argument as originally intended by the arguer surely does have at least some inductive force. Therefore, the arguer must be implicitly relying upon some further premise or premises, which we should try to make explicit. One proposition, which is surely relied upon by the argument, but which is not explicitly stated in the argument, is simply that Paddy Freaney claimed he saw a moa. The second sentence almost states this explicitly, but does not quite do so. So we should include this in our reconstruction:

P1)   Paddy Freaney has claimed he saw a moa.
P2)   Paddy Freaney climbed Mount Everest twice, and did not
        claim to see a yeti.

C)   Paddy Freaney saw a moa.

This is better. We now have in the premises, it seems, a statement of all the particular facts about Paddy Freaney from which the arguer is inferring that Paddy Freaney saw a moa. But still we have not made everything explicit. In order to see this, ask yourself, why does P2 – in view of the fact that Paddy Freaney claimed he saw a moa – support the conclusion that he did see a moa? It is something like this: the arguer seems to be responding to the charge that Freaney is liar, that he wishes fraudulently to claim credit for a certain sort of zoological discovery. As against this, the arguer points out that Freaney climbed Everest twice without claiming a yeti-sighting. But surely, reasons the arguer, if a person were the sort to go around making false claims about seeing strange creatures, then if he has twice climbed Mount Everest, he would probably have claimed to see a yeti (for such a person, having visited Everest, surely would not be able to resist claiming to have seen the notorious yeti). But Freaney climbed Everest twice without making such a claim, so he must not be such a person. If he is not such a person, then he didn't lie about the moa. So, if he *said* he saw a moa, he *did* see a moa.

What is missing from the preceding reconstruction, then, is an assumed generalisation: a person who has visited Mount Everest without claiming to see a yeti is not a person who would fabricate the sighting of a creature whose existence is disputed. This is a generalisation because it is not something said on the basis of knowledge about Paddy Freaney in particular. It is plausible to say, as a general fact about human nature, that a person who wishes to tell 'tall tales' about some particular kind of thing is unlikely to pass up a favourable opportunity to do so.

The argument implicitly depends upon this generalisation as a premise; hence in our reconstruction we should make it explicit:

P1)   Paddy Freaney has claimed he saw a moa.
P2)   Paddy Freaney climbed Mount Everest twice, and did not claim to see a yeti.
P3)   A person who lies about sighting creatures whose existence is disputed would claim to see a yeti, if he or she were to climb Mount Everest.

C)   Paddy Freaney saw a moa.

Note that, although we could have produced a valid argument by writing 'everything Paddy Freaney says is true' (or an inductively forceful argument by writing 'most of what Paddy Freaney says is true'), doing so would have failed to take into account the relevance of P2. If we had written that premise in place of the actual P3, then the conclusion could have been inferred from that premise along with P1, and P2 would have played no role in the argument. This is important, because the arguer clearly means to give us a very specific reason to believe this particular claim of Freaney's; he or she is clearly not simply relying on Freaney's general honesty or trustworthiness.

This reconstruction of the argument now seems to include the relevant facts about Paddy Freaney upon which the arguer is relying, and it includes the generalisation upon which the arguer is (implicitly) relying. We could make its structure a bit more explicit by making an intermediate conclusion explicit, and adding one further relevant point about the moa (note that we have had to change the numbering of the premises):

P1)   Paddy Freaney climbed Mount Everest twice, and did not claim to see a yeti.
P2)   A person who lies about sighting creatures whose existence is disputed would claim to see a yeti, if he or she were to climb Mount Everest.

C1)   Paddy Freaney does not lie about sighting creatures whose existence is disputed.

P3)   Paddy Freaney has claimed he saw a moa.
P4)   The moa is a creature whose existence is disputed.

C2)   Paddy Freaney saw a moa.

The argument is not deductively valid. To see this, suppose that the premises P1–P4 of the argument are indeed true. In that case, Paddy Freaney was not lying, making up a story, in saying that he saw a moa. But it does not follow that Paddy Freaney *did see* a moa, for he could have been *mistaken* rather than *lying*. In that case, his claim to have seen one was not a lie, but nor was it true. Thus the inference from C1, P3 and P4 to C2 is invalid. So the argument as a whole is invalid. In order to make this clear, we can represent the argument like this:

P1) Paddy Freaney climbed Mount Everest twice, and did not claim to see a yeti.

P2) A person who lies about sighting creatures whose existence is disputed would claim to see a yeti, if he or she were to climb Mount Everest.

C1) Paddy Freaney does not lie about sighting creatures whose existence is disputed.

P3) Paddy Freaney has claimed he saw a moa.

P4) The moa is a creature whose existence is disputed.

C2) Either Paddy Freaney saw a moa, or he was mistaken in believing he did.

C3) Paddy Freaney saw a moa.

This makes the argument's invalidity quite obvious: the inference from C2 to C3 is invalid. Might the argument be inductively forceful, then? What follows from the premises is that Freaney either saw a moa or was mistaken. In order to conclude that Freaney *probably* saw a moa we would thus need to know which of these alternatives is more likely. Since the argument does not give us any information relevant to this, we are not really in a position to judge the argument inductively forceful.

Note finally that having begun with an argument whose structure was like this:

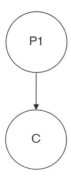

Figure 5.2

We arrived at a much more complicated one like this:

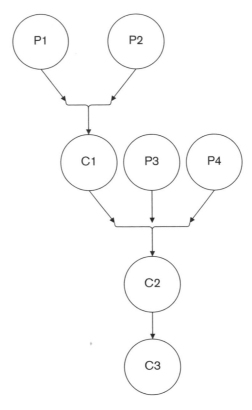

Figure 5.3

Let us now look at an example from down under (Australia this time), which shows how making a generalisation explicit can reveal the weakness of an argument:

> The suggestion that in order to protect children from sunburn, a rule should be instituted requiring all children at our school to wear a sun hat when they are outside after 11 a.m., is unacceptable. For clearly such a rule would be an infringement upon the freedom of the individual.

The conclusion, obviously, is that a sun hat rule at school would be unacceptable. The only explicit premise is that given in the second sentence. So we may begin with:

P1) A sun hat rule at school would infringe upon the freedom of the individual.

C) **A sun hat rule should not be instituted.**

Obviously a generalisation is being implicitly assumed. A first shot at making it explicit, and which might well seem to capture what the arguer must have been thinking, might be this: that no rule that infringes upon the freedom of the individual is acceptable. So we write:

P1) A sun hat rule at school would infringe upon the freedom of the individual.

P2) No rule that infringes upon the freedom of the individual is acceptable.

C) **A sun hat rule at school is unacceptable.**

Here is a deductively valid argument. If the premises are true, then certainly the conclusion is true. However, this does not establish that the conclusion is true. For that, we have to ask whether the premises are true – whether the argument is not only deductively valid but deductively sound.

Surely P1 is true, in a sense: by definition, a rule of any kind restricts, hence infringes upon, the freedom of those to whom it applies – in this case the children of the school in question. So let us grant that P1 is true. But look at P2. We often hear this sort of statement, and we are often so impressed by such a phrase as 'the freedom of the individual' that we accept the statement as true. We have the feeling that 'the freedom of the individual' is something important and valuable, therefore that anything which takes it away must be a bad thing. But, as stated here, this proposition is absurd. For as we just said, all rules 'infringe upon the freedom of the individual'. So what P2 amounts to is the absurd proposition that all rules are unacceptable. Unless you are a kind of radical anarchist, you have to conclude that this argument is not deductively sound.

Now there may be some less sweeping generalisation that the argument might employ instead of P2, which would be more plausible, yet sufficient to obtain the desired conclusion. But the arguer has not given any hint as to what generalisation this might be. So we cannot credit the arguer with actually having supplied a helpful argument on the issue. They may have something more plausible in mind, but they have not conveyed it.

This argument, by the way, is a good illustration of the importance of distinguishing between argument and rhetoric. It was by thinking carefully about the precise literal meanings of the words expressing the argument that we came to see that the argument is unsound. In order to do this, however, we had to have some courage: a phrase such as 'the freedom of the individual' is rhetorically powerful; nevertheless, it is just not literally true that every rule that 'infringes upon the freedom of the individual' is unacceptable; on the contrary, it is absurd to suggest it.

Connecting premises

Look back at the argument about successful politicians (p. 177). And now consider this argument:

> We can assume that inflation will increase, because we know that consumer confidence is increasing.

Reconstructing, we might write:

P1)   Consumer confidence is increasing.

_____

C)   **Inflation will increase.**

As it stands, the argument is neither valid nor inductively forceful. But we can see that the arguer is implicitly assuming that if consumer confidence is increasing, then inflation will increase. So we write:

P1)   Consumer confidence is increasing.
P2)   If consumer confidence is increasing, then inflation will increase.

_____

C)   **Inflation will increase.**

In each case – the inflation argument and the politician argument – the premise, which had to be made explicit in order to make the argument valid, is what we call a **connecting premise**. We have had to add connecting premises in many of the arguments we have so far considered. Usually, when people give arguments, the premises they give explicitly will be only those which pertain to the particular facts or subject-matter they are talking about. For example, someone might say 'My cat won't have kittens; she's been spayed'. The arguer explicitly sets forth the relevant fact about her particular cat, but doesn't bother to state explicitly the generalisation she assumes, that spayed cats can't have kittens. Probably she assumes this to be common knowledge; if she did not, then she would have made the premise explicit. The point then is that arguers very often leave implicit the more general assumptions they make. That is what happened in the inflation case and the politician case discussed earlier.

We cannot assume, however, that *whenever* an argument, as explicitly given, is neither valid nor inductively forceful, the *intended* argument *is* valid or inductively forceful. It is not always the case that the arguer is implicitly relying on an appropriate connecting premise. Sometimes people just do give bad arguments, ones that are neither valid nor inductively forceful. That is what may have happened in the Paddy Freaney case. In further cases, the implicit connecting premise is just not true, in which case the argument is unsound. That's what happened in the sun hat case.

Covering generalisations

In the politician case, the connecting premise was a **generalisation** (review the discussion of generalisations in Chapter 1 if you are not clear about what a generalisation is). Connecting premises are usually generalisations. But in the inflation case the connecting premise we used was a **conditional** (see Chapter 2). This is also common. However, there is an important relationship between conditionals and generalisations that must be appreciated. Consider the following propositions:

a   If Betty is a Siamese cat, then she has blue eyes.
b   All Siamese cats have blues eyes.

(a) is a conditional, (b) is a generalisation. The special relationship in which they stand is that (b) is a **covering generalisation** for (a). (We can also say that (a) is an **instance** of (b), as is common in logic.) Note that (a) may be inferred from (b); the argument from (b) to (a) would be valid. But covering generalisations need not be hard generalisations: 'If Jane's cat is Siamese then its eyes are blue' is an instance of 'All Siamese cats have blues eyes', but it is also an instance of '*Most* Siamese cats have blues eyes'. In such a case the inference from generalisation to instance is inductive rather than deductive.

There is one further aspect to the relationship between covering generalisations and their instances that should be appreciated. Another way to express the proposition expressed by the generalisation (b) is this:

c   If something is a Siamese cat, then it has blue eyes.

Or we could say, 'Whatever X may be, if X is a Siamese cat, then X has blue eyes. This is exactly like (a), except we use the indefinite pronoun instead of the name 'Betty'; this makes the conditional statement into a generalisation. In other words, generalisations of the 'All A are B' sort are themselves conditionals, except they are generalised. (b) and (c) are generalised forms of (a). The same goes for generalisations of the form 'No A are B', as in 'No ungulates are carnivores'. This says, in effect, that all ungulates are non-carnivores. So it could be expressed as 'If something is an ungulate, then it is not a carnivore'.

Very often, when people assert conditionals, they do so on the basis of some covering generalisation. It is important to be aware of this when reconstructing arguments. Suppose you are given the inflation argument, but without a connecting premise:

P1)   Consumer confidence is increasing.

C)   Inflation will increase.

Suppose you reply to the arguer by saying that you just have no idea whether or not P1 constitutes a reason to infer C, that inflation is going to increase. You point out that the argument, at any rate, is certainly not valid as it stands, and would not be inductively forceful. Suppose that the arguer now tries to satisfy you with:

P1)   Consumer confidence is increasing.
P2)   If consumer confidence is increasing, then inflation will
       increase.

C)   Inflation will increase.

Does this really improve the argument? It does make it valid. But this doesn't really help you. All that P2 says is that if P1 is true then so is C. You have already said that you have no idea whether P1 constitutes a reason to infer C. The arguer is not going to convince you merely by asserting P2; to do so is merely to assert that P1 is a good reason to infer C. So the new version is not really an advance on the first version; although you cannot deny that the new version of the argument is valid, you can't really say whether the argument is sound, even if you grant that the arguer does know that P1 is true.

Suppose, however, that you wished to find out whether or not to believe P2. Well P2 says that if consumer confidence is now increasing (which it is), then inflation will increase. So the only way to find out whether P2 is true would be to look into the future to see whether inflation does increase. But that you cannot do. So what do you do? What you need is to find out whether, *in general*, increases in consumer confidence bring about increases in inflation. And that you can find out, by doing some statistical research (consumer confidence is defined in terms of how much people buy, and how much they borrow in order to buy). So what you really need to know, and what it is possible to find out, is whether the following covering generalisation is true:

Whenever consumer confidence increases, inflation increases.

Probably it isn't, but the corresponding soft generalisation might well be true:

Usually, when consumer confidence increases, inflation increases.

This could be established by inductive inference from a survey of past cases in which consumer confidence increased.

So, the arguer giving the inflation argument gives a conditional premise rather than a generalisation, but if the arguer believes the conditional, he or she probably does so on the basis of believing the corresponding covering generalisation. Since that is what the arguer is assuming at bottom, that is what should be included in the reconstruction of the argument. If we do not do this, then our analysis of a given argument may be superficial. Indeed, it is easy to reconstruct an argument as valid in a completely superficial way, if we do not take pains to discover what connecting premises an arguer is relying on at bottom. For example, the following argument might have been given on the evening of the 28 June 1914:

P1) If the Austrian Archduke Ferdinand has been assassinated today, then a general war involving all the European powers will soon break out.

P2) The Austrian Archduke Ferdinand has been assassinated today.

C) **A general war involving all the European powers will soon break out.**

Now in fact this argument would have been sound: the Archduke was assassinated that day, and that single event touched off what would become known as the Great War, later as the First World War. But someone not well-apprised of the political situation in Europe at the time would have needed a lot of explanation in order to see why they should accept P1. P1 is a connecting premise that ensures validity, but it hardly begins to tell us why the arguer thinks that a single assassination will lead to a general war involving several countries. In reconstructing, we should try to bring out as much of this as we can. Connecting premises are almost always necessary, but they can fail to be sufficient to bring out the real basis of an argument.

Finally, you should take care to distinguish the relationship we have just been discussing between conditionals and generalisations from the following sorts of cases:

> If all men are mortal, then all women are mortal.
> If no men are mortal, then no women are mortal.
> If all men are mortal, then Socrates is mortal.
> If Socrates is mortal, then all men are mortal.

These are conditionals that have generalisations as antecedents, as consequents, or as both. They are quite common.

Relevance

This chapter began with a discussion of the necessity of eliminating extraneous material from argument-reconstructions. We turn now to some further aspects of this, and to some cases where the matter is more complex. Consider this argument:

> At *Les Champignons* they are usually fully booked (Professor Gilmour once took me to dine there). So we can safely expect *Les Champignons* to be fully booked tonight.

Without bothering to reconstruct, you can see that this would be an inductively forceful argument (of course it isn't deductively valid). You might try reconstructing the argument like this:

P1)   *Les Champignons* is usually fully booked.
P2)   Professor Gilmour once took me to dine at *Les Champignons.*

C)   **(Probably)** *Les Champignons* **will be fully booked tonight.**

But, if you think about it, there is no point in including P2 in the reconstruction of the argument. P1 alone is the basis for thinking that the restaurant will be fully booked; that the arguer once dined there with Professor Gilmour is irrelevant. When a proposition stated by the arguer is irrelevant to the reasoning that delivers the conclusion, that proposition should not be included in a reconstruction of the argument.

It might seem that the only reason not to include irrelevant material in an argument is that it would be distracting. But in fact it can affect our assessment of the argument in a more important way. For suppose P1 is true, but P2 is not; the arguer, wishing to boast of a greater intimacy with Professor Gilmour than they in fact enjoy, fibbed when telling us that they dined out with him. If we were to discover this, yet persist in the above reconstruction of the argument, we should have to pronounce the argument to be unsound. Indeed, upon discovering the lie and becoming annoyed with the arguer, we might well be eager to do just this. But this would be wrong, because P2 is irrelevant to the argument. The argument should be represented like this:

P1) *Les Champignons* is usually fully booked.

C) **(Probably)** *Les Champignons* **will be fully booked tonight.**

Since P1 is true, and the inductive inference is reasonable, the argument is inductively sound.

This is an obvious point, but some cases are more subtle. In such cases it is a point that is easy to lose sight of, especially when we wish to refute the argument. Consider this example:

> If the tuna industry is not regulated more stringently, it will collapse altogether, because tuna populations will vanish. The evidence is obvious: tuna catches have decreased significantly every year for the past nine years. Indeed, because of depleting stocks, the Mid-Pacific Tuna Company went out of business.

Suppose we initially reconstruct the argument as follows:

P1) Tuna catches have decreased significantly every year for the past nine years.
P2) Last year, the Mid-Pacific Tuna Company went out of business.

C) **If the tuna industry is not regulated more stringently, it will collapse altogether.**

For the moment, we leave out connecting premises. Here the arguer is claiming that P1 supports the conclusion by itself. But the arguer also seems to regard P2 as providing some additional evidence, in the form of an inductive inference from one case to the general proposition that tuna stocks have declined sufficiently to cause difficulty for the tuna industry as a whole. So surely P2 is not completely irrelevant to the argument. Both P1 and P2 support the conclusion. Suppose now you discover that although P1 is true, P2 is false, because the Mid-Pacific Tuna Company did not go out of business; rather, it was taken over by the larger Pan-Pacific Tuna Company. You might then conclude that since P2 is false, the argument is unsound, end of story. You might, indeed, exploit this mistake in attempting to discredit the arguer. If you were a person who opposed greater regulation of tuna fishing, drawing attention to this factual error might be a good rhetorical strategy to use in persuading people not to listen to arguments for increased regulation. Nevertheless, it would be a mistake from the point of view of critical thinking. This is simply because P1, by itself, constitutes a good reason for accepting the conclusion. To fixate upon the falsity of P2 simply diverts attention from the arguer's having cited P1. According to the principle of charity, we should simply omit P2 in our final reconstruction of the argument. More exactly: both P1 and P2, quite independently of each other, would support the conclusion. So really we should regard the arguer as having given two arguments for the conclusion, one of which we know to be unsound. So according the principle of charity, we should now focus on the other argument, the one utilising P1. Adding the needed connecting premises and an intermediate conclusion, we get:[2]

P1) Tuna catches have been decreasing significantly for the past nine years.

P2) If tuna catches have been decreasing significantly for the past nine years, then, if the tuna industry is not regulated more stringently, the tuna population will vanish.

C1) If the tuna industry is not regulated more stringently, the tuna population will vanish.

P3) If the tuna population vanishes, the tuna industry will collapse altogether.

C2) If the tuna industry is not regulated more stringently, it will collapse altogether.

This reconstruction makes for a plausible argument as it stands. There are two comments that it may be useful to make.

---

2   It might be more plausible to reconstruct this argument as inductive rather than deductive, but we have ignored this in order to maintain the focus on the point about relevance.

First, note that, as usual, we have deleted the phrase 'the evidence is obvious', which adds nothing to the substance of the argument. Second, note that we have applied our policy of logical streamlining fairly rigorously in this case. Most conspicuously, the argument contained a non-causal use of 'because', functioning in a way similar to 'since' (see pp. 170–1). We replaced it with a conditional and a statement of the antecedent of the conditional as a separate premise, thereby 'opening up' the logical texture of the argument.

It is easy to see that the argument from C1 and P3 to C2 is valid. Suppose that the tuna industry is not regulated more stringently. Then according to C1, the tuna population will vanish. But if so, then according to P3, the tuna industry will collapse. So it follows from C1 and P3 that if the tuna industry is not regulated more stringently, then the tuna industry will collapse; which is exactly what C2 says. (This is an example of a 'chain argument', as discussed near the end of Chapter 2.)

Returning now to the main theme of this section. The basic moral of this section is that the truth-values of the premises actually advanced by an arguer can be more or less relevant to the soundness of the argument. Sometimes it is highly relevant that a given premise is false, sometimes it is much less so. It depends upon the nature of the mistake, and upon the role played in the argument by the premise. The degree of **relevance** must therefore be taken into account in the process of reconstruction.

Ambiguity and vagueness

If our explanations of ambiguity and vagueness are not clear to you, then you should review the discussions of those concepts in Chapter 1. In this section, we explain how to cope with vagueness and ambiguity when you encounter it in arguments.

Ambiguity

In reconstructing arguments, we have to eliminate any ambiguities in the original statement of the argument. If the original statement contains an ambiguous sentence, we have to decide which of the possible interpretations was most likely intended by the arguer, and, in our reconstruction of the argument, rewrite the sentence, choosing a form of words that conveys the intended meaning unambiguously.

Let us take an example. Suppose that Jane, a Londoner, decides to invest some money in the share market. She decides to look for an investment adviser, and finds an advertisement which runs as follows:

The practice of argument-reconstruction

Sharemasters: London's leading personal investment advice service!

Suppose that this expresses a true proposition, and Jane accepts that what it says is true; she accepts that Sharemasters is London's leading personal investment service. Assuming that it would be fraudulent to publish such a claim if it were not true, Jane reasons as follows (for simplicity, we will ignore the reference to London in the advertised claim; this will not affect the point we are making):

P1) Sharemasters is the leading personal investment service.
P2) If I employ a personal investment service, then I should employ the leading personal investment service.

C) If I employ a personal investment service, then I should employ Sharemasters.

This looks to be a deductively valid argument. But this is not quite clear, because P1 is ambiguous. What does 'leading' mean, in this context? It could mean (and this is no doubt what the advertisers hope that people like Jane will think it means) that Sharemasters is the most *effective* personal investment service – that it secures better returns for its clients than other personal investment services. But it could also mean that Sharemasters is the *biggest* such organisation – in the sense of having the most clients (this is the sense in which McDonald's is the world's leading restaurant); it might even mean that Sharemasters is the most *profitable* personal investment service – that is, that it makes the most profits for the owners of Sharemasters itself, not necessarily for its clients (after all, this organisation is a business, and profitability can plausibly be said to be the measure of who is the 'leader' in a certain field of business). Suppose now that you wish to evaluate Jane's argument. You are aware of the ambiguity, so you rephrase P1 in each of the three ways, yielding three arguments:

A P1) (a) Sharemasters secures higher returns for its clients than any other personal investment service.
   P2) (a) If Jane employs a personal investment service, then she should employ the personal investment service that secures higher returns for its clients than any other personal investment service.

C) If Jane employs a personal investment service, she should employ Sharemasters.

B P1) (b) Sharemasters is the most profitable personal investment
service.

P2) (b) If Jane employs a personal investment service, then she
should employ the most profitable personal investment
service.

C) If Jane employs a personal investment service, she should employ Sharemasters.

C P1) (c) Sharemasters is the biggest personal investment service.

P2) (c) If Jane employs a personal investment service, then she
should employ the biggest personal investment service.

C) If Jane employs a personal investment service, she should employ Sharemasters.

Now all three arguments are deductively valid. But are any of them
sound? First of all consider arguments B and C. Even if we assume that
P1(b) and P1(c) are true, it does not seem that these are sound arguments,
because it does not seem that either P2(b) or P2(c) are true. Perhaps they
have some plausibility – since presumably if Sharemasters were highly
*un*successful at making money for its clients, then it would not have
grown so big or become so profitable. But these would not be very reliable assumptions; to reason in the manner of C, for example, would be
like concluding that since McDonald's is the biggest restaurant in the
world, it has the best food.

So you can conclude that Jane's argument has a good chance of being
sound only if argument A is what she had in mind. Suppose you inves-
tigate, and find that it is true that Sharemasters is the biggest as well as
the most profitable personal investment service in London. Suppose you
find, however, that it is not the most effective personal investment service
in London; its size and profitability are due to its high fees, its organisa-
tional efficiency, and effective advertising. Hence P1(b) and P1(c) are true,
but P1(a) is false. You must therefore conclude that although it is valid,
argument A is unsound. Since neither B nor C seems to be sound, you
must conclude that Jane's original argument is unsound; in *none* of the
three possible interpretations does it appear to be sound.

Eliminating the ambiguity of the original argument was crucial in
discovering this, for one could very easily think that the original argument was sound. Advertisements of this kind may be said to *exploit* this
sort of ambiguity. If Sharemasters is indeed the largest personal investment service in London, but not the most effective, then the slogan does
express something true; yet the advertisers might hope that readers will

interpret the claim along the lines of argument A (or possibly along the lines of B, making the questionable assumption that the biggest service of a given sort is likely to be the most effective).

Remember that a primary purpose of reconstruction is to represent the propositions that constitute an argument in the clearest possible way. Thus we should have no qualms about changing the language used to express those propositions; in changing it, we are only trying to gain a better grasp of what the arguer was thinking. There is no guarantee that we will not change or distort the arguer's thinking, but there is no point in allowing ambiguous language to remain unchanged. For we simply cannot evaluate an argument if we do not know exactly what argument we are evaluating. If we simply cannot decide between two interpretations of an ambiguity, then we must give both interpretations of the argument, and evaluate the two arguments independently.

Vagueness

As noted in Chapter 1, many words and phrases are vague in the way that 'bald' is vague. Examples include 'tall', 'orange', 'heap of sand' (i.e. we cannot draw a precise boundary between tall and not-tall, between orange and red, and cannot say exactly how many grains of sand you need to have a heap). Each such word pertains to a certain quality, such as height, region of the colour spectrum (which proceeds gradually from red through orange, yellow, green, blue and violet), or amount of sand, which has 'fuzzy' boundaries, but the *meaning* of the term is clear. The terms have vague *extensions* (range of things to which they apply) but the concepts or ideas they express are not vague.

These sorts of words seldom present problems for actual argument-reconstruction and assessment.[3] More important for critical reasoning are words whose actual *meanings* are vague. Indeed, many of the most

---

3   But they do cause trouble for logic. Consider the term 'sand dune'. There is no exact rule for how much sand is needed to constitute a sand dune, but here is one proposition about sand dunes that seems undeniable: if X is a sand dune and one grain of sand is removed from X, then X is still a sand dune. But now suppose that X is a sand dune. If we remove one grain of sand from X, then X is still a sand dune. But then if we remove one grain of sand from this, we still have a sand dune. And so on. But then eventually we run out of sand, so we have no sand dune. So at some point, X was a sand dune consisting of *n* grains of sand for some number *n*, such that X ceased to be a sand dune, upon the removal of one grain of sand. But that seems absurd; we cannot imagine a sand dune such that removing one grain of sand destroys its status as a sand dune. So we seem to have a contradiction. This paradox – Paradox of the Heap or Sorites paradox – was puzzled over by the ancient Greeks, and there is still no consensus as to how to avoid the apparent contradiction.

rhetorically powerful or emotionally provocative words in public (and private) discourse are vague in this way. Consider:

• politics/political	• radical
• liberal	• ideology
• elitism	• rights
• racism	• responsibility
• conservative	• love
• sovereignty	• weapons of mass destruction
• terrorism	• political correctness
• freedom fighter	

As pointed out in Chapter 1, we often have the feeling that these things are bad, or that they are good, without any precise idea of what we mean by them. What they signify is typically a whole group or cluster of things that are not unified in any exact way.

Let us take 'conservative' (in the political sense) as our example. There are various attributes often associated with someone's being 'conservative':

Conservative
▶ Believes in minimum government.
▶ Favours free market economics.
▶ Favours privatisation of government industries and services.
▶ Against the dole, welfare, etc.
▶ Supports 'traditional' values – pro-family, anti-gay, etc.
▶ Against government help for minorities, women, etc.
▶ Supports strong police, military, severe prison sentences.
▶ Supports business as against labour, environmental groups.

Someone could rightly be called 'conservative' without exhibiting all these attributes or tendencies. Exactly which attributes you must have, and which you must not have, to be a conservative, is simply not clear. So 'conservative' is vague.

Now, in reconstructing arguments, the best thing to do with vague words is simply to eliminate them. This can be seen from the following example:

MP Jeremy Price has made his conservative stance clear by favouring 'traditional values' and stronger sentencing for criminals. Therefore, we can certainly assume he will oppose any new laws protecting the environment.

It might occur to you to represent this as a two-stage argument, thus:

P1) Jeremy Price favours 'traditional values' and stronger sentencing for criminals.

C1) Jeremy Price is a conservative.

C2) Jeremy Price will oppose new laws protecting the environment.

The inferences from P1 to C1, and from C1 to C2, depend upon implicit generalisations, which, having learnt earlier lessons well, you know you would do well to make explicit:

P1) Jeremy Price favours 'traditional values' and stronger sentencing for criminals.
P2) All those who favour 'traditional values' and stronger sentencing for criminals are conservatives.

C1) Jeremy Price is a conservative.

P3) All conservatives oppose new laws protecting the environment.

C2) Jeremy Price opposes new laws protecting the environment.

The argument from C1 and P2 to C2 is deductively valid, but it might then occur to you that P3 is implausible. Surely not *every* conservative is so disdainful of environmental restriction. So you replace 'all' with 'most':

P1) Jeremy Price favours 'traditional values' and stronger sentencing for criminals.
P2) All those who favour 'traditional values' and stronger sentencing for criminals are conservatives.

C1) Jeremy Price is a conservative.

P3) Most conservatives oppose new laws protecting the environment.

C2) (Probably) Jeremy Price will oppose new laws protecting the environment.

Now this argument might seem plausible to the average person; it might seem to be inductively sound. But the argument appears better than it is, because of the presence of the word 'conservative'. And in fact, all the actual logic of the original argument can be reproduced without making use of that word at all. It is simple: The *actual evidence* the arguer has for their conclusion that Jeremy Price will oppose new environmental laws is that Price favours traditional values and stronger sentencing for criminals. The arguer supplies no further evidence, and the word 'conservative' plays no role at all. Thus, adding the necessary generalisation, we might just as well represent the argument like this:

P1)   Jeremy Price favours traditional values and stronger sentencing for criminals.

P2)   Most people who favour traditional values and stronger sentences for criminals oppose new laws protecting the environment.

C)   **(Probably) Jeremy Price opposes new laws protecting the environment.**

This remains inductively forceful, and it is no less inductively forceful than the previous version. But the inductive soundness of this argument is far from certain, because P2 is far from certain. This reconstruction thus makes the weakness of the original argument perfectly clear. It does so by removing the distraction created by the word 'conservative' (even if you do think that P2 is true, you have to admit that this reconstruction centres our attention on the real issue).

Since many of the most rhetorically highly charged words in public discourse are also vague, eliminating them from our argument-reconstructions achieves two things: it clarifies the argument, and, by eliminating emotionally provocative words, enables us to focus without distraction upon the logic of the argument.

The best thing to do with ambiguous or vague language, then, is simply to replace it with language that is not vague or ambiguous. The aim is to employ language that will express the intended propositions without ambiguity or vagueness. But this is not always possible. Where a sentence is ambiguous, we cannot always tell which of the different possible interpretations was intended by the arguer, even if we apply the principle of charity. In such a case we can assess each of the possible versions of the argument, but we may have to confess that we cannot tell which version the arguer intended. And – especially where the language used by the arguer is vague rather than ambiguous – we have to admit that the arguer's thinking may simply have been vague or confused, not just his or her language. Indeed, where vague words such as those listed above play a role in an argument, this is very often the case. In constructing your own arguments, such words are best simply avoided. They tend to obscure the issue rather than clarify it. However, not all vague language can be removed. We will return to this in the next chapter.

More on generalisations

As we noted in Chapter 1, only hard generalisations can rightly be conveyed by using a quantifier-word like 'all', 'no' or 'every'. Indeed, that is the usual function of those words – to make it perfectly explicit that a hard generalisation is what is intended. For example, someone at a meeting of Parliament might say, 'Every single MP in this chamber takes bribes', rather than 'MPs in this chamber take bribes'. Soft generalisations, indeed, are very often expressed without any quantifier at all, as in 'Children like sweeties'. Other times, we add a quantifier such as 'most' or 'almost all' to a soft generalisation, in order to make it clear that a soft generalisation is what is intended, and also to make it clear just how soft (or how close to being hard) it is meant to be.

Since there is often confusion over the difference between hard and soft generalisations, we should, when reconstructing arguments, always make it clear whether a generalisation is hard or soft (the one exception to this is the case of causal statements; this will be discussed near the end of this chapter). The confusion most often arises when the generalisation, as stated, lacks an explicit quantifier. The intended quantifier is merely implicit, so there is room for misinterpretation. A generalisation in which the quantifier is merely implicit is thus a kind of ambiguity. The way to eliminate the ambiguity is to add an explicit quantifier.

The scope of a generalisation

Consider the following hard generalisations:

1　All cows are herbivores.
2　All black cows are herbivores.

The **subjects** of these generalisations – what the generalisations are about – are cows and black cows, respectively. Both generalisations are true, and they stand in a special relationship. There are two aspects of this relationship. First, they attribute the same feature to their subjects (that of being herbivores). Second, the subject of the second is a subset of the first (all black cows are cows, but not all cows are black). Thus we say that the **scope** of (1) is **wider** than that of (2) and conversely that the **scope** of (2) is **narrower** than that of (1). Note that we can compare generalisations in this way only when the subject of one is a subset of the subject of the other. We cannot, for example, say that the generalisation 'All lions are carnivores' is narrower than, or wider than, either (1) or (2). Nor can we compare the scope of 'All sheep are herbivores' to that of either (1) or (2).

Figure 5.4 represents the situation expressed by (1) and (2). It can sometimes be important to adjust the scope of a generalisation, making it either narrower or wider. Usually, in reconstructing arguments, we have to narrow them; hardly ever do we have to widen them. Suppose, for example, you are a fervent environmentalist, and believe that radical measures must be taken immediately to protect the environment from air pollution. In particular, you believe that our reliance upon petroleum products – such as petrol for cars – must be halted as soon as possible. So you argue:

> Private vehicles that emit carbon monoxide should not be allowed.
> We must ban automobiles.

The reasoning here is pretty clear, but in reconstructing, some care must be taken with the generalisation implicit in it. The implicit generalisation, obviously, is that automobiles emit carbon monoxide. The argument might be reconstructed as follows:

P1) We should ban all private vehicles that emit carbon monoxide.
P2) All automobiles emit carbon monoxide.

C) **We should ban all automobiles.**

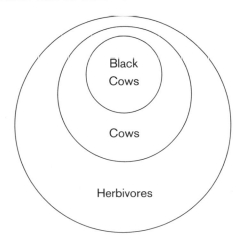

Figure 5.4 The scope of a generalisation

Note that in writing P1, we added the quantifier 'all'. Usually when someone speaks of 'banning' something they don't add the word 'all' (or any equivalent word), but they do mean that *none* should be allowed. Still, as always, it is worthwhile when reconstructing to make the quantifier explicit. Now assume you really do believe P1. This argument is deductively valid. However, you must admit that it has a weak point. For P2, as written, is clearly untrue. Some automobiles, for example, are electric, and run on batteries. Since they do not burn petrol (or any other petroleum product), they do not emit carbon monoxide (indeed they do not pollute the air at all, at least not directly). So even if P1 is true, you have failed to give a sound argument.

Now you could make the argument inductively sound by changing the word 'all' in P2 to 'most'. But you could do better, for two reasons:

First, it could become false that most automobiles emit carbon monoxide, without any reduction at all in the number of petrol-driven cars, in which case the pollution (and other problems) caused by the burning of petrol might not have been curtailed at all. For it would be possible that so many electric cars or other alternatives to be produced over a few years' time that they outnumber petrol-driven cars without any reduction in the number of petrol-driven cars. In that case, P2 would be false but you would still want to argue against petrol-driven cars, since they would still be emitting the same amount of pollution.

Second, changing 'all' to 'most', although it renders the argument sound, does not clarify the issue as much as another alternative.

This other alternative is to change the scope of the generalisation expressed by P2 – in particular, to **reduce its scope**. Instead of 'All automobiles emit carbon monoxide', we can more accurately write 'All petrol-driven automobiles emit carbon monoxide', rewriting the argument thus:

P1)   We should ban all private vehicles that emit carbon monoxide.
P2)   All petrol-driven automobiles emit carbon monoxide.

C)   **We should ban all petrol-driven automobiles.**

Assuming the truth of P1, this is a deductively sound argument. Even if you doubt P1, this is, at any rate, a much better argument than the earlier version; since the new P2 is a narrower generalisation than the old P2, its premises have a better chance of being true. Furthermore, by narrowing the generalisation, the issue is defined more exactly. We now have it explicitly before us that the point at issue is the use of petrol-driven automobiles, not automobiles in general.

Thus, when reconstructing arguments, we should take care not to employ a hard generalisation that is wider in scope than we need, if there is anything doubtful about the wider one that could be eliminated by employing a narrower one. If a narrower (but hard) generalisation will suffice for constructing an argument for the desired conclusion, then we should employ the narrower one. This is not to say we should *always* choose narrower generalisations whenever possible. For example, it would not improve the argument to rewrite P2 as 'All *green* petrol-driven automobiles emit carbon monoxide'. For adding the word 'green', besides not making the generalisation any more likely to be true (or at least not appreciably so), renders the argument invalid. The point is that if one generalisation is narrower than another and more likely to be true, then, provided that it is sufficient for obtaining the desired conclusion, the narrower one should be employed.

Note that in some cases there is no natural word or phrase for the class of cases we wish to generalise about. In such cases we have to reduce the scope of a generalisation by explicitly excepting a certain class of what would otherwise be counterexamples. For example, consider the inference 'That is a mammal; therefore it doesn't fly'. The generalisation needed is 'No mammals *except bats* fly', since 'No mammals fly' is false (and of course we would also need the premise that the creature in question is not a bat; we ignore flying squirrels).

Practical reasoning

The conclusion of the above argument about the automobile is one that has a *practical* conclusion: rather than saying that some proposition is true, it enjoins or commends a particular action. What the argument says, roughly, is that doing one thing (banning the petrol-driven automobile) is necessary if a certain desirable outcome or end (finding alternatives to vehicles that emit carbon monoxide) is to be achieved. Other arguments with practical conclusions are those that say that a certain action would be sufficient to bring about the desired end, and for that reason ought to be performed. Still others say that a certain action would lead to a certain *un*desirable outcome, and therefore ought not to be performed. Reasoning of this kind is often called **practical reasoning**, or means–end reasoning, and is normally based upon two sorts of considerations: First, an outcome is specified as being either desirable or undesirable (in this book we prefer to use 'must' or 'should' to specify the outcome, as illustrated below; normally, 'must' expresses a stronger demand or requirement than 'should'). Second, there is a proposition put forward that says either (1) that if such-and-such action is performed, the outcome will result; (2) that if the action is performed, the outcome will *not* result; (3) that if the action is *not* performed the outcome will *not* come about; or (4) that if the action is not performed then the outcome *will* come about.

This gives rise to eight different types of argument that concern a relation between action and outcome. Just for the purpose of illustration, then, suppose that the outcome is that the amount of chocolate in the world be increased, and the action in question is X. Then, using 'should', the eight types of practical reasoning can be sketched like this:

1 P1) The amount of chocolate in the world should be increased.

   P2) If action X is performed, then the amount of chocolate in the world will be increased.

   C) Action X should be performed.

2 P1) The amount of chocolate in the world should be increased.

   P2) If action X is not performed, then the amount of chocolate in the world will not be increased.

   C) Action X should be performed.

3 P1) The amount of chocolate in the world should be increased.

   P2) If action X is not performed, then the amount of chocolate in the world will be increased.

   C) Action X should not be performed.

4 P1) The amount of chocolate in the world should be increased.

   P2) If action X is performed, then the amount of chocolate in the world will be not be increased.

   C) Action X should not be performed.

5 P1) The amount of chocolate in the world should not be increased.

   P2) If action X is performed, then the amount of chocolate in the world will be increased.

   C) Action X should not be performed.

6 P1) The amount of chocolate in the world should not be increased.

   P2) If action X is not performed, then the amount of chocolate in the world will not be increased.

   C) Action X should not be performed.

7 P1) The amount of chocolate in the world should not be
increased.

P2) If action X is not performed, then the amount of chocolate
in the world will be increased.

C) **Action X should be performed.**

8 P1) The amount of chocolate in the world should not be
increased.

P2) If action X is performed, then the amount of chocolate in the
world will be not be increased.

C) **Action X should be performed.**

There is, however, an important complication that is most easily explained
in connection with type 1. Suppose that we believe that increasing the
number of doctors would improve the NHS. We might set out the argument like this:

P1) The NHS should be improved.

P2) If the number of doctors were increased, the NHS would
improve.

C) **The number of doctors should be increased.**

This is a start, but as it stands it is really not adequate. For if you
think about it, the argument is clearly not valid. It does not follow, from
the fact that such-and-such would bring about some desirable result, that
we should do such-and-such (also look again at the earlier argument about
the sun hat rule). There are two reasons.

First, we need to know that the **cost** of the proposed action does not
outweigh the **benefit** of the outcome. For example, it would certainly
improve the NHS if the Government were to increase its budget by ten-
fold. But that would not be a good idea, as the cost would be far too great.
This sort of thing – 'weighing the costs' – is clearest where money is at
stake, but it is not limited to monetary considerations. If you want
stronger muscles, for example, then you have to weigh the desirability
for you of stronger muscles against the 'cost' of exercising (the time
expended, the pain, etc.). Indeed, even in the argument about the NHS,
we are not assuming that the value of an improved NHS can be assessed
in monetary terms.

Second, we need to know that there is not some other means that
would bring about the same benefit but at a lower cost. We need to know,

that is, that the proposed action is the most *efficient* or *economical* way to bring about the desired outcome.

In reconstructing practical reasoning, then, we have to incorporate both of these points as premises. The argument concerning the NHS, then, would go something like this:

P1)   The NHS should be improved.
P2)   If the number of doctors were increased, the NHS would improve.
P3)   The benefits of improving the NHS would outweigh the costs of increasing the number of doctors.
P4)   Increasing the number of doctors would be the most efficient means of improving the NHS.

C)   **The number of doctors should be increased.**

This argument is valid.[4] Strictly speaking, P1 and P2 are now redundant, since they can be inferred from P3 and P4; but it is harmless, and it makes it clearer, to leave them in. Of course, the argument is a bit vague: it does not say to what extent the NHS should be improved, nor by how many the number of doctors should be increased. Someone actually advancing this argument would want to fill in these details.

In considering this issue we focused on an argument of type 1, but the weighing of costs and benefits may enter into four of the eight types of practical argument. Types 2, 4, 5 and 7 are valid as they stand, but types 1, 3, 6 and 8 are invalid types, and must always be supplemented by premises outlining costs, benefits and efficiency. For example, consider type 3. It might be that the cost of not performing action X would be greater than the benefit of increasing the amount of chocolate (that is to say, it might be that the benefit of performing it is greater than the benefit of increasing the amount of chocolate).

---

4   In endorsing this style of argument as valid we are assuming that all practical considerations can be subsumed under the categories 'cost' and 'benefit'. We do so for simplicity; but it should be acknowledged that many philosophers hold that *rights* and *duties* are practically relevant considerations that cannot be explained in terms of cost and benefit (cannot be explained, that is, from a *utilitarian* or *consequentialist* point of view). More generally, the relation of rule-theoretic concepts such as rights and duties to value-theoretic concepts such as cost and benefit is a central concern of the philosophical study of ethics. A way to accommodate this without complicating our argument-reconstructions is simply to think of rights and duties as entering into the calculation of cost and benefit in their own right, without any assumption that can be explained in terms of some independent conception of cost and benefit.

Balancing costs, benefits and probabilities

Someone giving the above argument about the NHS might concede that there is some possibility, even if the number of doctors were increased, that the NHS would not improve. Nevertheless, so long as he or she is reasonably certain that it would, it would be simplest to leave the conditional P2 as it is, rather than inserting 'probably' before its consequent, thereby making the argument inductive rather than deductive.

In other cases, however, practical arguments are more plausibly reconstructed as inductive. For we sometimes have to balance costs and benefits in a more complicated way. For example, suppose you are repairing a window. Having removed it, you are invited to a party, which is taking place now. You know the party would be a lot of fun, but although you could very easily repair the window tomorrow, there is no time to replace the window before going to the party; either you leave the window off and go to the party, risking the possibility of rain getting in (assume the window is too high up for there to be a risk of burglary), or you continue working on the window and miss the party. What should you do? Obviously the benefit of going to the party is high, but so would be the cost of rain getting in. If we assume that these are roughly equal, then clearly your decision should rest on the probability of rain: if the probability of rain is less than 1/2, then you should go to the party; if it is higher than 1/2, then you should not. But suppose the cost of rain getting in would be much greater than the benefit of attending the party. In that case you should not risk going to the party even if the chance of rain is fairly low. We can represent this in a table:

	Rain	No rain
Go to party	−10	+5
Not go to party	0	0

Here we are assuming that the unpleasantness of the rain, if you leave the window off, would be twice the pleasure of going to the party, and that not going to the party would be neither bad nor good (it does not matter that we used −10 and +5 to represent this relationship; we could just as well have used −4 and +2, or −2 and +1). In this situation, then, you should stay home, unless the probability of its raining is less than half the probability of its not raining. That is, you should stay home unless the probability of rain is less than one third.

What we are leading up to is the concept of **expected value**:

> Let $o_1, o_2 \ldots o_n$ be the possible outcomes of an action A; let V(o) be the value (cost or benefit) of each outcome o, and let P(o) be the probability of each outcome (given that action A was performed). Then the *expected value* of an action A is:
>
> $$[P(o_1) \times V(o_1)] + [P(o_2) \times V(o_2)] + \ldots [P(o_n) \times V(o_n)]$$

That is, for each possible outcome of the action, you multiply the probability of the outcome by its value (its cost or benefit, as the case may be). Then you add these figures together to get the expected value of the action. The idea behind this is that, given a range of possible actions, one should do whatever **maximises expected value**. If one's possible actions are $A_1, A_2, \ldots A_n$, and one of these – say A_k – has the highest expected value, then one should perform A_k. In the case of the window and the party, the possibilities are: stay and repair the window, or go to the party. If we assume that the probability of rain is 0.5, then the expected value of going to the party, according the values given in the chart above, would be:

$$0.5 \times (-10) + 0.5 \times 5 = (-5) + 2.5 = -2.5.$$

The expected value of not going to the party is:

$$0.5 \times 0 + 0.5 \times 0 = 0.$$

Since the expected value of staying to repair the window (0) is greater than that of going to the party (–2.5), you should stay to repair the window.

It is very helpful to have a firm grasp of the concept of expected value, because it is one of the areas in which people most frequently make mistakes in reasoning. For example, we sometimes see arguments like this:

> The bottom line is this: no matter how safe the Government says it is, they cannot rule out the possibility of a catastrophic accident. We should decommission all nuclear power plants as soon as possible.

If the arguer is right, then the expected value of decommissioning all nuclear plants should be greater than that of not doing so. But, although this may be true, the arguer has given us no reason to believe it. In order to reach that conclusion, we would need to know the actual probability of an accident; we would also need to know how the cost of an accident would compare with the benefits and other costs of continuing to use nuclear power, as well as the benefits and costs of relying on other sources of energy. The arguer has provided none of this, and the mere fact that an accident is not impossible is not disputed by anyone. Nor does anyone dispute that a nuclear accident would be a very bad thing. But the mere fact that something bad – no matter how bad – is a possible outcome of some action certainly does not establish that the action should not be performed.

It is somewhat controversial to suppose that the rationality of *all* action depends on its expected value. Suppose, for example, that there are ten people who will certainly die unless they are treated with a rare enzyme that happens to be present in your brain. It cannot be found anywhere else, and extracting it from your head will kill you. A doctor decides forcibly to extract it from your head – thus killing you – but justifies this on the grounds that since ten people will die if the enzyme is not extracted, and only one will die if it is, the expected value of the action is positive. (Assume that no other harm would result; e.g., the doctor would not be charged with murder or any thing like that.) It might be noble of you to volunteer for this, but it seems wrong to say that the doctor would be *right* or *justified* in extracting the enzyme from your brain. The reason is that his doing so would *violate your rights*. Alternatively, we might hold that there is an absolute moral rule, that (outside the context of war) it is *always wrong* to kill an innocent person, or to *use* a person's life against their will. Thus there is a certain limit to the application of expected value calculations: the expected value of a proposed action tells us whether or not it would be rational to do something, unless it is overridden by the existence of rights or moral rules. Normally, moral rules are invoked in a very straightforward way: x has property F; actions with property F must never be performed, therefore x must not be performed. The main difficulty faced by reasoning in terms of moral rules is that, at least on the surface, they sometimes come into conflict, as when one person's or group's rights seem to be incompatible with another's. Courses in ethics or moral philosophy are often concerned to find principled ways of resolving such dilemmas. Another central concern is the interplay between moral rules and expected value (or *utility* as it is often called), and the degree to which the former might be explained in terms of the latter.

Explanations as conclusions

In the first chapter, we took care to distinguish **arguments** from **explanations**. An argument supplies reasons why we should believe a certain proposition whose truth-value is in question. By contrast, an explanation tells us why it is that a certain proposition is the case, when the truth-value of that proposition is not in question. It is especially important to observe this distinction when dealing with arguments whose conclusions are themselves explanations. The aim of this sort of argument is to persuade the audience that such-and-such is the actual cause of a fact or event. Such arguments are very common. For example:

> We must not have fertilised that plant. It hasn't got a disease. We've watered it correctly, and it gets enough sun, but it still isn't growing well.

This passage does involve an explanation; but it is, nevertheless, an argument. The conclusion is that the cause of the plant's poor growth is that it wasn't fertilised. So we might reconstruct it like this:

P1) If a plant is not growing well, then either it has a disease, it is getting the wrong amount of water, it isn't getting enough sun or it has not got enough fertiliser.
P2) This plant is not growing well.
P3) This plant has not got a disease, it gets the right amount of water and it gets enough sun.

C) **This plant has not got enough fertiliser.**

This argument is valid. But it is not quite right, because the conclusion does not say that the plant's poor growth is caused by its not having enough fertiliser. It is a perfectly good argument, and indeed it is part of what the arguer is trying to establish; but it is not all of it. In order to display the full force of the argument, we need to use the word 'cause' in both the premises and the conclusion:

P1) If a plant is not growing well, then the cause is either that it has a disease, that it is getting the wrong amount of water, that it isn't getting enough sun or that it has not got enough fertiliser.
P2) This plant is not growing well.
P3) This plant has not got a disease, it gets the right amount of water and it gets enough sun.

C) **The cause of this plant's not growing well is that it has not got enough fertiliser.**

Or, as we might more naturally put it, this plant is not growing well *because* it has not got enough fertiliser – that would be the causal use of 'because' that was discussed in the first section of this chapter. Note that in order to obtain the desired conclusion, it was necessary to include the word 'cause' (or the word 'because') in P1. If we had left P1 as it is in the first version, then the inference to the conclusion in the second version would have been invalid. For it is certainly not true that if A is true (the plant hasn't enough fertiliser), and B is true (the plant isn't growing well), then A is the cause of B (though of course if A *is* the cause of B, then A and B must both be true).

In fact this is not quite the whole argument, but only a sub-argument. In order to get the final conclusion, 'This plant is not growing well because we did not fertilise it', we'd have to add another premise after the given conclusion: 'If we had fertilised this plant, then it would have had enough fertiliser.'

Note that the correct reconstruction is not like this:

P1) If a plant has got a disease, it is getting the wrong amount of water, it isn't getting enough sun, or it has not got enough fertiliser, then it doesn't grow well.
P2) This plant is not getting enough fertiliser.

C) **This plant doesn't grow well.**

In the passage, the arguer assumes that the audience agrees that the plant isn't growing well. This fact is not in question. The aim of the argument is to persuade the audience as to the cause, that is, the explanation, of this fact.

All such arguments begin with an accepted fact – some proposition that the arguer expects his or her audience already accepts. The arguer's aim is to answer the question, 'what is the correct explanation of this fact?' by giving an argument. In the above example, the arguer recognises that there are several possible causes of the agreed fact, and, by eliminating all but one, advances the remaining one as the correct explanation. The pattern can be represented like this:

P1) (The agreed fact).
P2) (The agreed fact), was caused by either A or B (or C, or . . .).
P3) B is not the case (nor is C, nor . . .).

C) **(The agreed fact) was caused by A.**[5]

---

5   A more complex kind of case is one where we know that the cause was A or B, and that A and B were both true, yet we still wish to determine which was the actual cause (e.g. we might know that the patient's death was caused by either heart disease or liver disease, and that both his heart and liver were diseased). But we shall not discuss these sorts of cases here.

Normally P2 will be backed by a covering generalisation, of the form 'Whenever such-and-such happens, it is caused by . . .'. But not always; sometimes we know what the possible causes of a given fact or event are, but are unable to articulate generalisations from which they may be inferred. In cases where we do know the appropriate generalisations, however, we should, as always, include them in the reconstruction. That is what we did in the plant example. Of course the list of possible causes listed in P2 may be of any length.[6]

The generalisations appealed to in arguments of this kind are often soft rather than hard. For example, a sudden increase in the temperature of an automobile engine's cooling system is usually, but not always, caused either by a leak in the cooling system or a broken fan belt. In such cases, we must insert 'usually', or 'probably' or some suitable variant, into the appropriate place in P2. Likewise, we may not be able to rule out with certainty the possible explanations listed in P3. Again, in such cases we should have to insert 'probably', 'usually' or some suitable variant, into the appropriate place in P3 (or perhaps 'probably not', etc.). In these cases the arguments will be inductive rather than deductive. Such an argument might look like this:

P1) The temperature of the engine's cooling system has suddenly increased.
P2) Almost always, a sudden increase of the temperature of an engine's cooling system is caused by a broken fan belt, or a leak in the cooling system.
P3) It is very unlikely that the fan belt has broken.

C) **(Probably) The increase of the temperature of the engine's cooling system was caused by a leak in the cooling system.**

In this case, P3 might be the conclusion of another argument; for example, it may have been inferred from the fact that the fan belt is new.

Causal generalisations

In the preceding examples we were concerned with causal relationships between particular events or states of affairs. We were concerned, for

---

6   It may, indeed, contain only one item, in which case there is no need for P3. For example: smoke is always caused by fire; therefore if we see smoke, then since we know that it is always caused by fire, and never by anything else, we can conclude immediately that the smoke we see is caused by a fire. Such cases of course are not very interesting.

example, with whether or not the particular event in a car's cooling system was caused by a particular fault. However causal statements often appear as generalisations about types of events or states of affairs, as in:

Powerful electric shocks cause the muscles to contract.

This sort of statement is relatively unproblematic. What it means, roughly, is that whenever powerful electric charges are applied to a living person's body, the muscles contract (unless there is something wrong with their nervous system). So it is a hard generalisation about events. However, the word 'cause' does not always, or even typically, indicate a hard generalisation of this kind. Consider:

Smoking causes cancer.

This is not a hard generalisation about events, persons or states of affairs. It does not mean, for example, that every act of smoking causes an outbreak of cancer, or that everyone who smokes gets cancer. It does not even mean that smoking usually causes cancer (since it is not true that most smokers develop cancer). The following argument, then, is not inductively forceful:

P1)   Smoking causes cancer.

C)   **If you smoke, then, probably, you will get cancer.**

What, then, does 'Smoking causes cancer' mean? Roughly, what it means is that each person is *more likely* to develop cancer if they smoke, than that person would be if they did not smoke. Smoking *raises the probability* of getting cancer. So this argument is deductively valid:

P1)   Smoking causes cancer.

C)   **If you smoke, you will be more likely to get cancer than if you don't.**

But note that the statement about smoking does not tell us to what degree smoking raises the probability of getting cancer. In that respect it is vague. A more precise causal generalisation would take the form: 'Smoking raises the probability of cancer by such-and-such per cent.'

This connects with another important issue regarding generalisations. Consider:

> A recent study of primary school children has discovered a strong correlation between diet and school performance: better diets were strongly linked to better test marks. One of the simplest things we can do to improve performance in primary schools, then, is simply to improve the foods on offer at school refectories.

To discover a 'correlation' between X and Y is to discover that the proportion of things that exhibit the feature Y is higher among things that exhibit feature X than it is among things that do not exhibit feature X. The arguer here seems to infer a causal relationship from the correlation of better test marks with better diets. As noted in Chapter 4, this is the fallacy of confusing *correlation* with *cause*. The inference goes like this:

P1)   X is strongly correlated with Y.

C)   **X causes Y.**

But this inference is no good. This can be seen easily by considering the following example of the same pattern:

P1)   High concentrations of bicycles are strongly correlated with air pollution.

C)   **High concentrations of bicycles cause air pollution.**

P1 is actually true, since high concentrations of bicycles and high levels of air pollution are typically found in the same place, namely large cities. But obviously C is false. This argument-pattern is evidently not valid, and not inductively forceful either.

Usually, when there is a correlation between X and Y without causation, what is going on is that some underlying factor causes both X and Y. In the case of bicycles and pollution, the common underlying cause is the presence of a large and concentrated population of human beings (the population density explains the presence of such sources of pollution as cars, which in turn cause the pollution). As for the case of children and test scores, it is certainly plausible to suppose that diet influences school performance, but there may be a common underlying cause in that case as well. For example, it might be that children from better-educated households tend to be more intelligent (if only because intelligent people are more likely to complete a university education), and that better-educated households tend to eat better diets (perhaps because they tend to have more money, and hence can afford a better diet). Or it might be that children from poor households tend to eat poorer diets, and that poor households tend to suffer from other sorts of family problems that tend to impair school performance. Thus the correlation is not sufficient to establish the causal relationship.

Under what circumstances, then, can we legitimately infer the presence of a causal relationship? The answer should be evident from the rough-and-ready definition of causation given above: in order to infer a causal relationship from a correlation between X and Y, we need to know that the correlation holds, or *would* hold, even when other possible causes of Y are absent or were absent. In other words, we need to know that Y exists more frequently when X exists than when it doesn't, *regardless of the circumstances in which we find X*. We need to rule out other possible causes. So what we would need to know in the case of the children, for example, is whether or not children from well-off households do worse at school if their diets are poor, and likewise for children from less well-educated households, and similarly for other alternative factors that might influence performance at school.

It is important to be aware of these issues, and especially to be able to point it out when a causal relationship is wrongly inferred from a correlation. But it would take us too far into the subject to give a general recipe for validly inferring causal relationships from correlations. Probably the most important single lesson to take away is that a causal relationship entails a correlation, but a correlation does not entail a causal relationship.

A shortcut

Where an argument contains a conditional among its premises, we have, in order to infer the consequent of the conditional, to write down its antecedent as a separate premise. This means that we have to write a certain sentence down twice. This can be cumbersome, and it often makes the structure of an argument more difficult to see than it need be. Consider again the first sub-argument in the argument about the tuna industry:

P1) Tuna catches have been decreasing significantly for the past nine years.

P2) If tuna catches have been decreasing significantly for the past nine years, then, if the tuna industry is not regulated more stringently, the tuna population will vanish.

C1) **If the tuna industry is not regulated more stringently, the tuna population will vanish.**

P2 is a conditional whose antecedent is P1. Instead of rewriting P1 out in full, we may abbreviate it simply as 'P1'. So we may rewrite the argument as follows:

P1) Tuna catches have been decreasing significantly for the past nine years.

P2) If (P1), then, if the tuna industry is not regulated more stringently, the tuna population will vanish.

C1) If the tuna industry is not regulated more stringently, the tuna population will vanish.

This is easier to read, and it saves you having to write things out unnecessarily. Henceforth, whenever an argument draws an inference from a conditional premise, feel free to abbreviate in this way.

CHAPTER SUMMARY

This chapter was concerned to address some of the main logical problems encountered in the **reconstruction** of arguments.

General aspects of this include **defusing the rhetoric** (rewriting so as to improve clarity by eliminating rhetoric) and **logical streamlining** (clarifying logical connections by using logically clear expressions such as 'if–then' for conditional relationships). In many cases, one or more premises upon which a conclusion depends is left **implicit** by the arguer. A necessary part of reconstruction is to make such premises **explicit**. Implicit premises are usually, though not always, **connecting premises**: these are either **conditionals** or **generalisations**. Where an argument contains a conditional among its premises, the conditional is often regarded by the arguer as being supported by a **covering generalisation**. In reconstruction, we should take care to include a suitable covering generalisation where appropriate. Covering generalisations may be either hard or soft generalisations.

Not everything explicitly stated by an arguer is **relevant** to the argument. A proposition asserted by an arguer may be completely irrelevant; that is, the arguer does not advance that proposition as support for the conclusion. Such propositions should not be included in the reconstruction. In other cases, a proposition explicitly stated does provide some independent support for the conclusion, but is such that if it were ignored, the arguer would still, by virtue of other propositions put forward, have given an argument

---

for the intended conclusion. In such a case, the proposition in question should be removed from the argument. If it is plausible to do so, it may be treated as a premise in a separate argument for the same conclusion.

Where possible, **ambiguity** and **vagueness** should be coped with by removing them. If it is possible to do so, the ambiguous or vague language should be replaced by language that is not ambiguous or vague. If a word in a premise or conclusion is ambiguous (can be read as expressing either of two meanings), and it is not clear which meaning is intended, then two reconstructions of the argument should be given, each reflecting one of the two meanings.

All **generalisations** in reconstructed arguments, whether hard or soft, should have explicit quantifiers. Where a premise is a generalisation, the **scope** of a generalisation should be as narrow as is needed to maximise its probability of being true, but not so narrow that the inference to the conclusion is no longer valid (or inductively forceful, as the case may be).

Practical reasoning, or **means–end reasoning**, is embodied in arguments that specify an **outcome** as being either **desirable** or **undesirable**, along with an **action** said to be either necessary or sufficient for bringing about that outcome. Such arguments can take any of eight basic forms. In order to reconstruct such arguments as valid or inductively forceful, we often have to add a premise stating that the proposed action is the most efficient means of bringing about the outcome, and a premise stating that the benefit of the outcome outweighs the cost of the action (or, in the negative case, that the cost of an action would outweigh the benefit of the outcome). But sometimes the outcomes of actions are only probable. This may require us to calculate the **expected value** of an action. The conclusions of arguments based on expected value may be overridden by **moral rules**.

Arguments are distinct from **explanations**, but many arguments have **explanations as conclusions**: such arguments attempt to establish which, of various possible causes of a given fact or event, is the actual cause. Arguments that attempt to establish **causal generalisations** present more difficulty. It is common to see causal generalisations fallaciously inferred from mere **correlations**. Causal generalisations are not as informative as one might be tempted to think: what they tell us is that one type of event or state of affairs increases the probability of another type of event or state of affairs.

EXERCISES

1   As given, the arguments below are invalid. But each can plausibly be thought to contain either a generalisation or conditional as an implicit premise – a proposition that the arguer is assuming but has not explicitly stated. The arguments can easily be made deductively valid by making the implicit premise explicit. (A) Identify the conclusion and explicit premises; then add the premise needed to make the argument valid. (B) Reconstruct the argument in standard form. Use a hard generalisation if you can think of one that is plausible; otherwise settle for a conditional. You should write all conditionals in the 'if–then' form.

a   Mr Bean is an idiot. You shouldn't marry him.

b   All men are idiots. You shouldn't marry one.

c   Johnny will like the Blandings Castle books; he likes the Jeeves books.

d   Pavarotti is going to sit in that chair! It's going to break!

e   Prices are not going to rise, because the savings rate is not decreasing.

f   Hakkinen won't win unless Schumacher's car breaks down. So Hakkinen won't win unless Schumacher's mechanic is inept.

g   Verdi was greater than Rossini, so obviously Verdi was greater than Puccini.

h   Since only democracies are just, no socialist countries are just.

i   If he doesn't accept the offer, then we will either withdraw the offer or raise it. If we raise it, then we incur financial risk. Therefore, if he doesn't accept the offer, then either we carry on with a second-rate manager, or we incur financial risk.

j   Unless John brought wine, there isn't any. John didn't bring wine. So we'll drink beer.

k   Cigarette advertisements don't encourage people to smoke? Ha. I think it safe to say that ads for chocolates encourage people to eat chocolates.

2   Rewrite the following in such a way as to defuse the rhetoric.

a   The democratic candidate's policy on the issues is that he jumps on the winning bandwagon.

b   The invasion of Iraq: the mother of all miscalculations.

c   If they impose trade tariffs then we don't have a level playing field.

d   She's been raking it in since she switched to writing chick-lit.

e   They can peddle that same ideology all they want, but we're not buying.

f   The Bio-tech shares offered by Ramsay? Just another fool's gold.

g   Our crusade against the junk-food mongers will not cease until the last junk-food ad has disappeared from children's television.

h   Blundering doctors killed 40,000 patients this year.

3   Logical streamlining: rewrite the following as single sentences using simple logical expressions such as 'if–then' and 'every'.

a   You threaten not to release prisoners? Then no cease-fire.

b   There is no way we're going to win the election without increasing our appeal to women.

c   There are places in which the most offensive speech is always deemed acceptable. They are called universities.

d   A leaf-blower is louder than a rake.

e   Embryo research is the thin end of the wedge towards human cloning.

f   He who laughs last laughs longest.

4   Find appropriate covering generalisations for the following conditionals. Choose a hard or soft generalisation as seems appropriate.

a   If John is under 18, then he cannot legally purchase alcohol in the UK.

b   If that is a scorpion, then it is poisonous.

c   If that wine is not French, then it is probably not overpriced.

d   That picture is not likely to be an oil painting, unless it was painted after 1500 or is Dutch or Flemish.

e   He is probably good at analysing arguments, if he is a successful lawyer.

f   If the patient is now haemorrhaging, then his blood pressure is decreasing.

5

a   Suppose you know that Doctor Bowes does not own or drive a Ferrari. Reconstruct the argument in accordance with the principle of charity.

> Doctor Bowes, the candidate, owns a majority share in a large and successful corporation. Furthermore, he drives a brand new Ferrari. Of course he is wealthy.

Exercises

217

The practice of argument-reconstruction

b   The following passage includes the assertion that the defendant has been addicted to cocaine for two years. Suppose you know this assertion to be entirely false (the defendant has never used any illicit drug). Reconstruct the argument in accordance with the principle of charity. In order to reconstruct it, you will have to rephrase some of the sentences, ignore some material, and also to make implicit premises explicit. The conclusion is also implicit.

> The evidence is very compelling. The defendant has been addicted to cocaine for over two years. Her blood and fingerprints were found on the murder weapon. She was seen emerging from the victim's flat not more than half an hour after the murder took place. She boarded a flight for Greece only twelve hours after the murder. And finally, the victim had recently ended the sexual relationship between himself and the accused.

6   We very frequently hear of claims or actions being criticised on the grounds that they are politically motivated. Sometimes this is put by saying that someone is 'playing politics', or using something as a 'political football'. What does this mean? Why is it a criticism? Find examples in the print media, and try to explain what the point is, in such cases in calling something 'political'.

7   Reconstruct the following arguments, taking care to eliminate vague or ambiguous terms. You will have to rewrite sentences, ignore some material, and make implicit propositions explicit.

a   Ms Jones has demonstrated her commitment to feminism by supporting an across-the-board pay rise for female academics. So no doubt she'll support a reduction of the evidential standard for rape convictions.

b   Make no mistake: whatever their keepers say, these so-called 'domesticated' wolves are *wild*. Wild animals are too dangerous to be kept as pets.

c   Researchers have found that heroin use in teenagers is linked to parents with histories of depression. Parents under psychiatric care for depression should therefore be told the symptoms of heroin use.

8   For this argument, reconstruct it twice: once retaining the vague term 'political correctness', and once eliminating it.

> When the Bunbury Women's Group proposes that the City Council bar men from the 'Women's Safe House', we realise that we must not allow them to have influence on the Council. For this makes it obvious

that the virus of 'political correctness' has infected the women's group, and we know what 'political correctness' stands for – they would promote such horrors as homosexuality being taught in schools and legal prohibitions against language deemed 'incorrect'.

9 Reconstruct the following arguments, making implicit propositions explicit as needed. If the argument is not deductively valid, increase its inductive force by decreasing the scope of the generalisation. If the argument is deductively valid, increase its chances of being sound by decreasing the scope of the generalisation.

a   Of course your new horse can be trained without much difficulty. Most horses can be.

b   Most men marry. Therefore most men have, have had or will have a mother-in-law.

c   No primates can learn to talk. Bobo is a chimpanzee, hence a primate; therefore he cannot learn to talk.

d   All countries can be attacked by sea. Thus all countries require a naval defence.

10 Reconstruct the argument about compulsory military service discussed at the beginning of this chapter (p. 169). Take into account the advice given in the section on practical reasoning (pp. 201–4).

11 Look at argument-pattern (1) in the section on practical reasoning (p. 204). In order for such arguments to be valid, we need to add two premises: first, that the benefit of increasing the amount of chocolate outweighs the cost of performing action X; second, that action X is the most efficient way of increasing the amount of chocolate. What similar premises are needed to make argument-patterns (3), (6) and (8) valid?

12 Reconstruct the argument below. Some guidance: you will need to remove some extraneous material and perhaps defuse some rhetoric. It is not easy to tell exactly what the conclusion is, and it may be implicit. Once you have decided, you may need to add implicit premises. You should also think about the role of the word 'deviant'; is it vague or ambiguous? Should it be avoided in the reconstruction of the argument?

Why has marriage always meant man and woman? Because other sexual relationships are *deviant*. Obviously homosexual relationships are deviant; that's just biological fact. And that's what the legalisation of same-sex marriage would mean: the legal protection of deviant sexual relationships – the legal protection of *all* sexual relationships, of *whatever kind*. Why not incest and bestiality too?

13 The following argument contains a fair amount of rhetoric, stage-setting and explanation, but also a practical argument. Decide which of the eight patterns of practical reasoning the central argument of the passage fits, and reconstruct it. Don't worry too much about including every point that might be relevant; your main task should be to get the central argument laid out before you (then you can add sub-arguments, if you find any). Part of the first paragraph is concerned to reply to a point made by the correspondent referred to; think carefully about whether, and in what way, this contributes to the writer's intended argument.

I despair of your correspondent who responded to the article on otters and mink (Letters, 9 July). Mink are certainly not playful and delightful animals. She must be confusing them with ferrets. While I agree it is no fault of their own that they are with us, it is not a question of survival. Mink are in paradise here in the wild: no harsh winter; no natural predators; a vast range of prey.

In the Mustelid family they have found a niche halfway between otters and pine marten with the aquatic ability of the former and the natural aggression of the latter. Mink are consequently able to reach nesting colonies of ducks and seabirds, formerly secure from predation, wiping them out and rendering the island sanctuaries untenable by birds. I would invite your correspondent to come to Argyll and see for herself. Mink are a scourge on our environment and should be eliminated at every opportunity.[7]

14 Another practical argument, this time giving you more practice identifying implicit premises and conclusion. Reconstruct as according to the instructions on practical reasoning. The letter is humorous, but contains a serious (though implicit) argument.

Sir, having read your report on how the police plan to test drivers for drugs, I and both my children in their early twenties attempted the tests described, without having taken any illegal substances.

We consistently failed the second test (on one leg, head tilted back, eyes closed, other leg off the ground, arms extended, touch nose with each index finger). Swaying and giggling helplessly at each other's attempts, we would have given every appearance of intoxication.

We have therefore decided that, if we are stopped and invited to perform these tests at the roadside, we will first ask the officer for a demonstration.[8]

---

7   Michael Murray, *Independent*, 16 July 2000.
8   John Tayler, *The Times*, 4 August 2000.

15 A friend offers you a wager: if you draw an ace out of a (normal) pack of playing cards, he'll give you £10. If you don't, you pay him £1. What is the expected value of accepting the wager? Should you do it?

16 There is a sweepstakes draw: all you have to do is post a letter with your name and address to the address given, and your name will go into the draw. The lucky winner, drawn from a barrel containing 400,000 names, will receive £100,000! Assuming that a second-class stamp costs 26p, what is the expected (monetary) value of posting your letter, thereby entering the sweepstakes?

17 Criticize the following argument: the purpose of the National Lottery is to earn money for the Government. Thus the amount collected from ticket sales exceeds the amount paid out in prizes. Therefore the expected value of buying a lottery ticket is negative. Therefore one should not buy lottery tickets.

18 The following passage contains an argument that can reasonably be construed as balancing costs, benefits and probabilities. Try to reconstruct it accordingly.

> Elimination of global hunger, prevention of deficiency diseases and protection of the world's threatened environments are within reach as bio-tech and genetically modified food research improves.
>
> The debate over food production has swung in favour of new high-tech methods. The benefits to consumers, producers and the environment from these new technologies are increasingly evident and vastly outweigh the risks. Every year millions of lives are lost to malnutrition. Thousands of hectares of precious habitat are sacrificed in the struggle to produce food using inefficient methods, namely conventional methods.
>
> For example, vitamin A deficiency is a serious worldwide problem. So it is hard to see the merit in eco-terrorists who destroy test crops of GM 'golden rice' – which contains high levels of beta-carotene to help fight rampant vitamin A deficiency and resulting blindness in developing nations.
>
> Meanwhile, too many people drastically overestimate the risks because they don't understand that GM crops are not essentially anything new. Genetic improvement has a long and venerable history, and with the exception of wild game, wild berries and the like, virtually all the foods in our diet are obtained from organisms that have been genetically improved. Scientists worldwide agree that adding genes

to plants does not make them less safe either to the environment or for humans to eat. Dozens of new plant varieties produced through hybridisation and other traditional methods of genetic improvement enter the marketplace each year without scientific review or scientific labelling. Many such products are plant varieties that do not and cannot exist in nature!

The scientific consensus is unequivocal: gene-splicing is more precise, controllable and predictable than other, 'traditional' or conventional techniques. For example, new insect-resistant varieties of grain crafted with gene-splicing techniques have lower levels of contamination with toxic fungi and insect parts than conventional grains. Thus, gene-spliced grain is not only cheaper to produce but is a potential boon to human health. Moreover, by reducing the need for spraying chemical pesticides on crops, it is environmentally friendly.

Florence Wambubu, and agronomist from Kenya, described how all farming there is 'organic' and has produced low yields and hungry people. She spent three years at Monsanto, in the United States developing a genetically modified sweet potato to help the farmers in her country, where the crop has been nearly destroyed by a virus. The engineered sweet potato is virus-resistant, and requires no pesticides. Wambugu is scornful of the environmental 'hooligans', whom she sees as trying to tear down many years of work on behalf of romantic notions and bad science.

19 The following are not simply explanations, but rather arguments that have explanations as conclusions. Reconstruct them, eliminating extraneous material and making implicit material explicit as needed.

a   At your last visit I said that the pain in your abdomen is caused either by a kidney infection, a musculoskeletal injury or cancer in the pancreas or liver. But no indicators for a kidney infection showed up in the urinalysis, and if it were musculoskeletal, the pain would have subsided, not grown, by now. I'm afraid you have cancer.

b   The stress of modern life is not because we work more than our parents did – we don't – but because we no longer go to church. Instead, we shop: the world's most stressful activity.

c   Nietzsche's going irrevocably mad was caused either by his tortured intellectual life – as romantically minded people would like to believe – or by the syphilis he contracted as a young man. But if it were his intellectual proclivities, then we should expect a great many other notable intellectuals to have gone irrevocably mad. The truth – again contrary to romantic fantasies – is that very few have.

d   We read with horror that the age of the onset of puberty in girls is getting younger. We don't believe this has to do with artificial hormones in the milk or anything like that – surely in these more environmentally aware times, there are fewer artificial hormones and suchlike in our food than there were say, twenty years ago. The real reason is the unprecedented onslaught of sexualised images to which children are now subjected, especially on television.

e   Mr Jenkins blames the high unemployment rate on Britain's high interest rates: these strengthen the Pound, making British exports uncompetitive, which in turn forces British manufacturers to cut costs by means of redundancies. We blame it on the ease with which people out of work can go on the dole. Jenkins' argument assumes that the non-manufacturing sector of the economy is not growing as fast as the manufacturing side shrinks. Manifestly, it is.

f   The president says that greenhouse gasses are mostly produced by trees, not by industry. That makes sense. Global warming is on the rise, and we all see how, all over the world, people are busy planting trees and closing down factories, getting rid of their cars, and so on. The world of our pre-industrial ancestors must have been a real hothouse.

20 Review the section on causal generalisations. Every example below is a case either of (1) assuming that a causal relation entails a hard generalisation or a generalisation of the 'most' type; or (2) too readily inferring a causal relationship from a statistical correlation. In a short paragraph, criticise the following arguments: say whether each argument is a case of either (1) or (2) and explain your answer.

a   It is just not true that prolonged exposure to the sun causes skin cancer. If it did, then everyone who has ever had a suntan or a sunburn would get skin cancer.

b   I am so tired of hearing that social and economic deprivation 'cause' teenage criminality. Plenty of teenagers suffer from social and economic deprivation without turning to crime.

c   Taking lots of vitamin C makes my colds go away. I always take vitamin C when I get a cold, and it always goes away.

d   A causal link between violent video games and juvenile violence has been demonstrated. A study has shown that the incidence of violence is much higher among teenage boys who play violent video games regularly than it is among those who do not.

e   Oxbridge representatives claim that their admission procedures are not biased against students from poor backgrounds. How can they maintain this obvious falsehood, when *their own figures* show that the proportion of Oxbridge undergraduates from impoverished backgrounds is far lower than the proportion of *applicants* from impoverished backgrounds? Oxbridge continues to exclude the poor because they are poor.

21 (A) Draw tree-diagrams for the following arguments as written. (B) Reconstruct them thoroughly, and draw tree-diagrams for the reconstructed versions. (C) Say whether they are valid, inductively forceful or neither.

a   The sharp increase in the death rate in ancient Antioch, in the year AD 364, has been ascribed to many factors: to famine, to an influx of disease brought by soldiers returning from the Persian campaign, and to problems with the city's water supply. It was probably the water supply: if it were food shortages, it is unlikely *both* that no contemporary historian mentions it, and that there should be no record of similar sufferings in the lesser towns of the area or the surrounding countryside. And if the soldiers had contracted disease in Mesopotamia, then, since they were seriously weakened by hunger and the strain of a long and arduous campaign, they would have died of disease in significant numbers. And then it is certain that Ammanius, an eyewitness, would have recorded those fatalities – so cruel after the humiliations and losses they had endured in battle – in his history. But he is silent on the point.

b   Jepsen's Neural Syndrome – JNS – seems to be caused in dolphins by an excessive intake of heavy metals. A genetic cause is ruled out, because if the cause were genetic, then the correlation discovered between JNS and the presence of abnormally high levels of heavy metals in dolphins would be extremely unlikely. True, the correlation between JNS and abnormally high levels of heavy metals is no greater than that of JNS with the consumption of large amounts of squid. But squid, as we know, tend to retain, over time, large concentrations of the trace heavy metals that pass through their bodies. Dolphins tend to eat the larger, therefore older squid. It is very probable that if squid did not retain heavy metals, then the correlation between JNS and squid consumption would not exist. Since there are no other significant correlations with JNS, the heavy metals diagnosis looks highly probable.

c   If alcoholic *behaviour* in parents – as opposed to genetic predispositions to alcoholism – caused alcoholism in children, then we would find that children whose parents are not alcoholic, and who are adopted at a very early age by alcoholic parents, were significantly more likely to become alcoholics. But our study shows that they are not. Therefore mere heavy drinking in parents does not, despite the well-known correlation, cause children to grow up to be alcoholic.

Chapter 6

Issues in argument assessment

Rational persuasiveness

It is plain common sense that the role of an argument is to give us reasons for accepting its conclusion as true. The aim is to give an argument that the intended audience *ought* to be persuaded by. But we have not quite defined what it is, exactly, for an argument to do this. You might think that we have done this with the notions of deductive and inductive soundness, but that is not quite right. The reason is that even if we have reconstructed an argument perfectly, we cannot always tell whether or not the argument is sound. And that is because a sound argument must have true premises. A deductively sound argument is one that has true premises and which is deductively valid; an inductively sound argument is an inductively forceful argument with true premises. Since we do not always know which propositions are true and which false, we cannot always tell whether an argument is sound or not.

What we want, rather, is to characterise the property of 'giving us good reasons to accept the conclusion' in such a way that when an argument has that property, we are always able to recognise it – just by virtue of whatever knowledge we do possess, along with our ability to assess arguments logically. This property cannot be the property of validity or inductive force, since the fact that an argument is valid or forceful does not give us a reason to accept its conclusion unless we already have reason to accept the premises. But neither can this property be the property of soundness, since being able to recognise soundness normally requires that we have factual knowledge that goes beyond the ability to analyse or reconstruct arguments.

Here is a very simple illustration. Suppose you are wondering whether or not you should expect that interest rates will increase in the next year, and someone presents you with the following argument:

P1)   Interest rates will neither decrease nor remain unchanged in
        the next year.

C)   **Interest rates will increase in the next year.**

Clearly this argument is of no use to you. It is logically correct – it is deductively valid – but such an argument could not persuade anyone of the conclusion who did not already accept it. For if you did not know whether or not to expect interest rates to increase, then of course you didn't know whether to expect them to decrease, or to remain unchanged. If you had had some reason to accept P, then you could not have been wondering whether to accept C.

Here is another illustration. Suppose Bert drops a coin into a cup of coffee, and it settles to the bottom 'heads up'. Neither Bert nor Barney can see it, so neither knows that it landed heads up. Neither has any idea which way the coin landed. Then Bert and Barney consider the following argument:

P1)   If the coin landed tails down, then it landed heads up.
P2)   The coin landed tails down.

C)   **The coin landed heads up.**

In the envisaged situation, the argument would be deductively sound, since it is deductively valid and the premises are true. But, although P2 is true, neither Bert nor Barney has any reason think so. So, although the argument is deductively sound, and Bert and Barney can see that it is deductively valid, it gets them no closer to knowing the truth-value of the conclusion.

In such a situation, we say that the argument is **rationally unpersuasive**. More exactly we must say it is rationally unpersuasive for Barney, and also for Bert. Why we must put it this way – why we must *relativise* the notion of the rational persuasiveness of an argument, can be seen from a variation of the story.

Suppose that Barney, but not Bert, knows that the coin is weighted in such a way that it almost always ends up tails down. Then Barney, but not Bert, has a good reason to accept P2. Therefore Barney has a good reason to accept that the argument is sound, but Bert does not. Therefore the argument is rationally persuasive for Barney, but not for Bert.

Now imagine a further variation on the story. Suppose that at a particular moment, Barney tells Bert about the weighting of the coin. If Bert had considered the argument before that moment, the argument would not have been rationally persuasive for him. But if he considers it after that moment, then it *is* rationally persuasive for him, because of Bert's acquisition of the relevant information. So rational persuasiveness is doubly relative: an argument is or is not rationally persuasive *for* a person *at* a particular time. Since different people are in different states of information at different times, an argument may be rationally persuasive for Barney but not for Bert, and it may be rationally persuasive for Bert at one time but fail to be at another time. In what follows, we will usually suppress this complication, but it is worth knowing that it can sometimes be relevant.

Before we give our official definition of rational persuasiveness, there is one last complication to be discussed. Looking over the example just given, you might think that an argument is rationally persuasive (for a person at a time) if (i) it is inductively forceful or deductively valid and (ii) the person reasonably believes the premises (at the time). But this is not quite right.

For consider now the following example:

P1) Almost all residents of Inverness own at least one item of woollen clothing.

P2) Jane is a resident of Inverness.

C)   **(Probably) Jane owns at least one item of woollen clothing.**

This is an inductively forceful argument. Suppose in fact you have good reason to accept both P1 and P2. Indeed, suppose you know with certainty that they are both true. Does it follow that you should accept C? Can you imagine a situation in which you know that P1 and P2 are true, but in which you could reasonably reject C? Yes. For suppose that, in addition to your knowledge of P1 and P2, you know that Jane is violently allergic to wool. In that case, you could quite reasonably expect C to be false. Someone who knew the truth of P1 and P2, but nothing else about Jane, could reasonably expect C to be true, but not you. The argument would be rationally persuasive for them, but not for you.

What we say, in such a case, is that the argument is **defeated for you** by other evidence that you have; in this case you have, in effect, two arguments: the argument as given, and also a more compelling argument for the falsity of the first argument's conclusion.

In particular:

> To say that an inductively forceful argument is *defeated* for a person is to say: The person reasonably believes the premises, but, nevertheless, reasonably rejects the conclusion.

An inductively forceful argument whose premises you have reason to accept is rationally persuasive only if your total evidence does not defeat the argument for you (we will say more about evidence in Chapter 7). Note that the definition pertains only to inductive arguments. The reason for this will be clear in a moment. Thus our definition:

> To say that an argument is *rationally persuasive* for a person (at a time) is to say:
>
> (i)   the argument is either deductively valid or inductively forceful;
> (ii)   the person reasonably believes the argument's premises (at the time); and
> (iii) it is not an inductively forceful argument that is defeated for that person (at that time).

There are six further points to bear in mind as regards rational persuasiveness.

1   It is not possible for the conclusion of a *deductively valid* argument to be *defeated* by a person's total evidence – this is only possible for inductively forceful arguments. Thus condition (iii) of the definition of rational persuasiveness only applies to inductively forceful arguments. The reasons for this are:

a   If you accept with good reason the premises of an argument that you recognise to be deductively valid, then you must accept the conclusion as well; for you know that if the premises are true, then the conclusion must be true as well. If a person has good reason to accept the premises of a deductively valid argument, then we may conclude that it is rationally persuasive for that person without further ado. Any further consideration that, for that person, casts doubt on the conclusion, must equally cast doubt on the premises.

   The reason for this comes from the **definition** of a **valid** argument: if its premises are true, then its conclusion must be true. Remember from Chapter 2: validity has nothing to do with the actual truth of the premises. Therefore, *if the premises are true and the argument is valid – the conclusion must necessarily (no exceptions) be true*. So if you have reason to accept the premises then those very same reasons are equally strong reasons to accept the conclusion. The only way that a **deductively valid** argument can fail to be rationally persuasive is if a person is without reason to accept the truth of one or more of the premises (remember that since the argument is deductively valid, condition (i) has already been fulfilled).

b   The adverb 'probably' (or similar term) before the conclusion of an inductively forceful argument allows the possibility that the premises are true and the conclusion false. When you have an argument that is inductively forceful, the third condition of the definition of rational persuasiveness becomes relevant; for the evidence that defeats the conclusion is precisely the evidence that shifts the balance of probability. Because the claim that an argument is inductively forceful only claims that if the premises are true the conclusion is likely to be true, there is room for situations in which the conclusion is actually false.

   Condition three of the definition of rational persuasiveness means that there are *two* ways in which an inductively sound argument can fail to be rationally persuasive. The first is when the person has no good reason to accept one or more of the premises (i.e. it fails condition (ii)). The second is when the argument is defeated for the person: the person has evidence that prevents him or her from accepting the conclusion even though he or she recognises that the premises are true and the argument is inductively forceful.

2   It is not part of the definition that the argument be *sound* (either deductively or inductively). The reason is simple: the notion of rational persuasiveness is intended to capture what it is about an argument that constitutes its rational claim on a person. It explains what it means to say: *this person ought to accept the conclusion of this argument*. It is the notion of an argument's giving a person good reason to accept its conclusion. Indeed, an argument can have a false premise, and hence be unsound (neither deductively nor inductively sound), yet be rationally persuasive for a person. To illustrate, go back to the second version of the weighted coin. Suppose that on this one rare occasion, the coin settles to the bottom of the cup heads down, so P2 is false. Still, in that case, Barney would still be quite reasonable in thinking that P2 is true (for he knows that the coin is weighted). So the argument would still be rationally persuasive for Barney, despite its having a false premise, and thereby being unsound. He would be quite right – in the sense of being rationally justified – to accept the conclusion of the argument, even though, in fact, it is false.

This point about rational persuasiveness illustrates an important fact to which we will return later in more detail: a person may reasonably believe a proposition that is, as it happens, false. In other words, there is such a thing as a reasonable mistake. This is an elementary point, but it is an easy one to forget – and hence, for example, you might inappropriately blame people when they make a mistake of this nature. Indeed, a useful way to put the point is to say that the word 'mistake' is ambiguous. To say that someone is 'mistaken' could mean either (i) that they have accepted a false conclusion, or (ii) that they have been persuaded by bad reasons – by an argument which is not in fact rationally persuasive for them (or they have *failed* to be persuaded by good reasons – by an argument that *is* rationally persuasive for them). Clearly we are responsible for our mistakes of type (ii); we ought to be persuaded by good reasons, and not by bad reasons. If we fail in this, then, typically, we are blameworthy. But it is much less clear that we are always responsible for mistakes of type (i). If someone believes a proposition on the basis of good reasons – on the basis of arguments that are rationally persuasive for him or her – then it might just be bad luck if the proposition turns out to be false. If so, then the person need not be to blame for having made a 'mistake'.

Suppose, for example, that you are a doctor. Suppose there is a drug X that you know to have cured a certain dangerous disease every single time it has been used, in over a million cases; furthermore, you know that it has never had a negative side effect, and contains no substances known to be dangerous in any way. A patient has the disease and you prescribe X. Unfortunately, instead of being cured by X, the patient is made ill by it. Were you mistaken in believing that X would safely cure the disease? Not if by 'mistaken' we mean a mistake of type (ii), and hence not in the sense required if you are to be blameworthy. Indeed, you would have been open to criticism if you had decided *not* to prescribe the drug, since you would have been going against a massive body of evidence.

3   It should be appreciated why we have named rational persuasiveness as we have. Remember that at the beginning, we said that there are various kinds of attempts at persuasion. This book is about trying to distinguish argumentative from non-argumentative – especially rhetorical – attempts at persuasion, and learning to evaluate them. An attempt at persuasion by argument is an attempt at rational persuasion, as opposed to other kinds of persuasion, which do not appeal to your reason (but rather to your emotions or prejudices). Directed at you, it is an attempt at providing you with a rationally persuasive argument. Note, again, that this does not mean that the argument must be a sound argument. The attempt depends upon what you reasonably believe regardless of whether or not those reasonable beliefs are in fact true.

4   Rational persuasiveness is a matter of degree; it is not all-or-nothing. This is evident from the fact that inductive force is a matter of degree.

5   'Rationally persuasive' does not mean merely 'persuasive' or 'convincing'. A rationally persuasive argument may fail to persuade anyone. Whether or not an argument is rationally persuasive for you does not depend upon whether you think it is. The crux of the matter is to understand this: an argument may be rationally persuasive for you even though you are not persuaded by it. This should not be regarded as paradoxical. All it means is that there are cases where you *ought* to be persuaded by an argument, but you are not. Likewise, there are cases where you *are* persuaded or convinced by an argument, but where you *should not* be, because the argument is not actually rationally persuasive for you. It is one task of rhetoric to cause people to overestimate the rational persuasiveness of an argument – to convince or persuade people without actually giving them good reasons.

To understand why this is so, examine Figure 6.1. You can see from this figure that when we examine the relationships between sound arguments, rationally persuasive arguments and the arguments that actually persuade people, it is possible for a given argument to be one, two or all three of them. The important point you need to note is that rational persuasiveness and soundness are properties that arguments can have independently of whether an individual or group actually finds them persuasive. Human beings are not always perfectly rational and part of the function of the concept of rational persuasiveness as we have defined it is to acknowledge this. If rational persuasiveness were defined so as to make all rationally persuasive arguments ones that actually persuaded people, we would have no way of accounting for the fact that sometimes people fail to be persuaded by arguments that they really should be persuaded by, and are sometimes persuaded by arguments that they should not be persuaded by.

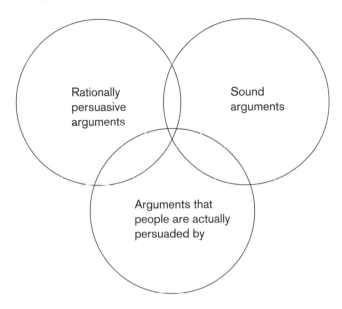

Figure 6.1

There are three ways in which one can be mistaken about the rational persuasiveness of an argument. Study them carefully, especially if the preceding paragraphs are mysterious to you.

First, we can make mistakes concerning whether or not an argument is valid or inductively forceful. Especially in the case of a logically complex argument, we may, for example, think the argument deductively valid or inductively forceful when it is neither (for example, when the argument contains a fallacy that is also an effective rhetorical ploy; see Chapter 4). If so, then even if we accept the truth of the premises, and are perfectly justified or reasonable in doing so, we may think that the argument is rationally persuasive for us when it is not. Equally, if we think an argument invalid when it is valid, or think it inductively unforceful when it is inductively forceful, it is possible to think an argument rationally *un*persuasive for us when in fact it *is* rationally persuasive for us.

Second, we can think we have good reason to accept a premise when we don't, or vice versa. For example, consider the following argument:

P1)   Next summer will be a hot one.

P2)   Hot weather is good for Cabernet Sauvignon grapes.

C)   **(Probably) Next year's Cabernet Sauvignon harvest will be good.**

This looks like an inductively forceful argument, and P2 is true. Now suppose Jane knows that P2 is true. She also thinks that P1 is true, but her reason is that she has the superstitious belief that whenever it rains on Winter solstice, the following summer will be hot (assume it really is unreasonable for her to accept P1; as we will see in more detail later, what are often called 'superstitious' beliefs are not always unreasonable). In that case, assuming she knows it did rain on Winter solstice, she may think her belief in P1 is reasonable or well-founded, but it is not. So in that case, having noticed its inductive forcefulness, she may well think that this argument is rationally persuasive for her, but she would be wrong. She may be persuaded, but she is not rationally persuaded.

Third, you can be mistaken about whether or not an argument is defeated for you. On the one hand, you might accept an argument for a given conclusion – thereby accepting the argument as rationally persuasive – without realising that you have information sufficient to construct another argument that defeats the conclusion of the first argument. You might, for example, accept an argument for the conclusion that Mr Jones will attend the meeting, momentarily forgetting that Mr Jones had scheduled a holiday today. On the other hand, you might think that an argument is defeated for you when it isn't. You might, that is, mistakenly think you have good reasons to reject the conclusion of an argument that is inductively forceful and whose premises you accept.

Obviously one can give arguments for various purposes, including deceitful ones. But the rational, non-deceitful motivation for giving an argument is surely this: *it is to give a sound argument that is rationally persuasive for oneself, and for its intended audience.* Different arguments may be required for different audiences. We cannot always know with certainty whether an argument is sound, but that is the human predicament. It is simply a consequence of the fact that we do not always know with certainty which propositions are true and which false. If we did, we would never need arguments.

6   In saying that an argument is rationally persuasive for a person only if the person reasonably believes the premises, we are not requiring that the person have, at his or her disposal, further arguments with those premises as conclusions. What we are requiring is that the person be justified in accepting the premises. Justification is a wider concept than rational persuasiveness: if one has a rationally persuasive argument for a proposition then one is justified in accepting it, but one may be justified in accepting it by means other than argument. In particular, some beliefs, especially **perceptual** beliefs such as 'I see a dog in front of me', are often justified – reasonable – even though they are not inferred from other beliefs. We will return to this in the next chapter.

Some strategies for logical assessment

Once we have an argument represented in standard form, we have to pronounce whether or not the argument is valid, and if not, whether or not it is inductively forceful. To do this, the basic technique is simple: ask yourself, can I imagine or conceive of a situation in which the premises are true, but the conclusion false? If under no conceivable situation could that be, then the argument is valid.

If you can think of ways in which the premises would be true but the conclusion false, then you must determine to what degree, if any, the argument is inductively forceful. What you do here is to imagine various situations in which all the premises are true. Of these situations, which are more likely, the ones in which the conclusion is true, or the ones in which it is false? If the situations in which the conclusion is true would be more likely than those in which it is false, then the argument is inductively forceful; if not, not. If it is forceful, it remains only to specify the degree to which it is so.

Here is an illustrative example:

P1)   The diamond thief wore size five high heels.

C)   **The diamond thief was a woman.**

This is not deductively valid, since it is not impossible that the thief was a man with very small feet wearing high heels, or even a child. This is readily conceivable. Is the argument inductively forceful? Not just as it stands, since the premises themselves do not tell us that children seldom steal diamonds and that men very seldom have such small feet. But these are items of general knowledge that we can add as premises, thus making the inductive force of the argument explicit:

P1)   The diamond thief wore size five high heels.
P2)   Very few men wear size five high heels.
P3)   Very few children steal diamonds.

C1)   **(Probably) The diamond thief was a woman.**

Whenever we find that an argument is not valid, we should always ask whether there are premises that (1) the arguer could reasonably be expected to know, or which we know to be true, and (2) would make the argument inductively forceful, if added.

Arguments with conditionals or generalisations as conclusions

The process described above, where we ask ourselves whether there is a possible situation in which an argument's premises are true but its conclusion false, can be mentally taxing, where the argument's conclusion is a conditional or a generalisation. Recall the argument from Chapter 5 concerning the tuna industry, rewritten to eliminate the use of 'unless':

P1) Tuna catches have been decreasing significantly for the past nine years.

P2) If tuna catches have been decreasing significantly for the past nine years, then, if the tuna industry is not regulated more stringently, the tuna population will vanish.

C1) If the tuna industry is regulated more stringently, then the tuna population will vanish.

P3) If the tuna population vanishes, the tuna industry will collapse altogether.

C2) If the tuna industry is not regulated more stringently, it will collapse altogether.

Concentrate on the argument from C1 and P3 to C2. It might be a bit difficult to imagine C1 and P3 true, and then ask whether C2 could be false in such a situation. But in fact, when we considered this argument earlier, we used a method that makes it easier. We shall now make this more explicit, as it is important when considering arguments that have as much logical complexity as this argument (or more). Note that C2 is a conditional. What a conditional asserts, roughly, is a certain relation between the antecedent and consequent – that if the antecedent is true then so is the consequent. So the question we want to answer is this: *if* the premises of the argument were true, then would this purported relationship hold? To answer this question we suppose, not only that the premises of the argument are true, but that the *antecedent of the argument's conclusion is also true*. And then what we want to know is whether, under all those suppositions, the consequent of the argument's conclusion would also have to be true. If that is so, then that conditional proposition does follow from the premises.

We can illustrate the matter like this, using the arrow '→' to indicate 'if–then' as we did in Chapter 2. Suppose we have an argument that looks like this, with capital letters standing in for sentences:

P1) ....
P2) ....
_____

C) P → Q

Such an argument is valid only if the following is also valid, where P1 and P2 are the same as before:

P1) ....
P2) ....
P3) P
_____

C) Q

That is to say, in order to determine whether P → Q follows from some premises, we ask whether Q follows from those premises together with P.

So back to the tuna fishing argument. Suppose C1 and P3 are true, _and_ that the tuna industry is not (going to be) regulated more stringently (this is the antecedent of C2). We can now reason as follows: we have assumed that the tuna industry is not regulated more stringently; therefore, according to C1, the tuna population will vanish. But in that case, according to P3, the tuna industry will collapse altogether. But that is precisely what the consequent of the C2 says. So we see that if C1 and P3 are true, then it does follow, from the antecedent of C2's being true, that the consequent of C2 is true also. So the argument is valid.

The same sort of technique is useful where the conclusion of an argument is a generalisation. Consider this argument:

P1) Every midfielder on the Italian national side is a good defender.
P2) No one is a good defender who does not tackle well.
_____

C) Every midfielder on the Italian national side tackles well.

Here, as before, we begin by supposing the premises true. But in this case the conclusion is a generalisation. Now recall from Chapter 5 that generalisations can typically be regarded as generalised conditionals. So the conclusion C can (somewhat awkwardly) be re-worded as: '*If* someone is a midfielder on the Italian national side, *then* that person tackles well.' Thus suppose that P1 and P2 are true. What we do in this case is to suppose that someone is a midfielder on the Italian national side; that is, we consider any midfielder on the Italian national side. What we now want to know is whether P1 and P2 force us to conclude that that person tackles well. They do: according to P1 this person is a good defender; but then according to P2, this person must tackle well. But this was just *any* Italian midfielder, not any one in particular. So we can conclude that every Italian midfielder tackles well (if P1 and P2 are true). Now consider a slightly different argument:

P1) Every midfielder on the Italian national side is a good defender.
P2) Every player who tackles well is a good defender.

C) Every midfielder on the Italian national side tackles well.

If we imagine our Italian midfielder again, P1 entails that he is a good defender. But P2 does not entail that he tackles well. It says that every player who tackles well is a good defender, but it does not tell us that if he is a good defender, then he tackles well. So P1 and P2, in this argument, do not allow us to conclude that our Italian midfielder tackles well. The argument is invalid.

Supposing the conclusion false

Another way to assess the validity of an argument is suppose the premises are true but the conclusion false. If we can see that this is impossible, then, according to the definition of validity, the argument is valid; if we can see that this is possible, then we know that the argument is invalid. So consider the first argument about the Italian footballers. To suppose the conclusion false is to suppose that there is at least one Italian midfielder who does not tackle well. If he does not, then by P2 he is not a good defender. But then he is an Italian midfielder who is not a good defender, which contradicts P1. So if the conclusion is false, it is impossible for the premises to be true. So the argument is valid.

Do the same with the second argument about the Italian footballers. We now imagine an Italian midfielder who does not tackle well. According to P1, he must be a good defender. But P2 does not force us, or enable us, to draw any further conclusion about this Italian midfielder. It tells us that if he tackles well, then he is a good defender, but it does not tell us anything about the case where he does not tackle well: it does not say that if he does not tackle well then he is not a good defender. So the falsity of the conclusion is perfectly consistent with the two premises being true. For all the premises say, our midfielder might be a good defender for other reasons – he might be very quick and energetic, good at clearances and so on. So the argument is invalid.

This method can be used on any argument, not just those whose conclusions are conditionals or generalisations. But it is especially helpful in those cases.

Refutation by counterexample

We move now to an important technique for showing that an argument is invalid or inductively unforceful. Normally, you would use this when you have already determined that the argument is not valid or inductively forceful, and, in an argument commentary, when you wish to explain why the argument is not valid or inductively forceful. It is grasped most easily by looking at an example. Consider this argument:

P1)   Almost all heroin addicts were marijuana smokers before becoming heroin addicts.

C)   **Marijuana smokers tend to become heroin addicts.**

This argument is sometimes given as a reason not to legalise marijuana (or cannabis). But it is definitely a bad argument. This can be seen very readily by comparing it with this argument:

P1)   Almost all heroin addicts were milk drinkers before becoming heroin addicts.

C)   **Milk drinkers tend to become heroin addicts.**

Obviously this argument would not give us a reason to outlaw the drinking of milk. Yet it has a true premise, just as the first argument, and more importantly, it embodies exactly the same reasoning as the first argument. In particular, both arguments assume that if almost everyone who does X did Y beforehand, then having done Y makes them more likely to do X (or, those who do Y tend to become people who do X). As the second argument above illustrates, that is clearly wrong.

If you were given the first argument, you could show that it is a bad argument by presenting the second as an example of the same reasoning. That is what we mean by refuting an argument by means of a counterexample. The second example is a counterexample to the belief in this form of reasoning.

Now in this case we have been able to lay bare the mistaken assumption upon which the mistaken reasoning rested. This can often be very useful, and according to our general policy of making everything explicit, we should make the assumption explicit, rendering the two arguments thus:

P1) Almost all heroin addicts were marijuana smokers before becoming heroin addicts.

P2) If almost everyone who does X did Y beforehand, then those who do Y tend to become people who do X.

C) Marijuana smokers tend to become heroin addicts.

And:

P1) Almost all heroin addicts were milk drinkers before becoming heroin addicts.

P2) If almost everyone who does X did Y beforehand, then those who do Y tend to become people who do X.

C) Milk drinkers tend to become heroin addicts.

In making this generalisation explicit, we make explicit exactly what is wrong with the original argument. For we have now represented the argument as a deductively valid one. But in this way we represent the argument as very obviously unsound, owing to the falsity of P2. The second argument shows this, because it is valid, yet P1 is true and C is false. According to the definition of validity, it follows that P2 is false.

The technique just discussed is this: if an argument is unsound due to an implicitly assumed but false generalisation, first make explicit the assumed generalisation, in such a way that the argument becomes deductively valid (or inductively forceful). Then find a true premise and false conclusion that are suitably analogous to the premise and conclusion of the original argument, and substitute them (as we did with P1 and C of the above argument).

Sometimes an arguer's assumed, faulty generalisation is perfectly obvious, but they seem not to notice that it is faulty. Here is an example:

> *The continuing carnage on our roads must be stopped. Since it will certainly reduce the number of fatal road accidents, I propose that we immediately reduce all speed limits by 25%.*

We can reconstruct this, making the generalisation explicit, as follows:

P1)   Reducing speed all limits by 25% would reduce the number of fatal road accidents.

P2)   Anything which will reduce the number of fatal road accidents should be done immediately.

C)   **All speed limits should immediately be reduced by 25%.**

This is deductively valid, but it can easily be refuted by counterexample:

P1)   Banning all motor vehicles would reduce the number of fatal road accidents.

P2)   Anything which will reduce the number of fatal road accidents should be done immediately.

C)   **All motor vehicles should be banned immediately.**

Since P1 is true and C false, and the argument is valid, P2 must be false. So the original argument, since its P2 is the same, is unsound. Of course, this does not mean that nothing should be done to reduce road fatalities. It means only that the fact that a given remedy would reduce them is not sufficient for carrying it out. As explained in the Chapter 5 section on practical arguments, we must, in such cases, show that the overall expected value of the envisaged remedy would be positive (i.e. that it would not cause other, worse problems), and also that no other remedy would have a higher expected value (no other would be more practical and effective).

Engaging with the argument I: avoiding the 'who is to say?' criticism

Sometimes an argument will contain a premise that no one would say can be known with certainty. Sometimes these will have to do with what a particular person was thinking, or with what motives people in certain circumstances are likely to have, or with the future, such as whether unemployment will increase or the Labour Party will win the next election. Consider this argument:

> If they close down the factory – making over 500 workers
> redundant – then unemployment in our town will immediately
> double, at the very least. This will surely lead to increases in family
> tensions, hence in domestic violence. Studies have found this
> happening in every case where there is such an abrupt and
> dramatic increase in unemployment.

The conclusion is that if the factory closes, domestic violence will increase. Without bothering to reconstruct further, you can well imagine someone reacting to this argument with: 'Well, who is to say what will happen? You don't *know* that increased domestic violence would result; you can't just assume that the people in our town are as bad as that.' But this is an empty criticism of the argument. The critic has given no reason to suppose that the people of the town in question are different from other people. The critic is just ignoring the argument, not analysing it. Assuming the premises to be true, the evidence that an increase in domestic violence tends to follow large increases in unemployment is very strong. Perhaps this sort of thing cannot be absolutely certain until it happens, but that is the nature of inductive inferences. Where an argument is inductively forceful, the person who says 'who is to say' that the conclusion is true is either repeating what nobody doubts – that the argument is not deductively valid – or expressing a seemingly unreasonable scepticism, like a person who refuses to believe that past observation supports the hypothesis that Spring will follow Winter.

Another variety of the 'who is to say?' response is illustrated in the following example:

P1) Our finest works of art are irreplaceable cultural assets.
P2) It is the Government's responsibility to protect our
irreplaceable cultural assets.

C) **It is the Government's responsibility to protect our finest works of art.**

Now the phrase 'finest work of art' is a vague term; no doubt the boundary between the finest works and the not-so-fine works is not clear. It is also what is sometimes called a 'value-laden' term, since what makes something a fine work of art depends at least partly upon whether, in fact, people do value it (more generally, a value-laden term is one whose application to things depends in some way upon our attitudes towards those things; for example, the word 'weed' is value-laden, since whether or not something is a weed depends on whether we like or tolerate it in gardens or among crops). So now suppose some opponent of the conclusion responds to this argument with: 'Well, who is to say what are our finest works of art? It's a matter of opinion.' But this is not an effective criticism of the argument. It may well be that there is some difficulty in achieving unanimity on such a question. But in order effectively to criti cise an argument – in order to *engage* with it – one must either (i) show that the argument is neither valid nor inductively forceful; or (ii) show or argue that one or more of the premises is false; or (iii) show, if it is an inductive argument, that it is defeated by some other argument. Merely pointing out that a term occurring in the argument is vague or value-laden is not sufficient. Certainly remarking the presence of vagueness is not sufficient. For example, 'bald' is a vague term, yet it is inductively forceful to argue 'Robin is female, therefore Robin is not bald'. Nor is remarking the presence of a value-laden term sufficient as a criticism.

To make this vivid, consider this argument:

P1)   Killing innocent children is immoral.
P2)   One should not do what is immoral.

C)   One should not kill innocent children.

This argument contains the words 'immoral', and 'innocent', which are certainly value-laden. It would certainly be possible for someone to say: 'Who is to say what is immoral, or what is innocent?'. But the fact that these terms can present problems of application does not detract from the evident soundness of this argument.

Of course, it might be that if the Government policy suggested by the argument about works of art were enacted, it would be very difficult to apply it, owing to the difficulty of identifying 'our finest' works of art. That might even constitute an argument against such a policy. But in order actually to engage with the argument, the critic must actually produce such arguments; merely to point out that an argument contains a problematic or vague term like 'fine work of art' is not enough, as shown by the murder example.

Engaging with the argument II: don't merely label the position

Here is a typical example of what we mean by this:

Freiberg argues that rape victims are 'peculiarly vulnerable' to emotional distress and therefore should be given special protections when questioned by defence lawyers. This is the usual

'politically correct' stance that gives every break to women or
so-called 'minorities'. A man being prosecuted for rape should
have the same rights as any other defendant, and that includes
the opportunity to question the alleged victim.

It should be clear that whatever Freiberg's argument was, the writer has
not engaged with it. The writer has not given a reason to think that the
argument is not sound: they have not criticised either its reasoning or its
premises. What the writer has done, in calling Freiberg's position 'politically correct', is indulge in a certain kind of prejudicial labelling. Used in
this way, the label invites the reader to think that Freiberg is merely biased
in certain ways, subscribing unreflectively to a certain perceived ortho-
doxy. Similar things happen when positions or arguments are labelled
'conservative', 'liberal' and the like.

Argument commentary

We have now completed our survey of our basic concepts and procedures of argument analysis. By 'argument analysis' we mean a two-stage
process; comprising first the reconstruction, then the assessment of the
argument. At this point, we need to say a bit more about the final product
of this process. When the analysis of an argument is undertaken, you
may sometimes want to produce a piece of written work that summarises
the analysis you have made. This should consist of three parts:

1 The argument (or arguments) as originally expressed.
2 The argument(s) expressed in standard form.
3 A *commentary* on the argument(s), written in ordinary prose.

Generating **2** out of **1** is the stage of argument-reconstruction; most of
what was said in Chapter 5 of this book is addressed to various sorts of
difficulties commonly encountered in making that step. The concepts
discussed in Chapters 2 and 3 also bear systematically upon the step from
1 to **2**, because, as explained earlier, the principle of charity enjoins us
to reconstruct the argument in the most favourable way, and we need
those concepts in order to determine exactly what that means.

What we have not yet discussed explicitly is **3**. What this comes to
is simply a written piece of work that covers the following points (either
all of them, or as many as seems relevant in the particular case):

(*i*) A general discussion of the argument, explaining, as appropriate: (1)
The *context* in which the argument is given, that is, whatever facts a reader

would need to know in order to understand the point of the argument. Often this will include a description of what the arguer's *opponents* are saying or arguing, especially when the arguer's primary intention is to rebut those arguments. (2) If needed, some discussion of the structure of what the arguer has written or said. For example, if the arguer gives several arguments, or devotes a great deal of space to explanation or rhetoric rather than argument, then it may be useful to explain this.

(*ii*)   A discussion of how and why the standard-form reconstruction was derived as it was, focusing especially on any problems encountered in the process. If any implicit premises (or any implicit conclusions) have been added, it should be explained why. If the conclusion or any premises have been re-worded, it should be explained why (for example, it should be explained why an ambiguous sentence has been rewritten, why a vague or highly rhetorical term has been replaced, etc.). It may also be useful to explain meanings of important words that appear in the reconstruction. In general, this section should ideally include everything necessary to justify the given reconstruction. You have to explain why you have reconstructed the argument in the way that you have (but there is no need to state points which are simply obvious). Frequently, this will mention the likely intentions of the author of the original argument, and the context in which the argument was given.

(*iii*)   A discussion of the validity or degree of inductive force of the argument. You have first to pronounce whether or not the argument is deductively valid. If it is not, you should explain why it is not (here, for example, you might use the method of refutation by counterexample). And if it is not, you should pronounce and explain to what degree, if any, the argument is inductively forceful. If the argument commits a fallacy, then you may identify it at this point, especially if the fallacy is a formal one.

(*iv*)   If the argument is either valid or inductively forceful, a discussion and verdict concerning the truth-values of the premises. This will amount to a verdict regarding the soundness of the argument. It should be explained in detail which premises are most debatable, and why. Except where it is more or less obvious, these explanations must be substantive; actual reasons for accepting or doubting particular premises must be given. One should avoid the 'who is to say?' criticism, for example. If the argument commits a substantial fallacy, then you would explain this here.

(*v*)   In the case of an inductively sound argument, you should also say whether or not the argument is defeated for you. An argument's being defeated for you is a fact about your relation to the argument, not a fact directly about the argument itself. By contrast, an argument's validity or inductive force (or lack of it), and its soundness (or lack of it), are matters concerning which there is a single right answer, a fact about the argument which is independent of the state of knowledge of particular people. Nevertheless, when our ultimate concern is with the truth-value of the conclusion of an argument, it is obviously relevant, when the argument is defeated for you, to point this out in your argument commentary. In other cases, however, we may be interested, not so much in the truth of the conclusion, but in the merits of the argument as given by the arguer. For example, Napoleon may have advanced an inductively sound argument for the conclusion that his army would prevail at Waterloo. That argument would be defeated for us, since we know that his army did not win. But if our concern were to assess Napoleon's reasoning, then we would not fault it on the grounds that his argument is defeated for us.

We might rest with showing that the argument was inductively sound. Still, this leaves open whether the argument was rationally persuasive for *Napoleon*. In order to find this out, we would need to know more about what Napoleon knew or might have known. As historians or military strategists, we might be interested in this question. And depending on the answer, we might find Napoleon open to criticism in either of two ways. First, even if the argument was inductively sound and rationally persuasive for Napoleon, its *degree* of inductive force may not have been sufficient to risk the battle. In other words, the expected value of fighting the battle may have been negative, or insufficient to justify the risk. Second, the argument may have been defeated for Napoleon, and hence not rationally persuasive for him despite being inductively sound. That is, the argument may have been defeated by some fact that he knew but failed to take into account.

If an argument is defeated for you, you may be perfectly justified in saying: the conclusion is false. For if an argument for a conclusion is defeated for you by a more powerful argument against that conclusion, then you have a good reason for asserting that the conclusion is false. In that case, you can say something stronger than 'this argument is defeated *for me*'; you can say: 'the conclusion of this argument is false.'

We cannot always reach a definite verdict concerning a valid or inductively forceful argument. In some cases your belief in the premises may not be strong enough for you to pronounce confidently that the argument is sound. In such a case you would say that you think that the argument is probably sound. In other cases we fail to have a belief either way with respect to an argument's premises. What we should do in such a case, rather than arbitrarily committing ourselves to a soundness verdict, is to say that we cannot determine it because we are too ignorant of the truth-values of the premises (note that one is in such a case showing that one finds the argument rationally unpersuasive). We should also explain, if we can, what we would need to find out in order to alleviate that ignorance

Ideally, it is helpful to keep the discussions (*i*)–(*v*) separate. However, this is not always practical. For example, we may justify a given reconstruction on the grounds that it is inductively more forceful than another possible reconstruction (following the principle of charity). So we would be jumping ahead to (*iv*) in the midst of (*ii*). That is all right. The main thing is to ensure that all three tasks are completed, with as much clarity as possible.

A complete example

What follows is a complete reconstruction with commentary of some arguments appearing in a London *Times* editorial piece by Mick Hume. Many members of the public, and some tabloid newspapers, had expressed outrage that a convicted rapist who had served 15 years of his sentence had won £7 million in the UK National Lottery, having purchased a ticket while out on weekend furlough (he was due to be released the following year). We have assigned letters to paragraphs and numbered sentences within in order to facilitate discussion, but this is not always necessary, provided that you can clearly indicate which parts of the argument as originally presented you are talking about.

Part 1 The arguments as presented

(A) ① LIFE, they say, is a lottery. ② But life has taught me that some things, other than death and taxes, are dead certainties. ③ It seems a safe bet, for instance, that as soon as newspapers stir up public outrage over something, the Home Secretary will promise a law to ban it. ④ When it comes to new legislation, David Blunkett's knee jerks so fast and often that his guide dog might need to wear a riot helmet.

(B) ① Mr Blunkett's latest example of made-to-order law and order is a pledge to stop prisoners who win the National Lottery benefiting from their winnings in jail, and make them pay compensation to the official victims' fund. ② This comes after the public uproar over Iorworth Hoare, a convicted rapist serving a life sentence, who won £7 million while on release from an open prison.

(C) ① The Home Secretary considers this so important that he has written an article in *The Sun* promising to 'find a way to stop this happening again'. ② Given that it has never happened before, there seems no reason to imagine that it ever will. ③ Yet Mr Blunkett's article protests that 'this is not a knee-jerk reaction'.

(D) ① Hoare is obviously a horrible specimen deserving of public contempt, and I could not care less about his 'human right' to buy a Lotto ticket. ② I am worried, however, about this irrational outburst of national outrage.

(E) ① Everybody seems to be up in arms about such a bad man enjoying such good fortune. 'And he's not the only undeserving winner', moans one newspaper. ② Indeed he is not. ③ I am also an undeserving lottery winner. ④ And if, like me, you have picked up the occasional tenner, then you are one, too. ⑤ As Clint Eastwood tells Gene Hackman in *Unforgiven*, 'Deserves got nothin' to do with it'. ⑥ Life may or may not be a lottery, but Lotto definitely is. ⑦ To win it, nobody has to prove his moral worth, simply that he has the price of the ticket.

(F) ① Some complain that they are outraged by Hoare's windfall because they play the lottery to give money to good causes. ② Come off it. ③ When I buy a ticket it is no more an act of charity than when I bet on the dogs or football. ④ It gives me (and my young daughters who pick the numbers) a quick frisson of excitement on a Saturday evening. ⑤ But when we don't win, what difference can it make to us who does?

(G) ① Now Mr Blunkett says that 'there's no justice' if Hoare can win the lottery while his victims suffer. ② Since when, Home Secretary, has criminal justice had anything to do with who wins a raffle? ③ I always thought justice involved criminals paying their debt to society, not repaying their lottery winnings to the Home Office. ④ That is why Hoare was sent to prison. ⑤ No doubt there is an argument to be had about whether he should have been on release. ⑥ But the widespread suggestion that his victims should start suing him for compensation is likely to make matters worse. ⑦ What price do you put on a rape that happened 20 years ago, anyway? ⑧ It is entirely understandable that the women he attacked in the seventies and eighties should feel aggrieved at this turn of events. ⑨ But exactly how are they supposed to benefit from seeing their past ordeals dragged across the national media today?

(H) ① Lotto can be neither a force for good nor evil in society, whether that overblown raffle is won by a convicted rapist or a conviction politician. ② And there cannot be a new law to ban everything that we don't like in life.

Part 2 The arguments reconstructed

Argument 1

P1)   Something should not be banned if it is unlikely to happen.

P2)   It is unlikely that another imprisoned criminal will win the lottery.

C)   **Imprisoned criminals should not be banned from winning the lottery.**

Argument 2

P1)   Very few lottery winners deserve their winnings.

P2)   Most lottery winners are entitled to collect their winnings.

C1)   **Some lottery winners who do not deserve their winnings are entitled to their winnings.**

C2)   **In order to be entitled to lottery winnings, it is not necessary to deserve them.**

Argument 3

P1)   Most people, when playing the lottery, are not motivated primarily by the desire to support good causes.

P2)   Most lottery winners are entitled to collect their winnings.

C1)   **Some lottery winners who are not motivated by the desire to support good causes are entitled to their winnings.**

C2)   **In order to be entitled to lottery winnings, it is not necessary that one's playing the lottery should be primarily motivated by the desire to support good causes.**

Argument 4

P1)   If a someone convicted of a crime has served the sentence prescribed for that crime, then, if the sentence was sufficient for the crime, the person has been sufficiently punished for the crime.

P2)   Mr Hoare has served the sentence prescribed for the crime for which he was convicted.

C)   **Either Mr Hoare's sentence was not sufficient for the crime, or he has been sufficiently punished for it.**

Part 3 Commentary

Iorworth Hoare, a convicted rapist, purchased a lottery ticket while on weekend furlough from prison. He has served 15 years and is due to be released shortly. The ticket was the winning ticket for a prize of £7 million. The author, Mick Hume, appears to be responding to claims that Hoare should not be given the money, which seem to be supported by arguments based on the following premises. First, that imprisoned criminals should be banned from winning the lottery. Second, that only people who 'deserve' to win the lottery are entitled to lottery winnings. Third, that only people who play the lottery with the intention to contribute to 'good causes' (the causes funded by lottery ticket sales) can be entitled to lottery winnings. Hoare is an imprisoned criminal, is not a 'deserving' person, and presumably did not play with the intention of contributing to good causes. Thus if these premises are true, then we have three sound arguments for the conclusion that Hoare is not entitled to the £7 million. Hume provides separate arguments against each of these premises, and also provides a further argument whose relevance will be explained below.

Argument 1 is derived from paragraph C. Paragraphs A and B are largely stage-setting and rhetoric. Hume also criticises Home Secretary[1] David Blunkett for having reacted too quickly to newspaper-induced outcry over the issue by pledging to stop prisoners from receiving lottery winnings. He does not, however, support this claim, except possibly by claiming in paragraph A that Blunkett often reacts hastily to such public outcry. This *ad hominem* point about Blunkett would not be relevant to Hume's central question of whether or not prisoners should be allowed to win the lottery. Blunkett has, however, pledged to disallow it in the future, presumably by getting a law passed preventing it. Sentence 3 of paragraph C, then, seems to argue that no such law should be passed. P2 reiterates the statement made explicitly by that sentence; P1 is an implicit premise, and C the conclusion that Hume seems to invite us to draw.

Paragraph D, sentence 1 makes it clear that Hume is not contesting that Hoare is a 'horrible specimen'. Sentence 2 expresses a vague worry about an 'irrational outburst of national outrage', but it is never made clear what this worry is.

---

1   In the British system of government, the Home Secretary is a member of the Prime Minister's cabinet who is responsible for various domestic matters, especially law and order and immigration policy. Blunkett was Home Secretary in 2004 when this argument was given.

Argument 2 is derived from paragraph E. Some people, Hume says, complain that Hoare is an 'undeserving' lottery winner, and therefore that he should not be entitled to collect the prize. However, Hume says that he too is an 'undeserving lottery winner'. By this, as sentences 4–5 make clear, he means to present himself as a *typical* case. The typical lottery winner does not 'deserve' the money they win; thus, as represented in the reconstruction, very few winners 'deserve' the money. The word 'deserve' is important here. To *deserve* something does not simply mean that one is *entitled* to it. For example a person who merely finds money on the street does not thereby *deserve* it even though he or she is entitled to keep it. On the other hand a person who does appropriate labour may have earned the money and thereby deserve it. We also say, for example, that a man who has worked hard for several months in succession 'deserves' a holiday. In general, 'deserves it' seems to mean 'is owed it', or 'has earned it, by virtue of work or other valuable actions'. So in this sense (P1) very few lottery winners *deserve* their winnings. Yet we do accept that most winners are entitled to them: typically, if your ticket is the winner, you have the right to collect. C1 of argument 2 thus follows. In fact, it is probably true and accepted by most people that all but a few winners are entitled to the prize, in which case it would follow that *most* lottery winners do not deserve their prize but are entitled to it. But all we need here is the weaker P2 as written. C2 follows from C1, which establishes Hume's point: one cannot argue that Hoare is not entitled to the lottery prize from the premise that he is undeserving. For the needed premise, that winners are entitled to the prize only if they deserve it, is false.

Argument 3, derived from paragraph F, is similar to argument 2. Again, some people claim that those who do not play the lottery with the intention of contributing to good causes by purchasing lottery tickets are not entitled to the prize. Since Hoare is a bad person, they reason, he cannot have had that intention, so he is not entitled to the prize. Hume contests the first premise of that argument. Hume points out that he and his daughters are not motivated in this way when they play, and again assumes that he and his daughters are typical in this respect. Hence P1. P2 is as in argument 2; from these follow C1, from which follows C2, contradicting the idea that only those who intend to support good causes by purchasing lottery tickets are entitled to collect winnings.

Argument 4 is directed against the quoted claim by David Blunkett that 'there's no justice' if a criminal such as Hoare wins the lottery. Hume interprets this as meaning that if the criminal wins the lottery, then the requirements of *criminal* justice will not have been satisfied. That is to say, it will not be the case that the criminal has received a legal punishment appropriate to the crime. As against this, Hume poses what is written in the reconstruction as P1, and which seems to be what is expressed by sentences 2–4. The condition 'if the sentence was sufficient for the crime' seems necessary. For suppose we wrote simply: 'if someone convicted of a crime has served the sentence prescribed for that crime, then the person has been sufficiently punished for the crime.' This is surely not true, since at least some prescribed sentences are too lenient. Hume's point seems to be that it is the purpose of penal sentences to satisfy the demands of criminal justice. Provided that the sentence fits the crime, a criminal who has served the prescribed sentence has satisfied the demands of criminal justice. Although Hume does not do so, it might be added that it is *wrong* to punish a criminal further, when the criminal has already satisfied the demands of criminal justice, and thus it would be inappropriate to deprive him of money (the lottery winnings) that would otherwise legally be his. Since Hume does not assert that Hoare's sentence was appropriate to the crime, and I do not know whether it was, I have stated Hume's conclusion (which is only implicit in his presentation of the argument) as a disjunction: 'Either Mr Hoare's sentence was not sufficient for the crime, or he has been sufficiently punished for it.'

All four of the arguments are valid, and arguments 2–4 seem to me to be sound. Argument 1 does not seem to me to be sound because P1 seems to me to be false. If something is highly unlikely, then still it might be that it should be banned, especially if its consequences would be extremely bad. Also, it is not clear whether P2 is true. Perhaps it is not likely that *another* prisoner will win £7 Million, but if it has happened once, it cannot be so unlikely that we can assume it won't happen again. Also, it is not so unlikely that prisoners will win smaller prizes, which would raise the same issue.

Finally, some mention should be made of paragraph H. Hume's opponents think that something is *morally* wrong if bad people win the lottery. Hume's main point seems to be that it is the whole purpose of the lottery that the winner should be determined by pure luck – not moral considerations or anything of that sort. So argument 2 seems to be the most important one. Since it is sound, I conclude that Hume has been successful in his main task.

Commentary on the commentary

In work of this kind, there is always the question of how much detail to go into. In this case we have included quite a lot of detail, largely in order to be highly illustrative. Still, we could have gone into a lot more. In other cases – especially where it seems important or interesting to do so – even more detail may be appropriate; more likely, less detail may be appropriate. Also you should bear in mind that this case only illustrates a handful of the techniques and issues that have been raised in this book; no one case is going to illustrate very many of them, and every argument presents its own problems of interpretation and reconstruction. There is certainly no need to copy the style of the foregoing commentary slavishly – what is important is that the reconstruction be *explained* and *justified* in a way that it is *informative, clear, non-rhetorical* and *balanced* (that is, you should aim to be judicious and disinterested, in the sense of being neutral or unbiased). Any technique, style or approach that serves these aims may be appropriate. Note also that although the ability to analyse arguments is a highly transferable skill – that is, it can exercised on arguments on any subject, and does not typically require specialised knowledge of the subject – knowledge of the subject is often helpful, especially for understanding the *context* in which the argument is given. This is often crucial, since so many key components of arguments are often only implicit.

CHAPTER SUMMARY

A **rationally persuasive** argument must be either deductively valid or inductively forceful. A deductively valid argument is rationally persuasive for you (at a time) if you have good reason to accept its premises (at that time). An inductively forceful argument is rationally persuasive for you (at a time) provided that you have good reason to accept the premises (at that time), and the argument is not **defeated** for you (at that time). An inductively forceful argument is defeated for you (at a time) if you have some other argument for rejecting the conclusion that is more rationally persuasive for you than the one in question.

Unlike validity, inductive force and soundness, rational persuasiveness is not a feature of arguments in themselves. It is also a matter of a given person's relationship to an argument (at a time). An argument may be rationally persuasive for one person but not for another, and for a person at a given time but not for the same person at another time. An argument may be sound but not rationally persuasive for you, for the premises might be true even though you lack good reasons to accept them, or you may accept the premises of an argument that you recognise to be inductively sound, yet the argument is defeated for you. Moreover, an argument may be rationally persuasive for you but not sound. For you may have good reasons for accepting a set of premises, even when one of the premises is false. But the question of whether or not an argument is rationally persuasive for you is not simply the question of whether or not you find it persuasive, or whether you are in fact persuaded by it. For unlike the question of whether we are actually persuaded by an argument, we can be mistaken about rational persuasiveness: an argument may be rationally persuasive for you even when you think it isn't, and fail to be when you think it is. The importance of the concept of rational persuasiveness is that it captures what arguments are intended to do: the distinctive aim of persuasion by argument is to persuade people rationally, that is, by actually giving them good reasons to accept a given conclusion, and not just seeming to. The person *ought* to accept the conclusion, even if they do not.

There are various informal methods of **logical assessment**, and of demonstrating that an argument is not valid or inductively forceful. The principal task is simply to apply the definitions of deductive validity and inductive force, but there are some strategies to facilitate this in more difficult cases. One strategy that is almost always pertinent is to suppose the conclusion of the argument to be false, and then to ask whether it would still be possible for all the premises to be true. Another strategy, where the conclusion of an argument is a conditional, is to suppose that the antecedent of that conditional is true, and then to determine whether the remaining premises force one to conclude that the consequent would also be true. If the conclusion of an argument is a generalisation, an analogous strategy is to suppose that the antecedent of an arbitrary instance of the generalisation is true. Finally, an effective way of demonstrating that an argument is invalid, or inductively unforceful, is the method of **refutation by counterexample**. This involves giving an argument that employs the same type of inference as the one in question, but which is obviously invalid or unforceful.

It is important to avoid the '**who is to say?**' criticism. One form this takes is to complain that the conclusion of an inductively forceful argument has not been 'proven', that it 'might' be false. Another is to object to an argument on the grounds that it contains a value-laden term. It should be clear that these are not genuine criticisms from a rational point of view. One must also avoid merely **labelling** an argument or position, for example, as 'politically correct', 'socialist' or whatever; the applicability of such a label does not in itself show why the argument or position should be rejected or accepted.

EXERCISES

1   For questions a–i, consider this argument:

P1)   If Rangers won the match then the pub will sell pints for £1 tonight.

P2)   Whenever Rangers are ahead at halftime of a Scottish Premiership match, they almost always win the match.

P3)   Rangers were ahead at halftime, and this is a Scottish Premiership match.

C)   **(Very probably) The pub will sell pints for £1 tonight.**

Suppose that the premises are true. Suppose that both Andrew and James know that the premises are true (they have both seen the sign in the pub window about the £1 pints, they both saw the halftime score of 1–0 in favour of Rangers announced on television, and both know that Rangers have won every Scottish Premiership match in the past three years when leading at halftime). Andrew has no other information relevant to the truth of the conclusion; but unlike Andrew, James saw on television that the opposing side scored twice in the second half to win the match 2–1.

a   Is the argument deductively valid?

b   Is the argument deductively sound?

c   Is the argument inductively forceful?

d   Is the argument inductively sound?

e   Is the argument rationally persuasive for Andrew?

f   Is the argument rationally persuasive for James?

g   Should Andrew be persuaded by the argument?

h   Should James be persuaded by the argument?

i   If the argument is not rationally persuasive for either Andrew or James, explain why.

Issues in argument assessment

2 Now consider this argument:

P1) The majority of well-educated Germans speak English.
P2) Jacob is a well-educated German.

C) **(Probably) Jacob speaks English.**

Assume this time that P1 is true and that the conclusion is true; but assume that P2 is false: Jacob is Austrian, and not very well educated either. Still, he did learn English quite well from his American mother. Assume that Catherine, Jane, Mary and Anna all know that P1 is true. *Catherine* believes P2 is true because her friend David told her it is; David is a reliable person who knows Jacob, and Catherine has no reason to doubt him. In fact David's mistake was quite reasonable: Jacob lied to him, telling him he completed a university degree in history; further, it was reasonable for David to infer, from Jacob's accent, that Jacob is German. For, although German is the national language of Austria, the vast majority of native German speakers are German. Catherine knows nothing else about Jacob, and accepts C. *Jane* also believes P2, but for different reasons: she fancies Jacob, having seen him, at a distance, at a party, and thinks he's well-educated because she saw Jacob wearing glasses and a tie. Jane also accepts C, but has no other information relevant to the truth of C. *Mary* believes both P1 and P2, for the same reasons as Catherine; but she does not accept C, because she heard Jacob speaking German to David at the party, and inferred, quite reasonably, that Jacob does not speak English. She has no other information relevant to the truth of C. *Anna* does not believe P2. She heard what David said to Catherine, and believes that David is always sincere and well-informed; but Jacob is athletic and handsome and she has a stupid irrational prejudice according to which athletic, handsome men are almost always stupid, and therefore not well-educated. She has no other information relevant to the truth of C.

a Is the argument inductively forceful?

b Is the argument inductively sound?

c Is the argument rationally persuasive for Catherine? Why or why not?

d Is the argument rationally persuasive for Jane? Why or why not?

e Is the argument rationally persuasive for Mary? Why or why not?

f Is the argument rationally persuasive for Anna? Why or why not?

3   Consider the following argument:

George W. Bush's apparent obsession with Saddam Hussein may have the *appearance* of paranoid schizophrenia: the fear that someone is out to get us (paranoia) and the belief that only we can save the world (grandiosity). But Bush's beliefs wander into dangerous mental territory only if they're wrong. If he's right about the danger presented by Saddam and our role in ending that danger, then he's perfectly rational.

Harry Sorenson, San Francisco Chronicle, 17 March 2003

(i)   The last two sentences embody a serious confusion. Explain this confusion in terms of the distinction between the *rational persuasiveness* of an argument and the *truth* of an argument's conclusion.

(ii)   What do you suppose is the intended conclusion of the argument? Reconstruct the argument. Is it sound? Why not?

4   The conclusions of the following arguments are conditionals or generalisations. Reconstruct them. Then, using the technique discussed earlier of supposing the antecedent of a conditional conclusion to be true, explain why the argument is, or is not, valid. (In h the conclusion is a generalisation; trying supposing 'x is a Roman', whatever x may be.)

Example

This man is either a Russian spy or a criminal. No Russian spy wears a Rolex. Everyone who enters this repair shop wears a Rolex. Therefore, if this man enters this repair shop, then he is a criminal.

> ✎   P1)   No Russian spy wears a Rolex.
>   P2)   Everyone who enters this repair shop wears a Rolex.
>   P3)   If this man is not a Russian spy, then he is a criminal.
> ───
>   C)   **If this man enters this repair shop, then he is a criminal.**

Suppose the man enters the repair shop. Then according to P2, he wears a Rolex. Then according to P1, he is not a Russian spy. Then according to P3, he is a criminal. So if he enters the repair shop, then he is a criminal.

a   If the Lena is polluted, then the Ob is polluted. But if the Ob is polluted, then the Dneiper is polluted. Therefore if the Lena is polluted, then so is the Dneiper.

b   The Lena is longer than the Ob. Therefore if the Danube is longer than the Lena, it is longer than the Ob.

c Every Russian spy wears a Rolex. Everyone who enters this repair shop wears a Rolex. Therefore if this man enters this repair shop, then he is a Russian spy.

d If this man is not a spy, then he is a detective. But all detectives wear trench coats, and he is not wearing one. If he is a spy, then either he is Russian or American. But no American spy knows how to order dessert wines, unless he is from New York. But all spies from New York wear trench coats. Therefore, if this man knows how to order dessert wine, then he is a Russian spy.

e If the ancient Allemani were both vicious and loyal, then the Romans would have purchased their allegiance. If they had done so, then the Franks would never have challenged the Allemani. But they certainly did. Therefore, if the Allemani were vicious, they were not loyal.

f All Roman citizens were literate. Therefore if some ancient Visigoths were literate, then some ancient Visigoths were Roman citizens.

g All Roman citizens were literate. Therefore if some ancient Visigoths were Roman citizens, then some ancient Visigoths were literate

h Every educated Roman knew Homer. But anyone who knows Homer knows the story of Achilles. Therefore all Romans knew the story of Achilles.

i If God is unwilling to prevent evil, then God is not good. If God is unable to prevent evil, then God is not omnipotent. God exists only if God is both good and omnipotent. If God is willing and able to prevent evil, then evil does not exist. Therefore if evil exists, then God does not exist.

j If God is unwilling to prevent evil, then God is not good. If God is unable to prevent evil, then God is not omnipotent. If God exists, then God is good and omnipotent. If God is willing and able to prevent evil, then evil does not exist. Therefore if evil does not exist, then God exists.

5 The conclusions of the arguments in Exercise 3, a–e and i–j, are conditionals. Split them into two statements: antecedent and consequent. Now add the antecedent to the premises, regard the consequent as the conclusion of the argument, and rewrite the argument accordingly in standard form.

Example

P1) All Roman citizens were literate.

_____

C) Therefore if some ancient Visigoths were Roman citizens, then some ancient Visigoths were literate.

✎ P1) All Roman citizens were literate.
    P2) Some ancient Visigoths were Roman citizens.

_____

C) Some ancient Visigoths were literate.

6 Reconstruct the following arguments, then refute them by counter-example – that is, by giving arguments that embody the same pattern, but which have true premises and false conclusions. It may help to extract the logical form of the argument (as according to Chapter 2, pp. 65–7).

a A significant increase in the rabbit population would bring about an increase in the number of foxes. And sure enough, the number of foxes has increased lately. This must, therefore, be due to an increase in the rabbit population.

b If free will is impossible, then the concept of responsibility is nonsense. If so, then the existing justice system is legitimate. Therefore if free will is possible, then the existing justice system is legitimate.

c Many people have tried to prove that Nessie does not exist. But they have failed. You should by now admit it: Nessie is real.

d You admit that the Loch Ness monster has not been seen in recent years. If so, then it must be very secretive. But if it is secretive, then, obviously, it exists. Therefore you have admitted that Nessie exists.

e Why don't we do what we know will stop these evils? We should give drug-dealers and paedophiles life prison sentences.

7 For Exercise 3, a and c–j, extract the logical form. Use capital letters for sentences or general terms. (See Chapter 2, p. 65). Some are difficult! It may help to choose letters that remind you of what you're replacing them for. For example, in d, you could use S for 'spy', D for 'detective', T for 'trench coat wearer', R for 'Russian', A for 'American' and Y for 'from New York'.

8 Draw tree diagrams for the arguments in Exercise 3.

Issues in argument assessment

9 List the *explicit* premises and the conclusions of the arguments in Exercises 16, 18 and 19 of Chapter 5. Draw tree-diagrams for these, including only the explicit premises. Now add the needed implicit premises to the list, and draw new tree-diagrams for the complete arguments.

10 Could one give an argument that (i) one knows to be sound (ii) is rationally persuasive for its audience, and (iii) is not rationally persuasive for oneself? If not, why not? If so, would that be deceitful, or otherwise naughty in any way? Why or why not? Make up an example.

Chapter 7

Truth, knowledge and belief

In this final chapter we will delve deeper into some philosophical issues underlying the principles of good critical thinking. We begin the chapter by extending the discussion of truth that appears in Chapters 1 and 2 and attempting to dispel what in our experience is a deep seated myth – that what is true depends upon nothing more than personal opinion or taste. As we will explain, this is the myth that **all truth is relative**. Later we examine the relationship between **believing** that something is the case, being **justified** in believing that it is the case and **knowing** that it is the case. These relationships are important for critical thinking because they are concerned with the **adequacy of evidence** for beliefs. Thus they are at the root of our determinations of whether or not premises are true, whether or not the conclusion of an inductively forceful argument is defeated for a person, and whether or not an argument is rationally persuasive for a person. Further, the concepts of truth, knowledge and evidence are such frequent sources of confusion in argumentative contexts that clarity about them is extremely valuable in its own right.

Truth and relativity

When we say something, claim something such as 'The kettle has boiled', we **assert** something; we express a **belief**. A belief is an attitude we take towards a **proposition**: to believe a proposition is to accept it as **true**. Assertion is a truth-claim, and belief is a truth-attitude. Assertion, belief and truth are internally related in this way. From the outset we have been working with an intuitive understanding of truth such that to say that a claim is **true** is simply to say that things are as the claim says they are: *to assert that a proposition is true is equivalent to asserting that very same proposition*. What this means is that a pair of sentences such as the following:

▶ Maria Sharapova was the Wimbledon Women's Singles Champion in 2004.

▶ It is true that Maria Sharapova was the Wimbledon Women's Singles Champion in 2004.

must have the same truth value; if one of them is true, then so is the other. This necessary equivalence is the fundamental fact about the ordinary meaning of the word 'true'. Suppose, then, that Julie says that Maria Sharapova was the Wimbledon Women's Singles Champion in 2004. To say that Julie's claim is true, at bottom, is just to say that Maria Sharapova did win the Women's Singles at Wimbledon in 2004. Thus, although truth is a feature of claims that people make (of some claims, of course, not of all of them), whether or not a claim is true has nothing at all to do with the person who makes it; nor with that person's beliefs, culture or language (except when the proposition is explicitly about those things). Whether or not Julie's claim about Maria Sharapova is true depends *only* on whether or not Maria Sharapova won the Women's Singles at Wimbledon in 2004, and does not depend in any way on anything about Julie. In particular, the mere fact that Julie *believes*, and *has claimed*, that Maria Sharapova won Wimbledon, has nothing to do with whether or not her belief or claim is true.

Notice also the following consequence of the equivalence noted above. If John responds to Julie's claim by saying 'That's true', then what he does, in effect, is to assert the very same thing that Julie did. He agrees with her. Her claim is true if Maria Sharapova won Wimbledon and false otherwise; likewise with John's.

These points are quite straightforward, but they can be easy to lose sight of in other contexts, and these contexts can create confusion about truth generally. In order to dispel the myth that truth is relative, we first explain the concepts of **indexicals** and **implicit speaker-relativity**. Consider the following sets of claims:

1.
   ▶ Bill Clinton was the US President immediately before George W. Bush.

   ▶ Water is H$_2$O.

   ▶ Neptune is larger than Venus.

   ▶ La Paz is the capital of Bolivia.

2.
   ▶ It's raining here.

   ▶ She's 35 years old.

   ▶ That book is too expensive for most students to afford.

   ▶ The boss is visiting our office today.

3.
   ▶ Algebra is hard.

   ▶ Chocolate ice cream tastes better than vanilla ice cream.

   ▶ George Clooney is more handsome than Brad Pitt.

   ▶ Gone with the Wind is a highly entertaining film.

   ▶ It is more fun to play Monopoly than it is to play football.

The claims in each of the three sets are expressed using the same **assertoric** form. Assertoric form is generally used to express a belief that such and-such is true (except when someone is lying or play-acting); but the fact that someone has made an assertion does not establish that the assertion is true, only that the speaker believes it to be so. Thus, if someone asserts 'Neptune is larger than Venus', they express their belief that one planet is larger than another, that it is fact that the one is larger than the other. But whether or not the assertion is true depends only on whether or not Neptune really is larger than Venus. Similarly with 'Bill Clinton was the US President immediately before George W. Bush' and 'La Paz is the capital of Bolivia'. Note that although someone making one of these statements asserts their own belief, they are certainly not talking *about* themselves; someone who asserts that La Paz is the capital of Bolivia asserts one of their beliefs, but the statement, and their belief, is only about La Paz and Bolivia.

Now look at the second set of claims, which, as we have noted already, are expressed in the same assertoric form. Each claim includes an **indexical** – 'here', 'she', 'that' and 'today', respectively. An indexical is a word that picks out a particular thing (in philosophers' terms, it is a 'referring term'), but precisely *which* thing it picks out depends upon the context of utterance, and sometimes on the intention of the speaker. Thus what it picks out can change from utterance to utterance. This has the effect of making the truth-value of the sentence **context-relative** too. 'It's raining here' uttered in Glasgow might be true, whereas uttered in Madrid at the very same moment it might be false. So determining to what location 'here' refers to in a given context is crucial to determining the truth-value of the sentence in which it occurs. Similarly 'She's 35 years old' might be true if uttered about Jones, yet false when uttered about Smith; while it might be true that the boss is visiting today when 'today' refers to Tuesday, it might be false if 'today' is Friday; and if 'that book' is a 100-page paperback that costs £50, then it is indeed too expensive for most students, if, on the other hand, 'that book' refers to a 300-page edition at £5, then it is false to claim that it is beyond the means of most students.

Sentences are often context-relative in a certain respect without *explicitly* containing an indexical that signifies it as such. Consider 'It's raining here' again. That might be true if uttered in Glasgow *today*, but false if uttered in Glasgow *tomorrow* (one can always hope). The sentence does not *contain* the indexical word 'now', but it is context-sensitive with respect to the time of utterance. It is exactly as if the sentence were 'It's raining here now'. That is how it is with many typical uses of present-tense verbs: if you say 'I'm hungry', or 'The car needs a wash', you are saying that these things are so *now* (similarly with past and future tenses – 'She used to be married', etc.). Location is also a contextual feature that is often left tacit. For example, we usually say 'It's raining', reserving 'It's raining here' for the case where speaker and hearer are in different places, as on the telephone. So 'It's raining' involves *two* implicit indexicals: 'here' and 'now'.

More generally, a sentence containing indexicality (explicit or implicit) *expresses different propositions in different contexts of utterance*. A **context** is simply a collection of factors relevant to determining what is said by a given utterance. This will include the identity of the speaker (*who* is speaking), the time and place of utterance, and other factors such as what a speaker happens to be pointing to. Thus if Groucho says 'I'm hungry' at 3:00 and Chico says 'I'm hungry' at 5:00, then they express different propositions – Groucho says *that Groucho is hungry at 3:00*, whereas Chico says *that Chico is hungry at 5:00*. If they both speak truly, they report *different facts*.

Since what is expressed by a sentence involving indexicality depends on the context of utterance, its truth-value depends on context of utterance. But such sentences are still fact-stating: once we have determined the relevant features of the context, we have a complete proposition with a fixed truth-value. The truth-value of the *proposition* is not context-relative: either Groucho was really hungry at 3:00 or he wasn't, end of story (ignoring the possible vagueness of 'hungry'). Other indexical terms include personal pronouns such as 'I', 'he', 'we', 'you' and 'they'; impersonal ones such as 'this' and 'there' (often accompanied by a pointing gesture or suchlike); expressions employing possessive pronouns such as 'my house', 'your car', 'our dog', 'their holiday'; and temporal expressions such as 'tomorrow' and 'yesterday'.

Turning to the third set of claims, if we consider the first claim:

Algebra is hard.

It appears to assert a fact about the difficulty of algebra. But imagine Jane – who has had no end of tutoring and has certainly tried her best – saying this to Mary; Mary replies, 'No it's not! It's easy!'. Must they really be disagreeing? It seems not. In such a case, it seems that what Jane might really be saying is that algebra is hard *for her*; Mary is saying that *she*, Mary, finds it easy (unless Mary is telling Jane that she's so dim she can't even do something that is in fact easy – but let's assume she isn't!). Since the sentence expresses a different proposition depending on who utters it, the sentence is implicitly indexical and hence context-relative. In this kind of case, we say that the claim is **implicitly relative**. A claim is implicitly relative when it states a comparison or other relation to something it doesn't explicitly mention (see Chapter 1, pp. 30–1, for a review of this concept). For example, said of an adult man, 'John is tall' states a *comparison*, a *relation*, between John and other men; it really says that John is taller than the average man.[1]

Furthermore, what Mary says about algebra is implicitly **speaker-relative**. Unlike 'John is tall', the fact expressed is implicitly *about the person making the assertion*. Mary, we are assuming, is really expressing the proposition that *Algebra is hard for Mary*. Similarly, suppose that John has very fair skin, and says 'The sun is too strong' during a walk on a Mediterranean beach. He alludes to the danger of sunburn. Julie, whose darker skin is less sensitive to the sun, says 'No it isn't'. In such

---

1   Of course there is no such thing as 'the average man', as if, in addition to Tom, Dick, Harry and the rest, there were another chap, the average man. To say that John is taller than the average man is to say that if you take the average (the mean) of the heights of all men, then John's height exceeds that figure.

a case, John might only be saying that the sun is too strong for him, and Julie saying that it isn't too strong for her.

Implicit speaker-relativity is most common in the expression of attitudes, preferences and the like, as illustrated by the remainder of the examples in the third set. If Julie says 'Chocolate ice cream tastes better than vanilla', then what she is really saying is that *she* prefers chocolate to vanilla. Similarly, if John asserts this very same sentence, then he is saying that chocolate ice cream tastes better to *him* than vanilla does. So Julie and John are saying different things, despite the fact that they use the same sentence to say it. These two speakers' assertions are statements of fact about their respective preferences, not statements of fact about the superiority of chocolate over vanilla ice cream independent of anyone's preference.

To sum up the discussion of the third group: the sentence by means of which we express such a proposition – 'Chocolate ice cream tastes better than vanilla' – is an incomplete expression of the proposition we express by means of it. The statement actually expresses a fact about the person making it, but the sentence does not explicitly mention this; that is why the statement is **implicitly speaker-relative**.[2]

The importance of these differences emerges when we consider what happens when people appear to disagree over claims that are implicitly speaker-relative in this way, and compare this with genuine factual disagreement. Suppose now that Julie and John disagree about the capital of Bolivia. Julie says:

La Paz is the capital of Bolivia.

But John denies it. He says: 'La Paz is not the capital of Bolivia' (perhaps he thinks it's the capital of Columbia). In this case, there is exactly one proposition – that La Paz is the capital of Bolivia – such that Julie asserts it and John denies it. That is what genuine factual disagreement is: genuine disagreement is when there is one proposition that is asserted by one person but denied by another. If Julie and John value the truth, they will want to know whose claim is true.

Contrast with the case when Julie says 'I am wearing wool socks', and John says 'I am not wearing wool socks'. The sentence that John asserts is the negation of the sentence that Julie asserts, but obviously

---

2   There is one slight complication, however: statements of this kind may mean that something is preferred or liked by *most people*. For example, this is plausibly what someone means who says: 'soured milk does not taste good.' Nevertheless, these statements are still implicitly relative, because they still depend for their truth on an implicit reference to people's preferences. In such a case, the statement is a generalisation about people's actual preferences rather than a statement of one person's preference.

they are not disagreeing about anything. Due to the explicit context-relativity introduced by the indexical 'I', the proposition asserted by Julie is not the proposition denied by John.

But when context-relativity is implicit rather than explicit, there can appear to be genuine factual disagreement when there isn't. Suppose that Julie and John seemingly disagree about the relative merits of chocolate and vanilla ice cream: Julie contends that chocolate tastes better, while John is on the side of vanilla. As we have seen, in order to make her meaning perfectly explicit, Julie would have to say 'Chocolate ice cream tastes better than vanilla to me'; John would have to say the same in order to be explicit. So what Julie is really saying is that chocolate tastes better to *her*, John that vanilla tastes better *to him*.

The proposition that Julie expresses can equally well be expressed as:

(1) Chocolate ice cream tastes better than vanilla to Julie.

Whereas John's proposition is:

(2) Vanilla ice cream tastes better than chocolate to John.

These are two different propositions. There is certainly no logical conflict between them: they could both be true. But in that case, Julie and John do not really disagree: there is not one proposition here that either Julie or John asserts, and that the other denies. They are not really disagreeing about the truth-value of the same proposition. That is, they do not dispute the facts of the matter; their claims are simply expressions of different preferences. To continue to dispute such an issue would be a waste of time. Indeed, notice that (1) and (2) are no longer implicitly speaker-relative; they are *explicitly* speaker-relative. So there should be no temptation to say that the truth of either (1) or (2) depends on who is making the claim. If you say 'Chocolate ice cream tastes better than vanilla', then you are implicitly talking about yourself, and the truth of what you say depends on facts about you (your preferences). If you assert (1), however, the truth of your assertion depends only on facts about Julie, not on facts about you.

Having discussed the concepts of indexicals and implicit speaker-relativity, we are now in a position to confront the myth that truth is relative.

True for me, true for you

Often, people who have succumbed to the myth that 'the truth is always relative' respond to a disagreement about the facts by saying something like: 'Well, that may be true for you, but it's not true for me.' In doing so, they use a common ploy to avoid proper engagement with the argument. Unless the matter under discussion is one that is actually implicitly speaker-relative, as it is in the ice cream example, this is not a legitimate move to make within an attempt to persuade rationally. It is a refusal to argue any further.[3] A similar refusal to engage in debate occurs when someone responds to others' claims by saying, 'that's just your opinion' as though expressing one's mere opinion is not an attempt to make a true claim about a matter but, rather, tantamount to expressing a preference for chocolate rather than vanilla ice cream. But when we express our opinion on a matter – the best way of reducing crime rates, say – we *are* expressing our beliefs about the truth of a matter. It is really a kind of self-deception not to face up to this: that when we express our opinion, we are making a claim to truth. So criticising someone's contribution to a conversation by saying, 'that's just a matter of opinion' is another attempt to hinder rational persuasion or debate, and unjustifiably denies that there is any such thing as disagreement.

The 'true-for-me' phraseology, however, is not just a device for evading arguments. It is a characteristic way of expressing the relativity-myth (though the relativity-myth may itself be motivated by the wish to avoid the sometimes unpleasant reality of disagreement). Thus we shall try to dispel the myth by considering it in more detail. Consider again the sentence:

Chocolate ice cream tastes better than vanilla.

The implicit speaker-relativity of a sentence like this might be described by saying that the sentence is true for Julie, and not true for John. Upon hearing Julie assert this sentence, John might say: 'Well, that may be true for you, but it isn't true for me.' John might, in this case, simply be making the point about implicit speaker-relativity. If so, then that is all right; he is quite right to do so. However, phrases such as 'true for me' are sometimes used in what appear to be factual contexts where implicit speaker-relativity is not in play. For example, suppose that Julie believes in astrology, and says:

Scorpios tend to be luckier than Libras.

---

3   When you think about it, it is very hard to see exactly what this claim amounts to. It seems to say that truth is relative to persons; yet it is odd that the only way that this can be the case is for that statement itself to be true in just the way that the statement itself denies – thus it seems that relativism about truth may be contradictory.

John does not believe in astrology, and therefore does not believe that one's character depends on what the part of the year one is born. So he thinks this proposition is false. But John, wishing to avoid a painful disagreement, expresses himself by saying. 'Well, that may be true for you, but it isn't true for me.'

As we have just seen, where implicit speaker-relativity is involved, the use of such phrases as 'true for you' is perfectly legitimate. But in the astrology case, the use of this phrase is misleading. Is this sentence implicitly speaker-relative? Is the sentence *about* a preference, belief or other attitude? It certainly does not seem to be. It is like the sentence about La Paz: it purports to state a fact about the respective fortunes of Scorpios and Libras. Someone asserting the sentence about La Paz expresses their belief concerning La Paz, but they are not talking about themselves, they are talking only about La Paz and Bolivia. This is shown by the fact that the truth of what they say depends only on how things are with La Paz and Bolivia, its truth does not depend in any way on the beliefs of the speaker. Likewise, someone asserting the astrology sentence *expresses* their own attitudes about Scorpios and Libras, but is not saying anything *about* their own attitudes towards Scorpios and Libras. So when John says, of the astrology sentence, that it might be true for Julie but not for him, he cannot be saying that the sentence is implicitly speaker-relative, and could therefore be true when Julie says it but false when he says it.

What, then, could John reasonably mean by 'true for you' in this context? As we noted, when someone sincerely asserts a declarative sentence, they express a belief. By 'true for you', then, John could simply mean that *according to Julie*, the sentence is true. That is to say, he could mean simply that Julie *believes* the proposition expressed by the sentence: that she believes that Scorpios tend to be luckier than Libras. John, of course, denies this very same proposition. So this is a straightforward case of genuine disagreement over the same proposition. In suggesting that the sentence is true for Julie and not for himself, all that John is doing is pointing out the fact that he and Julie do disagree: Julie believes, and John disbelieves, the very same proposition. Unfortunately, by using the phrase 'true for you', he makes it sound as if it's a case of implicit speaker-relativity, in which case there is no actual disagreement. Since that is the sort of case where 'true for me' has a legitimate point to it, he makes it sound as if there is no actual disagreement, thus smoothing over his difference with Julie. This is perhaps polite of him, but it is really just an evasion.

With these points in mind concerning 'true-for-me', we can now dispel the myth that all truth is relative. The myth is often expressed by saying that we cannot legitimately speak simply of what is *true*, but only of what is *true for me*, or *true for you*, or more generally true-for-X, where X is some person (or perhaps culture). If this is explained as the claim that all statements are really implicitly speaker-relative, then this is clearly not so, as we have seen: a statement like the one about La Paz just isn't speaker-relative. However, the claim that all truth is truth-for-X might also be understood in accordance with the way that John employed the phrase in his dispute with Julie about astrology. According to this interpretation of 'true-for-X', to say that a proposition is true for X is to say that X believes it. Could all truth really be truth-for-X, in that sense?

Let us work out the implications of supposing that it is. Consider these two sentences:

(3) Scorpios tend to be luckier than Libras.
(4) It is true that Scorpios tend to be luckier than Libras.

According to what we said about the word 'true' at the beginning of this chapter, (3) and (4) are *necessarily equivalent*: it is *impossible* for one of them to be true and the other false. That is why we can always register our agreement with a claim simply by saying, 'that's true'. And that, we might say, is the point of having the word 'true': that is how the word is used. However, according to the version of the myth we are considering, if Julie asserts (4), then she would be speaking more accurately if she were to say: 'It is true for me that Scorpios tend to be luckier than Libras.' Thus, as we ourselves would express it, what she says by means of (4), according to the myth, is really:

(5) It is true for Julie that Scorpios tend to be luckier than Libras.

And this, as we said, is more accurately expressed by:

(6) Julie believes that Scorpios tend to be luckier than Libras.

So according to this version of the relativity-myth, Julie's utterance of (4) is equivalent to (5), which is equivalent to (6). So according to the myth, (4) is equivalent to (6). But (6) is certainly *not* equivalent to (3). (3) Makes no reference to Julie; it would be possible for (3) to be true but (6) false, or the other way round (in fact, if (6) were true, then since presumably (3) is false, they would actually differ in truth-value). *Thus, according to this version of the myth, we would have to say that (4) is not equivalent to (3)*. But that cannot be right, for that is simply *not* how the word 'true' is used. This version of the relativity-myth violates the

actual, ordinary day-to-day meaning of the word 'true' according to which
(3) and (4) are equivalent. According to that meaning, Julie is right when
she says (3) if, and only if, she is right when she says (4). So (3) and (4),
whoever utters them, cannot differ in truth-value. If so, then since (5)
and (6) mean the same thing, (5) cannot be what is meant by (4), in which
case 'true' cannot mean 'true-for-X'.

There is no getting around it, then. There is no way to make satis-
factory sense of the relativity-myth. So truth is not relative. It is *objective*,
and the truth of a proposition is *independent* of our desiring or believing
it to be true. Just as thinking or desiring cannot make the moon be made
of green cheese, thinking or desiring cannot make it *true* that the moon
is made of green cheese. To believe is to believe something to be true,
but truth is not the same thing as belief. This means that truth is independent of *all of us*; it does not mean that one powerful person or being
could hold the key to all that is true about the world. Thus in saying that
truth is objective, we are certainly not taking any kind of political stance,
saying that certain cultures or institutions have or might have a monopoly
on truth. The aim of good reasoning and argument is to get at the truth,
at the way the world is, irrespective of how people think or feel it to be.
Rationality is a great leveller. In the pursuit of truth, we are all equally
placed before the world, and no amount of political power can provide an
advantage.

Truth, value and morality

So far we have been tackling the myth that all **truth** is relative. Many
people are also tempted to think that **values** like those central to
moral issues are relative to personal or cultural preferences. It is possible
that people are tempted to think that *truth* is relative because they think
that *value* is relative. In fact, however, the non-relativity of truth does
not imply the non-relativity of value. The question of the relativity of
value is a different sort of question, and it is important to see how and
why. By way of example, we'll take the claim:

> Doctor-assisted suicide is immoral.

According to the relativist view, when opponents of doctor-assisted suicide
say it is morally unacceptable and their opponents contradict them and
say that it is morally acceptable, there is no real disagreement; rather the
two sides do not share the same moral preferences. Thus, for the relativist, value-statements are always speaker-relative, whether implicitly or
explicitly. Thus the incoherence of relativism about all truth does not

entail that value-statements are not relative in this way: the relativist can claim that all value-statements are speaker-relative without claiming that all statements are speaker-relative. An apparent disagreement over a value is in this respect like that between Julie and John concerning chocolate versus vanilla ice cream. One reason why this relativistic view of moral issues is so tempting is that we feel uncomfortable about being seen to dictate morals to other people because we (rightly) value tolerance of different opinions.[4]

We cannot prove, and would not try to prove, that moral relativism is false. It is conceivable that all claims about values are implicitly speaker-relative, or perhaps implicitly relative in some other way. We will, however, try to explain why there is good reason to resist moral relativism. While moral issues are almost always complicated and can be difficult to agree upon, the problem with this simplistic relativist approach is that it leaves no room for genuine disagreement about moral issues. It enjoins us to say, 'You feel OK about doctors helping their patients to die, I don't, end of story' without attempting rationally to persuade one another of the truth of our beliefs. The poverty of such a view of morals is illustrated by the following case: suppose there emerged a terrible fascist regime that murdered millions of people on grounds of race, religion or political beliefs. Simplistic relativists who desire to remain consistent with their relativist commitment would be unable to hope that the fascists are wrong, and that, therefore, others could rationally be persuaded that the fascists are wrong; for the fascists' views about the moral status of their victims would be nothing more than preferences that just happen to be different from most other people's. In the same way that many people prefer ice cream to carrots, this regime prefers murdering people who are different from them to living tolerantly alongside them. This is a very extreme example, but the point is well made. To adopt naive relativism about moral matters, to deny there can be a truth of the matter; and to say that claims such as the claim that torture is wrong have a similar status to the claim that chocolate ice cream tastes best, is to deny ourselves the opportunity to attempt rationally to persuade others that their moral beliefs are false and to persuade them not to follow courses of action that would be harmful to others. It places fundamental moral issues outside of the ambit of critical thinking.

Yet the critical thinker does not have to give up hope. While people may continue to believe that moral relativism is true, they must also be

4   This repudiation of moral relativism is aimed only at the very naive type of relativism that holds that moral questions are simply a matter of personal or cultural preference and therefore not the subject of genuine disagreements. There are various more sophisticated versions of moral relativism. It is not our intention to repudiate such theories.

consistent in their judgements. For example: it is irrational to hold that murderers are bad people, and at the same time, in full knowledge of his crimes, hold that Jack the Ripper was not a bad person. Thus, the critical thinker can at least demand logical consistency of the relativist: they can show that there is a valid argument from a premise accepted by the relativist to the conclusion that Jack the Ripper was bad. This means that it is possible to refute the relativist's moral views if it can be established that they are incoherent. In moral arguments a good way to do this is to find a general principle that the relativist accepts and go on to show how it is inconsistent with the belief that you wish to challenge. For example, if a relativist is pro-abortion and you discover that they are also against any form of killing, then you could force them to revise their beliefs if you could establish by argument that abortion was a type of killing.[5]

Belief, justification and truth

It is not the case that for any given proposition, we either believe it to be true (believe it), or believe it be false (disbelieve it). We may simply have no attitude towards it, either because it has never come to our attention, or because we choose not to consider the question. Or we may have an attitude that is midway between belief and disbelief: we may suspend judgement, because we find upon reflection that we lack sufficient evidence to make the judgement. This happens when we lack an argument either for or against the proposition that is rationally persuasive for us. The issue of the existence of a single deity who is said to have created the world provides a good example with which to illustrate the point. Consider the claim:

The world was created by an omnipotent and omniscient being.

Some people, let's call them 'theists', believe the proposition expressed here. Others, atheists, disbelieve it. Others, agnostics, are not sure whether or not to believe it so they have suspended judgement until such time as they acquire sufficient evidence (or faith) to support a belief either way. These three positions probably cover most adults in our society. But consider the position of most pre-school children. They do not believe

---

5   See Louis Pojman's essay 'Ethical relativism versus ethical objectivism' in his *Introduction to Philosophy: Classical and Contemporary Readings* (New York: Oxford University Press, 2004) for an excellent critical analysis of moral relativism and a convincing case for a version of moral objectivism. This very accessible paper is aimed at beginning Philosophy students.

that a deity made the world. They do not believe that a deity didn't make the world. However, it would not be accurate to say that they have suspended judgement on the issue. For they have not considered the issue, indeed they are probably too young to understand the claim that is the subject of debate. Of course, when assessing an argument's soundness and rational persuasiveness, the stance of having no opinion about the truth of the premises is not an option for critical thinkers. Either we consider ourselves to have sufficient evidence to believe or disbelieve the proposition expressed by the premise(s) or we recognise that we lack such evidence, and suspend judgement until such evidence is available. And even if we believe the argument to be inductively sound, we may find that having accepted its premises, the argument is not rationally persuasive for us because its conclusion is defeated by some further evidence that we have.

It is crucial to bear in mind that in saying that someone does not hold a certain belief, we are not saying or implying that they hold the opposite belief. If someone tells you that they don't believe that the Prime Minister is a bad person, they are not thereby saying or implying that they *believe that the Prime Minister is not a bad person*, let alone that the Prime Minister is a good person. They may not know the Prime Minister very well and may want to learn more about the Prime Minister before making a judgement, or they may simply not care and have no intention of ever forming a belief about the Prime Minister's moral standing. Or perhaps they have never even heard of the Prime Minister. As we saw in Chapter 4, an argument that assumes that someone who does not believe a proposition believes its negation commits a version of the **epistemic fallacy**.

Of the **four stances** we can take towards a proposition – **believing it**, **not believing it**, **suspending judgement**, **not engaging with it** – two, believing and not believing, admit of degrees. Smith and Jones may both believe that the Conservative Party will form the Government after the next general election, but they may not hold the belief with the same degree of confidence. Smith may be nearly certain, while Jones, an arch-sceptic when it comes to predicting voting behaviour, still believes it but to a lesser degree. Similarly Jack and Jill may both disbelieve the proposition that the Conservative Party will form the next Government, but the strength of Jack's disbelief may be such that he'll bet two weeks' wages at odds of 20 to 1 on a Conservative defeat. Whereas Jill, normally a keen betting woman, would not risk nearly as much money (if offered the same odds).

Given that someone holds a certain belief, we can ask whether or not the belief is *justified*, and whether or not it is *true*. Suppose Smith works for a national polling organisation and has seen the results of several methodologically sound top-secret polls that predict the Conservative Party will gain 80 per cent of the vote on election day. In the absence of any evidence that goes against that prediction, Smith is in possession of an argument that is highly rationally persuasive for him. He would thus be well-justified (other factors such as the reliability of the data notwithstanding) in believing the conclusion of the argument with a strong degree of certainty. As critical thinkers we may conclude that Smith's belief is reasonable or **justified** given what we know about the evidence available to them. Whenever someone's belief is backed by an argument that is rationally persuasive for them, it follows that they are justified in believing the conclusion, precisely to the extent that the argument is rationally persuasive for them.[6]

However, the fact that Smith is perfectly rational and justified in holding this belief does not establish that the belief is *true*. That depends upon whether the Conservative Party do in fact form the next Government. A belief's being true is a matter of its fitting the facts, not of there being good reasons to think that such-and-such is the case. We see this clearly when we consider the possibility of being justified in holding a belief that is actually false. Suppose I form the belief that the Government has just been deposed in a military coup. I am led to form this belief because while writing this chapter, I have been distracted into reading electronic newspapers and I find the same story appearing on several previously reliable and reputable internet sites. I track down one or two colleagues, they look at their own favourite sites and sure enough, find the same story. Given the widespread coverage of the coup and the fact that the sources are reliable and reputable, I would be justified in believing that the Government had been deposed by a military coup. But in fact, despite my good reasons for having formed this belief, it turns out to be false. A clever computer hacker has managed to hack into several UK-based internet news services and post this false story. So I have a justified but false belief. I may be in possession of an argument that is rationally persuasive for me, but my belief in its conclusion still need not be true.

---

6   This is not to say that a belief is justified only if one has a rationally persuasive argument for it. According to many theorists, some beliefs, especially those that arise in perception, are justified but not 'inferentially' – not, that is, by means of arguments or reasoning. Others deny this, holding that even the justification of perceptual beliefs depends upon underlying premises or assumptions. Since this is a fundamental open question in the theory of knowledge (epistemology), we have avoided taking a stand on it here. See the concluding section of this chapter. For detailed discussion see Robert Audi, *Epistemology: A Contemporary Introduction to the Theory of Knowledge* (2nd edition, Routledge, 2002).

Justification without arguments

In order to be justified in holding a certain belief, must one be in possession of a (rationally persuasive) *argument* for that belief? No – or at least not in any ordinary sense. There are forms of justification that do not involve having reasons in the usual sense. The obvious case is that of **perception**. If you perceive, under normal circumstances, that the cat is on the mat, then you are normally justified in believing that the cat is on the mat. If you say 'The cat is on the mat', and someone asks 'How do you know?', it is a perfectly adequate answer to say 'Because I see it'. The question of exactly how perception is related to justification is a complicated philosophical problem, but for our purposes it is sufficiently straightforward that a normal person in normal circumstances who perceives that such-and-such is justified in believing it; put another way, perceiving something is good reason for believing it. That is why, in our discussion of rational persuasiveness in Chapter 6, we said that in order for an argument to be rationally persuasive for a person, they must be justified in accepting the premises – having rationally persuasive arguments for those premises in turn is one way for that requirement to be satisfied, but it is not the only way.

Other, less obvious non-argumentative forms of justification include **introspection**, or reports of one's own thoughts, feelings and emotions (though these might be regarded as 'perception' in a somewhat extended sense of the word). Thus if you report that you are hungry, happy or afraid of failing the exam, then, except in bizarre circumstances, your belief that you are hungry, happy or afraid of failing the exam is surely justified, and does not stand in need of an argument.

Knowledge

Truth and knowledge are intimately linked. Our desire to accumulate knowledge stems from a desire to get at the truth. And certainly if one knows something, then the proposition known must be true: one cannot rightly be said to know that the cat is on the mat if the cat is not on the mat. The truth of a belief is certainly one necessary condition of that belief's being knowledge. So it may seem reasonable to suppose that if Jones believes that the Government has been deposed in a military coup, and the Government *has* been deposed in a military coup, then Jones knows that the Government has been deposed in a military coup. This is to say that *knowledge* that such-and-such is the case is simply having a *true belief* that such-and-such is the case.

However, this is not correct. Having a belief that is true is necessary, but not sufficient for knowledge. Suppose that Smith has been given LSD. He is hallucinating like mad, and his reason has gone completely haywire. The conviction suddenly impresses itself upon his unhinged mind that evil leprechauns have set fire to his mother's house in Sydney, 15,000 miles away. So he believes that his mother's house is on fire. In fact, Smith takes LSD every day, and believes, every time, that his mother's house is on fire (though for a different reason each time). But this time, it just so happens that his mother's house *is* on fire. Just by chance, the belief, this time, was true. No one would say that Smith, in this situation, *knows* that his mother's house is on fire. It was true belief, but not knowledge. He is like a person who shoots at a target blindfolded, dozens of times, and finally hits it, despite not having had any idea where the target was.

So knowledge cannot be identified simply with having a true belief. A further ingredient must be added to true belief, if it is to be knowledge. In particular, a true belief counts as knowledge only if we arrive at that true belief via the *right route*: we have knowledge only if we have *good reasons* for a holding belief that turns out to be true. We have to be **justified**; we need to have solid **evidential support**. We must, if you like, earn the right to be sure. Lucky true beliefs do not count as knowledge.

This third requirement is incorporated into the traditional philosophical account of knowledge, which is called the **tripartite account**:

For any subject (S) and any proposition (P), S *knows* that P if and only if:

(i)   S believes that P.
(ii)   P is true.
(iii)   S is justified in believing that P.

According to this account, to know that P is to have a justified true belief that P. It amounts to saying, then, that *knowledge is identical with justified true belief*. If I have a justified true belief that Tony Blair is UK Prime Minister then I *know* that Tony Blair is UK Prime Minister.

Justification failure

There are two ways in which belief can lack the justification, the evidential support, required for knowledge: it can either be genuine but insufficient, or simply not genuine, that is, mistaken.

Insufficiency

Consider Mrs Green, the greengrocer, who discovers that a customer has left their shopping behind. She has served five customers so far that day – Mr Red, Mrs Pink, Mr Orange, Mr Yellow and Mrs Blue. She has no reason to suppose that any one of them is any more forgetful than any of the others. None of them is in the habit of forgetting their shopping, for instance. Mrs Green concludes that one of the men left the shopping behind. She does have some justification for forming this belief: of the five customers three were male, so on the balance of probability the forgetful shopper is more likely to be a man. That is to say, she does have an argument for that conclusion which is somewhat **rationally persuasive** for her. But, intuitively, we may feel that this probability is somewhat slim justification for her belief. Even if it turns out that the shopping belongs to Mr Orange, we don't feel inclined to say that she arrived at her true belief via the right route; that is, that her true belief is really *justified*. So even if she's right, we don't feel that she *knows* that the forgetful shopper is a man. This is not to say that probability as a justification for true belief should be ruled out per se. The problem here is that the probability is not strong enough. If there had been four male shoppers and one woman, we would be more inclined to allow that Mrs Green's belief is justified. If there had been 99 men and 1 woman, we would certainly be so inclined.

There are occasions when there is far more at stake in having the proper justification for forming a true belief than simply making sure that someone gets their groceries. An obvious case is where principles of justice are involved, where evidence is required to demonstrate beyond reasonable doubt that a defendant is guilty of an alleged crime. Suppose Jones is accused of the murder of Brown. In fact, Jones is guilty: he strangled Brown to death. Smith is called as a prosecution witness to Jones' crime. He is called as a witness because he has given a police statement in which he claims to have seen Jones emerging from Brown's house carrying a knife. If this is all the evidence the jury has, is it, by itself, sufficient reason for jury members to form the true belief that Jones is guilty of Brown's murder? Clearly not, even though Jones is in fact guilty of the murder. So although the jury members may have reached their true belief about Jones' guilt on the basis of Smith's evidence, they do not have a **justified** belief about Jones' guilt. If this is the only evidence they have for reaching their verdict, then they should not convict Jones of Brown's murder. Again, note that this holds even though Jones happens to be guilty.

How strong must our evidential support be, if a belief is to be justified? How strong must it be if a true belief is to qualify as knowledge? Unfortunately, there is no precise answer to this question. The terms 'justified' and 'knowledge', like 'bald', are somewhat vague: just as there is no exact quantity or proportion of cranial hairlessness required for baldness, there is no exact strength of evidence for a belief short of which it is not knowledge, and beyond which it is knowledge. But this should not trouble us too much. In practice, we are adept at recognising the cases where our degree of justification is borderline. This does not change the nature of our task as critical thinkers: we know that our task is to fashion sound arguments that are rationally persuasive for ourselves or for their intended audiences. By paying attention to the reasons why we are entitled to form true beliefs, we are able to achieve the firmest possible grasp upon what we can legitimately claim to know.

Mistakes about justification

Sometimes misevaluation of evidence leads us to form **irrational beliefs**, even in cases that are not so extreme as Smith and his hallucinations. In such cases we overestimate our evidential support, or we think that the evidence supports a belief when it doesn't. This is an error that people who attempt to persuade by devious means can often exploit to their advantage (indeed we noticed in Chapter 4 that some **fallacies** actually work well as **rhetorical ploys**). For instance they might describe one or two vivid examples of some alleged phenomenon with the aim of getting us to form generalisations for which the examples do not provide adequate support. An example that should be familiar to readers and observers of the UK tabloid press is that of a vivid description of a recipient of state benefit or of an asylum seeker, which apparently supports the claim that they enjoy an undeservedly luxurious lifestyle. Such examples are rolled out in an attempt to persuade readers to believe that the majority of benefit recipients and asylum seekers are undeserving cheats. Often, the details of such examples and the manner of their presentation are so rhetorically powerful that they cause us to misevaluate the significance of the evidence presented to us. In particular, we make an unjustified **inductive inference** (one with very low force). When we are led to make such mistakes and form irrational beliefs, we allow ourselves to be distracted by factors other than principles of good reasoning.

There is another type of irrational belief. Sometimes we allow ourselves to accept a false belief because we believe that accepting it will benefit us in some way. In such cases we not only lack evidence for the belief, but we also seem not to care that we have none. For instance, someone might believe that the predictions of their astrologer will come true; they might believe in faith-healing; ESP; life after death; that everything in the Bible is literally true; that their terminally ill grandparent will make a recovery; that a certain alternative healing method will cure cancer. We often feel that it would be unfeeling to point out that such a person's beliefs are irrational. Indeed, we often admire their faith and sincerity. However, it would be a mistake to retreat into relativity and conclude that their belief is 'true for them'. The belief is false, that's that. Indeed, such people can sometimes paradoxically be described as believing that which they know to be false – self-deceived.

However, we should not be too cold-blooded. It's not usually the case that such people are intentionally deceiving themselves, but rather that they are trying to deal with their plight by having faith that their hopes (however unlikely) will be borne out.[7] So it's rather unfair and unfeeling to accuse such people of being irrational, even though strictly speaking they are. While we should try to avoid irrationality, we must also accept that as human beings, it is sometimes psychologically better for us if our beliefs and behaviour fall short of rationality.

Knowledge and rational persuasiveness

Rational persuasiveness requires that you be justified in accepting the premises of an argument. If the argument is deductively valid, then if you are justified in accepting the premises, you are equally justified in accepting the conclusion. If the premises of such an argument are actually true, and you know that they are, then if you recognise that the argument is valid, you know the conclusion to be true.[8]

However, there are two complications. First, a rationally persuasive argument can be unsound: rational persuasiveness does not itself require that the premises of the argument actually be true. It requires that one be justified in accepting the premises; but, we have seen, it is perfectly possible to have good reasons, to be justified, in holding a false belief. Thus one can be rationally persuaded by an argument but not know the argument's premises to be true. In such a case, one can be rationally persuaded by an argument without thereby acquiring knowledge. *Knowledge* that an

---

7   There are, of course, cases where people *are* guilty of self-deception. A classic case is the person who knows (for their clothing has become too tight) that they have gained weight, but refuses to believe that their scales are functioning properly.

8   In epistemology this is called the 'closure principle'. It might seem undeniable, but in more advanced philosophical treatments of these issues, it is called into question.

argument is sound, on the other hand, makes a stronger demand on our epistemological relationship with its premises. To *know* that an argument is sound, we have to know that its premises are true. To know that an argument is sound, we need justified true beliefs in the premises. Whereas for rational persuasiveness, we need only the justification; the belief need not be true.

Second, in the case of an inductively forceful argument that is not defeated, the degree of justification transmitted from known premises to the argument's conclusion may be insufficient to establish the conclusion as knowledge. For the degree of inductive force may be too weak. One might, for example, know with certainty that 51 of 100 stones in a bag are black; one would thus have an inductively sound argument that is rationally persuasive for the conclusion that the next stone drawn at random from the bag will be black. But the argument is only slightly rationally persuasive. Even if that conclusion turns out to be true, the belief in it would be insufficiently justified by the argument, and so would not count as knowledge. More generally, the degree of justification one has for the conclusion of an argument that is inductively forceful but not deductively sound will be smaller than the degree one has for the premises (unless one has some other source of justification for the conclusion).

Finally, here is a case that displays what knowledge is, as opposed to what it isn't. The following scenario provides an example of the fulfilment of the requirements placed on knowledge claims:

> Tabitha Tabloid, a journalist, is at a restaurant one evening and sees a prominent politician at an adjacent table with a person she knows not to be their spouse. 'Perhaps there's a story in this', she thinks. Later, as she walks to her car, she notices a couple locked in a passionate embrace in a parked car that just happens to be parked under a street lamp. On discreet but close inspection she sees that the couple is the politician and their companion. She forms the belief (which happens to be true) that the politician is having an illicit affair with this person. In fact, she believes that the evidence for her belief is sufficiently strong that she persuades her editor that her story should be the next morning's front-page lead.

Here we have the three components that are apparently required for legitimate knowledge claims: a true belief that the politician is having an affair and a rational justification for that belief based upon what Tabitha witnessed in the restaurant and subsequently in the parked car, that is, the criteria provided by the tripartite account of knowledge are all met and it is reasonable to say that Tabitha *knows* that the politician is having an intimate relationship (or at least a one-off passionate embrace) with the person in question.[9]

Philosophical directions

In this final section, we mention just a few questions that arise naturally out of some of the main topics of this chapter, answers to which require more detailed or strenuous philosophical analysis than would be appropriate here. This may help you to see why philosophical inquiries are not always 'irrelevant' to real life: they arise inevitably when we reason critically about things, or try to determine exactly what is involved in doing so. We will quickly sketch these issues and recommend some sources for further reading. They are all issues in **epistemology** and the theory or science of **knowledge**.[10]

Foundationalism vs. coherentism

We said that unlike other sorts of beliefs, we do not normally think of beliefs based on perception as standing in need of *reasons*, that is, arguments. We think of normal perceptual beliefs as justified just as they stand, just by virtue of being grounded in perception. So long as we think so, then it is natural to think of *other* beliefs as ultimately being *based* on perception. Scientific theories, for example, seem to be ultimately based upon *observation*, that is, perception. Thus for each non-perceptual belief P, it seems plausible that it is justified – and hence potentially knowledge – only if we can trace it back along a chain of reasons to some perceptual belief or set of beliefs. Since perceptual beliefs are *self-justifying*, they can transmit justification along the train of reasons back up to the belief P that was in question.

This way of conceiving the structure of knowledge fits common sense very well, and is known as **foundationalism**. There is, however, a contrary point of view that – strangely enough – also appeals to common

---

9   In a famous essay Edmund Gettier described cases that appear to be justified true belief but not knowledge, thus casting doubt on the intuitive theory that knowledge is justified true belief. If you'd like to learn more, see Robert Audi, *Epistemology, A Contemporary Introduction* (2nd edition; Routledge, 2002). Gettier's original paper, along with notable attempts to solve the problem, is reprinted in Michael Huemer, *Epistemology: Contemporary Readings* (Routledge, 2002).

10   For further reading on these and other issues in epistemology see Robert Audi, *Epistemology, A Contemporary Introduction* (2nd edition, Routledge, 2002), and Michael Huemer, *Epistemology: Contemporary Readings* (Routledge, 2002).

sense. As everybody knows, perception is not 100 per cent reliable. We are subject to visual illusions (the man outside the train seems to be moving – no, it's the train beginning to move) and other less exotic perceptual mistakes (the referee honestly but mistakenly sees the player as offside). More dramatically, we *dream* and even *hallucinate*; aren't we then having false perceptions, or at least, experiences that are indistinguishable from true perceptions? Of course much or most of the time our perceptions are correct – we are quite certain we're not dreaming or otherwise mistaken. But even so, aren't we *implicitly* assuming that the circumstances are favourable? Aren't we reasoning something like this: this is the experience I would have if I were really seeing the cat on the mat under favourable circumstances. Circumstances are favourable. Therefore I really am seeing the cat on the mat. If so, then the question arises: what are the premises of *that* little argument based upon? The anti-foundational position known as **coherentism** claims that if we always insist on a foundation in self-justifying perceptual beliefs, then we can never get it, and no belief is ever justified. Since that is absurd, the foundationalist demand must be misconceived. Instead, we should think of our whole network of beliefs as mutually supporting: each belief – even if it is a perceptual belief – is justified just insofar as it *fits with* or *coheres* with the network we already have. Perceptual beliefs typically do pass this test, but not always: it looks like the magician saws the woman in half, but that does not cohere with other things we already know, so we don't believe it. On the other hand, coherentism has its problems too. Most conspicuously, surely a whole set of beliefs could be mostly false (the person is deluded about almost everything!); if another belief coheres with that set, does that *justify* it? It seems not.

Both theories have problems, but they are the only obvious options.

Internal vs. external justification

Exactly how is it that perceptual beliefs are justified? One answer is that perception is *reliable*. That is, in normal circumstances, when a perceptual belief arises in a normal, properly functioning human being, the belief is almost always correct. Perception is in this way *truth-conducive*. Thus we might suppose: if a person has a perceptual belief, then so long as the person is functioning normally and the perceptual circumstances are normal, the belief is justified; if not, then the belief is not justified.

On the other hand, you might wonder: surely it is not enough for the circumstances to *be* favourable in that way; doesn't the person have to *know* that the circumstances are favourable? Otherwise, by what right would he or she accept the belief? This might seem like a reasonable demand, until you recognise how much it requires: for how are we supposed to know that the circumstances are favourable, except by perception? But if we need more perceptions in order to justify the first perception, don't we need yet more to justify these? And so on; we are off, it seems, on what philosophers call a *vicious regress*. It is *vicious*, because unless we can put a stop to it, it seems we are unable to justify any perceptual beliefs.

Again, both sides have their advantages and disadvantages. The view that beliefs may be justified simply by having been acquired in the right way – whether or not we know them to have been so acquired – is called, for obvious reasons, **externalism**; the view that one must always be aware of the means of justification is **internalism**. The issue between them is by no means merely academic. For example, in 2002, British military forces participated the US-led invasion of Iraq at least partly on the grounds that Iraq was concealing so-called weapons of mass destruction. There turned out not be any. But the British Prime Minister Tony Blair defended the decision on the grounds that at the time of the invasion, the evidence available to him suggested that Iraq was concealing such weapons. Many people who granted Blair's sincerity on the issue were nonetheless unsatisfied. Plausibly, such critics were thinking that however Blair's decision may have been justified on *internal* grounds, it was not justified from an *external* point of view, because the means of justification was not in fact reliable.

Probability and justification

Where our reason for believing something is an argument with inductive force, is the question of justification simply the same thing as the degree to which the argument is rationally persuasive for us? In most cases, it is correct to assume so. But not, in seems, in all. Suppose that a few minutes ago you filled and switched on the electric kettle. So you know there's hot water in the kettle. Now compare this case. Your sister tells you she's got a lottery ticket. You happen to know that the chance that her ticket is a winner is one in ten million. As it happens, the draw has already taken place; neither of you know it, but her ticket is not a winner. In such a case, you naturally *believe* that your sister's ticket is a non-winner; this belief is *true*, and its *probability* of being true was *very high*. But do you *know* that her ticket is a non-winner? It seems wrong to say so. Yet the probability of this belief's being correct is much higher than that of your belief about the kettle! The failure rate of kettles is much higher than one in ten million. To repeat: both beliefs are true. The kettle-belief constitutes knowledge but the lottery-belief does not, *despite the fact that the kettle-belief had a greater chance of being wrong.*

One could respond to this seeming paradox in different ways. At first, you might think maybe you *do* know that the lottery ticket is a loser. But that seems wrong: every purchaser of a lottery ticket is in exactly the same position, has exactly the same evidence as to whether or not they've won: everyone knows their chance is miniscule, namely one in ten million. So everyone would be equally justified in claiming to have lost. But one such person would be wrong to claim this, namely the winner. If we say that the losers knew they were losers, then *knowledge* seems to be a matter of mere *luck*, which seems wrong; it also makes it seem completely irrational to play the lottery – why would you buy lottery tickets if you *know* that you're not going to win?

Another response is to suppose that standards for what counts as justi-fication – *criteria of justification* – shift depending on the subject-matter. So in some cases we demand a higher probability of being right than in others. Or perhaps probability can *never* suffice for justification: perhaps if the only reason for accepting a certain proposition is its probability of being true, then we cannot be justified in believing it, even if in point of fact it is true. But this seems to fly in the face of the notion of probability itself, which we explained as *degree of rational expectation*; probability just is a measure of the degree to which it is reasonable to believe some-thing. Yet another tack is to suppose that only what is *certain* – 100 per cent probable – can properly be said to be *known*. The problem with that route is that it leads swiftly to *philosophical scepticism*, the view that nothing, or very little, can actually be known. It remains one the defining endeavours of philosophy to formulate a consistent theory of knowledge that does not result in scepticism.

CHAPTER SUMMARY

It is crucial for critical thinkers to recognise that **truth is objective** and **not relative**. Otherwise the critical thinker's objective of analys-ing and assessing arguments with the aim getting at the truth of a matter is deeply undermined. Some sentences that appear to be straightforward assertions are in fact implicitly relative expressions of subjective preferences and tastes: they are **implicitly speaker-relative**. In such cases there cannot be genuine disagreements about the facts of the matter, whereas when a non speaker-relative propo-sition is asserted, a genuine disagreement can occur because a truth is at stake. To deny this, to accept the myth that all truth is relative, is to accept something of which it seems impossible to make sense.

In the case of **moral beliefs**, or beliefs about **value**, relativism may not be readily refutable, but (1) the consequences of denying that there is truth in this realm appear to be extremely pernicious and (2) relativism does not completely close the door to rational persuasion, because we may still demand consistency of the relativist.

If our stance is not that of not considering it, or refusing to consider it, which one of the three remaining **stances** we choose to take towards a given proposition depends upon the evidence available to us. We require sufficient evidence for the truth or falsity of a proposition in order to justify believing or rejecting it. If such evidence is unavailable, we should suspend our judgement. It is perfectly possible to be justified in holding a false belief. The evidence available to us might make it rational for us to accept a proposition despite the fact that it turns out to be false.

Some forms of justification do not involve arguments or reasoning. **Perception** is the obvious case. Merely having a true belief in a proposition is not sufficient to count as **knowing** the proposition, though it is necessary for knowledge of it. Traditionally, philosophers have concluded that knowledge requires a true belief arrived at via the **right route**; that is, via good reasoning based upon sufficient evidential support. This leads to the formulation of an account of knowledge known as the **tripartite account** according to which *to know that P is to have a justified true belief that P.* Knowledge is a stronger requirement than having a rationally persuasive argument. One may have a rationally persuasive argument for a proposition without thereby knowing it, if the degree of rationally persuasiveness of the argument is not sufficiently high.

EXERCISES

1 Without looking back at the relevant section of the book, write a paragraph explaining the difference between indexical sentences and implicitly speaker-relative sentences and then give an example of each.

2 For each of the following sentences, say whether it is indexical, implicitly speaker-relative or neither. If it is implicitly speaker-relative, explain also whether it could be implicitly relative to the preferences of the person asserting it. Explain your answers. Note that in some cases, there is room for reasonable disagreement as to the correct answer. So don't worry if you are not sure of how to answer; the important thing is to try to explain the answer you do give.

a   The maximum speed limit on UK roads is 70 miles per hour.

b   Yorkshire is nearby.

c   Maria Sharapova did not win the 2004 US Open Tennis Championship.

d   It's raining there.

e   Euthanasia is morally acceptable.

f   The climate in Southern Italy is too warm.

g   Haggis is delicious.

h   Bill Clinton was a great President.

i   I am in pain.

j   Drink-driving should be punished by a prison sentence.

k   The Government should cut the tax on petrol.

l   Bitter tastes better than lager.

m   I like bitter better than lager.

n   Robbie Williams has sold more records than Coldplay.

o   Robbie Williams' music is better than Coldplay's.

p   If you eat more fruit and vegetables you will be healthier.

q   It's going to snow tomorrow.

r   Tchaikovsky wrote the 1812 overture.

s   We all live in a yellow submarine.

t   That hurts!

u   France and Great Britain were Second World War allies.

v   10 is the square root of 100.

w   All pop/rock music is pathetic cacophony and a waste of any intelligent person's time.

x   All triangles have three angles totalling 180 degrees.

y   Blood is thicker than water.

z   This one is better than that one.

3   Without looking back at the relevant section of the book, write out the tripartite account of knowledge. Then, using your own example, explain why simply having a true belief that P is insufficient for knowledge that P.

Exercises

4   Suppose you are justified in believing a proposition that is in fact false. Could there be an argument for that proposition which is rationally persuasive for you? Would the situation change if the proposition were actually true rather than false? Explain your answer, using examples – your own examples – if you find it useful.

5   It is sometimes held that testimony – what people tell you – is like perception, in that one is normally justified in accepting the proposition without having an argument for it. The alternative view would be that in accepting something on the basis of testimony, one is implicitly doing some reasoning, relying on an argument. What would the argument be?

▇ Glossary

Words written in **bold** indicate references to relevant further glossary entries.

Ambiguity   A sentence is ambiguous in a given context if there is more than one possible way to interpret it in that context. A word is ambiguous in a given context if there is more than one possible way to interpret in that context. See also **lexical ambiguity**, **syntactic ambiguity**. Compare **vagueness**.

Antecedent   A **conditional statement** asserts a relation between two propositions, the antecedent and the **consequent**. When the antecedent of a true conditional statement is true, the consequent must also be true. Thus the antecedent of 'If John wins then Mary will cry' is 'John wins'; if one accepts both this conditional and its antecedent as true, then one must also accept that Mary will cry.

Argument   An argument is a system of propositions comprising one or more **premises** advanced by the arguer in support of a **conclusion**. Arguments may be evaluated as **valid**, **inductively forceful**, or neither, but not as **true** or **false**.

Argument commentary   An argument commentary is a short essay that discusses an **argument-reconstruction**, covering the following points: (i) how and why the argument was reconstructed as it was; (ii) the **validity** or degree of **inductive force** of the argument; (iii) the **truth-values** of the premises; (vi) the degree of **rational persuasiveness** of the argument for relevant audiences, where this is not already addressed by (iii).

Argument-reconstruction A presentation of an argument in **standard form** in which premises may be added, made explicit or clarified in order to make the argument either **valid** or **inductively forceful**.

Argument trees A graphical representation of the structure of an argument. See pp. 67–71.

Causal generalisation A causal generalisation is a **generalisation** to the effect that things of one kind tend to cause things of another kind. Such a generalisation is true if the presence of a thing of the first kind raises the probability of things of the second kind, even when other possible causes are absent.

Conclusion An argument's conclusion is the proposition that its **premises** are intended to support. The distinctive aim of giving an argument is to persuade an audience rationally that the conclusion is true.

Conclusion indicators These are words such as 'therefore', 'so' and 'thus' that are often used to indicate the conclusion of an argument. Such words sometimes serve other purposes, however, such as indicating a causal relationship.

Conditional A conditional proposition is single proposition that joins two propositions, the **antecedent** and **consequent**. Its usual function is to assert that if the antecedent is true, then so is the consequent. It is most characteristically expressed by means of 'if–then'. Conditionals, unlike **arguments**, may be evaluated as **true** or **false**.

Conditional probability The conditional probability of a proposition **P**, given evidence (set of premises) **A**, is the **probability**, if **A** holds (that is, if all the premises in **A** are true), that **P** is true. Conditional probabilities are to be assessed ignoring any evidence not included in **A** that might be relevant to the truth-value of **P**.

Connecting premises These are **conditionals** or **generalisations**, usually **implicitly** assumed by an arguer, that are needed in order to infer the argument's conclusion. For example, if the argument is 'Mary is a doctor, therefore Mary has a university degree', a suitable connecting premise is 'All doctors have university degrees'.

Connotation, primary/secondary The primary connotation of a term is the condition that is necessary and sufficient for something's being a member of the **extension** of the term: it is the rule that determines whether or not a given thing is or is not correctly designated by the term. The secondary connotation of a term is the range of further attributes that a thing is commonly assumed to possess if it is thought to be correctly designated by the term. The primary connotation of 'mink coat', for example, is 'coat made from the furs of minks'; its secondary connotation might include 'expensive', 'posh', 'old-fashioned', 'warm' and 'beautiful' or 'immoral', depending on opinion. Unlike a term's primary connotation, its secondary connotation can vary from person to person.

Consequent   See **antecedent** and **conditional**.

Context   The context of an argument is the set of circumstances in which an argument is actually advanced by an arguer. Context is significant because in order to **reconstruct** an argument we often have to fill in **premises** that are only **implicitly** assumed by the arguer. To determine what an arguer is likely to have assumed, we usually need to know the circumstances in which the argument is advanced. We also need to know the context in order to know the meaning of indexical (context-relative) expressions used.

Counterexample   (i) A counterexample to a **generalisation** is particular statement – a statement that is not a generalisation – that is the negation of an **instance** of the generalisation. For example, 'Darcy Bussell is a great ballerina who is tall' is a counterexample to 'No great ballerinas are tall'. (ii) A counterexample to an argument is an argument of the same form or pattern as the first argument that is clearly invalid or inductively non-forceful. It is used as an illustration to make it clear that the first argument is invalid or inductively non-forceful.

Covering generalisation   Often, where a premise of an argument is a conditional proposition of the form 'If Mary is a doctor, then Mary has a university degree', it is **implicitly** inferred from a **generalisation** of which it is an **instance** – in this case, 'All doctors have university degrees'. This relation is made more conspicuous if we express the generalisation in the form 'For any given person, if that person is a doctor, then that person has a university degree'.

Credibility   The degree to which someone's having said something constitutes a reason to think it **true**. While critical reasoning requires us to focus on an argument and not on the person putting it forward, a person's character and actions are certainly relevant to their credibility.

Deductive validity Validity can be defined according to either of the following, equivalent formulations: (1) An argument is valid if and only if it would be impossible for its premises to be true but its conclusion false. (2) An argument is valid if and only if necessarily, if its premises are true, then its conclusion is true.

Defeated argument An **inductively forceful** argument, whose premises a person reasonably believes, is defeated for that person if he or she has good reasons to think the conclusion false.

Expected value The expected value of a given action depends on the values and probabilities of the possible outcomes. In particular, if o_1, o_2, ... and so on are the possible outcomes of an action, $V(o)$ is the value of a given outcome, and $Pr(o)$ is the probability of a given outcome, then the expected value of the action is:

$$V(o_1) \times Pr(o_1) + V(o_2) \times Pr(o_2) + \ldots$$

The value of each outcome must be assigned a number, but the purpose of the numbers is only to indicate the comparative values of the possible outcomes. For example, if one outcome is judged to be twice as good as a second, we could assign them any two numbers so long as the first is assigned a number that is twice that assigned to the second. Expected value is the central concept of cost/benefit analysis. The idea is that, given a range of possible actions, one should perform the action with the highest expected value.

Explanations We give an **argument** for something when we seek to persuade an audience that that proposition is true. By contrast, when we give an explanation of something, we know, or assume, that the audience already accepts that the proposition to be explained is true. Our aim is not to give reasons for believing that proposition, but to specify, for example, the causes of the event that it mentions. Both arguments and explanations can be described as answering 'why' questions, but there is a crucial difference: whereas the question in the case of explanation is 'why is it so?', or 'why did it happen?', the question in the case of argument is 'why should I believe it?'. Potentially confusing is that in order to establish that an explanation is the correct one – e.g. that it specifies the actual cause of an event – we often have to give reasons why it should be believed, i.e. an argument. That is, we sometimes have to argue *for* an explanation.

Extended arguments An extended argument for a proposition is one containing more than one **inference**: a **conclusion** is used as a

premise for a further argument, the conclusion of which may be used as a premise for a further argument, and so on. Conclusions used as premises for further inferences in an extended argument are called **intermediate conclusions**

Extension   The extension of a general term such as 'cat' or 'red car' is the set or group of things designated by the term.

Factual assessment   The stage in the assessment of an argument in which we determine whether or not the argument's premises are true. If the argument is either **valid** or **inductively forceful**, then the argument is **sound** if and only if all its premises are true.

Fallacies   The term 'fallacy' encompasses certain commonly encountered failures of argumentation; it is partly because they are often effective as **rhetorical ploys** that they are commonly encountered. *Formal* fallacies are simply logical mistakes; that is, arguments that fail to be valid or inductively forceful in certain characteristic ways. *Substantive* fallacies are arguments that implicitly assume some quite general premise of a kind which, when more closely and explicitly considered, can readily be seen to be false. Some other common defects in argumentation fit neither classification; but since they involve fooling the audience in the context of argument they can be appropriately classified as fallacies.

Generalisations   A generalisation is a proposition concerning a class of things, either explicitly or implicitly involving a **quantifier** such as 'all', 'every', 'no', 'some', 'most', 'twelve', 'at least twelve' and so on. For example, whereas 'That dog is black' is not a generalisation, replacing 'that dog' with 'every dog', 'no dog', 'at least one dog' and so on, yields a generalisation. Sometimes the verb must be changed to the plural form, and likewise the predicate if it involves a noun rather than an adjective.

Gettier cases   Gettier cases are cases in which someone satisfies the conditions for knowing a proposition that are set down by the **tripartite account of knowledge**, yet fails to know it. This is usually because the person is only accidentally **justified** in believing a **true** proposition.

Good reasons   For someone to have good reasons for believing a proposition is for that person to possess an argument for that proposition that is **rationally persuasive** for them.

Hard generalisation   A hard generalisation is one that is correctly conveyed by using a quantifier such as 'all', 'every', 'each' and 'no'. Unlike **soft generalisations**, such generalisations are true only if there are no **counterexamples**.

Implicature (conversational implicature)   A proposition is said to be **implicated** or **conversationally implicated** by a statement (asserted utterance of a declarative sentence) when the proposition (i) is not explicitly stated by the utterance and (ii) is such that a listener who knew the relevant facts about the context would reasonably take it to have been intended by the speaker. Example: a tailor asks whether you want your jacket made in this particular fabric; you say 'That's ugly'. The tailor reasonably takes you to be intending to convey that you don't want it made in that fabric.

Implicit   A **premise** is implicit in an argument if it has been assumed but not actually stated by the arguer. **Conclusions** may also be implicit, though this is less common. Whether or not, as a matter of psychological fact, a given premise has been assumed by an arguer is often beside the point. In general, implicit propositions are those not stated by the arguer that would be included in a **reconstruction** produced in accordance with the **principle of charity**.

Implicit relativity   A statement is **implicitly** relative when the type of fact it expresses involves a relation to something that is not explicitly mentioned in the statement. For example, 'John is tall' is implicitly relative because what it really means is 'John is taller than the average man' (if John is a man). The relation to the average man is not explicit in the original statement.

Implicit speaker-relativity   An implicitly speaker-relative statement is one that is **implicitly relative**, where the implicit term of the relation is the person making the statement. Thus the statement is **speaker-relative**, but only implicitly so. For example, 'Chocolate ice cream tastes better than strawberry ice cream' is implicitly speaker-relative because what it really means is 'Chocolate ice cream tastes better to me than strawberry ice cream does'. (Some might say that the implicit term here should not be 'me' but something like 'most people'.)

Inductive force   The inductive force of an argument is the **conditional probability** of its conclusion relative to its premises.

Inductive inference   To draw an inductive inference is to conclude, on the basis that a certain proportion of a **sample** of a population possesses a certain feature, that the same proportion of the whole population possesses that feature. The inference is **inductively forceful** to the degree that the sample is representative of the population.

Inductive soundness   See **soundness**.

Inference   An inference is a step in reasoning from one or more premises to a conclusion. All **arguments** contain at least one inference. Inferences are evaluated not as **true/**false, but as **valid**/invalid and **inductively forceful**/inductively non-forceful.

Inference bar   In an **argument-reconstruction**, an inference bar is a line written between a **premise** and **conclusion**, indicating that the proposition expressed below the line has been inferred from one or more of the propositions above it. It can be read as 'therefore'. Every reconstructed **argument** contains at least one inference bar.

Instance   An instance of a **generalisation** is a proposition about an individual that is directly implied by the generalisation. Normally this will be a **conditional**. For example, 'If Socrates is a philosopher, then he is wise' is an instance of 'All philosophers are wise'. The **inference** from a hard generalisation to a corresponding instance is always **deductively valid**. That from a soft generalisation to an instance is **inductively forceful**.

Intermediate conclusion   In an **extended argument**, an intermediate conclusion is a **conclusion** inferred from some set of **premises** that is used, in the same argument, as a premise for a further **inference**.

Invalid   Synonymous with 'not **deductively valid**'. An argument may be invalid yet **inductively forceful**, or neither valid nor inductively forceful.

Justification   One's degree of rational justification for believing a proposition is the degree to which one is entitled to think it true. In many cases this will depend on whether or not one has good reasons – arguments that are **rationally persuasive** – for thinking so. In other cases – especially beliefs acquired by *perception* – one may be justified without being able to give further reasons. Rational justification can be distinguished from pragmatic justification, according to which one is justified in believing something if believing it has desirable consequences. Rational justification and pragmatic justification do not always coincide.

Knowledge   See **tripartite account of knowledge**.

Lexical ambiguity   An **ambiguous** sentence is lexically ambiguous if it contains an ambiguous word.

Logic   Logic is the systematic study of arguments, especially deductive validity and inductive force.

Logical assessment   Logical assessment is the stage of argument assessment at which it is determined whether the argument is **valid** or **invalid**, and at which the degree of **inductive force** of invalid arguments is determined. Except where **inductive inferences** are concerned, it is sharply to be distinguished from **factual assessment**.

Practical reasoning   Practical reasoning is the use of arguments whose conclusions recommend an action. See **expected value**.

Premise   A premise in an **argument** is advanced as a reason for **inferring** the argument's **conclusion**.

Premise indicators   These are expressions such as 'since, 'because' and 'for the reason that', which are often used to indicate a **premise** in an **argument**. As in the case of **conclusion indicators**, however, such words sometimes serve other purposes, such as indicating a causal relationship.

Principle of charity   According to this principle, if our aim is to discover the truth about a given issue, then we should reconstruct arguments so as to yield the maximum degree of rational persuasiveness for the relevant audience (which normally will include ourselves).

Probability   The probability of a proposition is the degree to which it is likely to be **true**, where this degree is expressed as fraction or decimal between 0 and 1. There are different ways of explaining this, such as proportion and frequency; but in this book the degree to which a proposition is likely to be true is taken to be the degree to which it would be perfectly rational to expect it to be true. Since this obviously depends on the evidence one has, the key concept is that of **conditional probability**: the degree to which it is rational to expect a proposition to be true given such-and-such evidence.

Proposition   A proposition is the factual content expressed by a declarative sentence on a particular occasion of using (writing or uttering) the sentence. In particular, it is what is expressed that admits of being **true** or false. Different sentences can express the same proposition. For example, 'Antony kissed Cleopatra' expresses the same proposition as 'Cleopatra was kissed by Antony'. Different propositions may be expressed by means of the same sentence. For example, if Antony and Cleopatra each utter the sentence 'I'm hungry', they express different propositions, since they talk about different people. A sentence's propositional content is independent of its rhetorical or emotive content.

Quantifiers Quantifiers are expressions such as 'all', 'some', 'every', 'many', 'twelve', 'not very many' and 'no', used in the explicit statement of **generalisations**. Often, where both hard and soft generalisations are concerned, they are left **implicit**.

Rational persuasiveness This is the concept we use to characterise a person's having 'good reason' for accepting a **conclusion**. An **argument** is rationally persuasive for a person if, and only if: (i) the person accepts its **premises**, and is **justified** in doing so; (ii) the argument is either **deductively valid** or **inductively forceful** and (iii) if it is inductively forceful, the argument is not **defeated** for that person.

Refutation by counterexample This is a method of criticising an argument. One fabricates an argument that embodies the same form or strategy as the argument one means to criticise, but which is clearly **invalid**, not **inductively forceful**, or **fallacious**. This shows that the strategy or form of the argument one means to criticise is defective in the same way.

Relevance The falsity of a premise can be more or less relevant, where the aim is to discover reasons for or against the conclusion in question. Sometimes a false premise can simply be removed from an argument without destroying its **validity** or degree of **inductive force**; the resulting argument may thus be sound. Other times the false premise can be replaced by another, similar premise that is true, again without compromising validity or inductive force. For example, the **scope** of a generalisation may be reduced.

Representative See **samples**.

Rhetoric A verbal or written attempt to persuade someone to believe, desire or do something that does not attempt to give **good reasons** for the belief, desire or action, but attempts to motivate that belief, desire or action solely through the power of the words used is an instance of rhetoric.

Rhetorical force   Not part of the **proposition** that a sentence expresses, but the emotive or otherwise suggestive window-dressing that surrounds that **proposition** and is used to persuade us to believe or do something by appeal to our non-critical faculties.

Rhetorical ploys   Commonly encountered instances of rhetorical use of language, these include: appeal to novelty, appeal to popularity, appeal to compassion, pity or guilt, appeal to cuteness, appeal to sexiness, appeals to wealth, status, power, hipness, coolness, etc. appeal to fear (also known as scare tactics), the direct attack and hard sell, buzzwords, scare quotes, trading on an equivocation and smokescreen (changing the subject).

Rhetorical question   An interrogative sentence that is not really intended as a question, but as a statement, usually of a **proposition** with which the speaker or writer assumes the audience will agree.

Samples   An **inductive inference** is inductively forceful if, and only if, the sample cited in the premise of the inference is representative of the population cited in the conclusion of the inference. Suppose that n is the proportion of the sample known to bear a certain trait. We can reasonably conclude that the proportion of the population bearing that trait is n only if we have good reason to think that nothing has caused that proportion in the sample that does not equally affect the population as a whole.

Scope   To speak of the scope of a generalisation – for example, one of the form 'All X are Y' – is a way of discussing the size of the class X. For example, the scope of 'All dogs are friendly' is wider than that of 'All beagles are friendly'. See **relevance**.

Sham-reasoning   Attempts to persuade which appear to give reasons for accepting/rejecting a claim but in fact do not give us any reason for doing so are instances of sham-reasoning. **Fallacies** and **rhetorical ploys** are types of sham-reasoning, the former argumentative sham-reasoning, the latter non-argumentative.

Soft generalisation   A soft generalisation such as 'Most dogs are friendly' is contrasted with a **hard generalisation** such as 'All dogs are friendly'. Unlike hard generalisations, soft generalisations cannot be refuted by a single counterexample. Soft generalisations are frequently expressed without an explicit **quantifier**, as in 'Siamese cats meow a lot'.

Soundness   An argument is sound if, but only if, its premises are all **true**, and it is either **deductively valid** or **inductively forceful**.

Speaker-relativity A kind of statement is speaker-relative if it expresses a different **proposition** depending on who makes the statement. For example, if John says 'I am left-handed' he says that *he* is left handed, whereas if Mary says 'I am left-handed' she says that *she* is left-handed. The two propositions, then, could have different **truth-values**.

Stances (towards a proposition) There are four possible stances that can be taken towards a **proposition** with which one is presented: believing it, not believing it, suspending judgement, not engaging with it. Believing and not believing a **proposition** admit of degrees dependent upon the evidence available to provide **justification** for belief in that **proposition**.

Standard form This is a style of displaying an argument's **premises**, **conclusion** and inferences, in which each **proposition** is enumerated, and each **inference** indicated by an **inference bar**. For example:

P1) If Mrs McFee were murdered, there would be signs of a struggle.
P2) There are no signs of a struggle.

C1) Mrs McFee was not murdered.

P3) If Mrs McFee was not murdered, then Inspector Radcliffe ought to leave the premises.

C2) Inspector Radcliffe ought to leave the premises.

Syntactic ambiguity An **ambiguous sentence** is syntactically ambiguous when the arrangement of its words is such that the sentence could be understood in more than one way (as expressing more than one proposition.) See also **lexical ambiguity**.

Tripartite account of knowledge According to this account of knowledge, someone counts as knowing a proposition if and only if (i) they believe it, (ii) it is true and (iii) they are justified in believing it. See also **Gettier cases**.

Truth To say, of a **proposition**, that it is true, is to say that things are as the proposition says it is. For example, to say that it is true that snow is white is to say that snow is as that proposition says it is, namely white. Another way to put the point: to say that it is **true** that snow is white is equivalent to saying that snow is white. Unless a statement is **speaker-relative**, the proposition that it expresses cannot be true for one person but false for another.

Truth-value   Sometimes it is convenient to speak of the truth-value of a **proposition** (see, for example, **speaker-relativity**): the truth-value of a **true** proposition such as 'snow is white' is truth, and that of a false proposition such as 'snow is green' is falsity.

Vagueness   An expression is vague if (i) its extension is indefinitely bounded, e.g. 'bald', 'tall' or (ii) in a given context it is unclear what is meant by it. In the first case the meaning of the term may be clear, but the extension is 'fuzzy' because there is no clear point at which things arranged on a single dimension (e.g. degree of baldness) cease to have the quality denoted by the term. In the second case particular uses of a term such as 'political' are vague: it may not be clear exactly what is meant by calling something political in a given context. Because of this, a word such as 'political' may be vague in both senses: because its meaning is vague, so is its extension.

Validity   See **deductive validity**.

Answers and hints to selected exercises

Chapter 1

1 (*a*) Argument. (*b*) N/A it's a conditional. (*c*) Argument. (*d*) Argument. (*e*) N/A it's an explanation. (*f*) Argument. (*g*) Argument. (*h*) N/A it's an unsupported claim. (*i*) Argument. (*j*) N/A it's a statement about something that happened. (*k*) N/A it's a conditional. (*l*) Argument (*hint*: if you insert a conclusion indicator such as 'therefore', you see more clearly that this is an argument of a similar structure to that in (*d*). (*m*) Argument. (*n*) N/A it's a statement. (*o*) Argument. (*p*) N/A it's a conditional (*hint*: don't be misled by the long consequent.) (*q*) Argument. (*r*) Argument (*hint*: the conclusion appears before the premise). (*s*) Argument (*hint*: compare with (*b*), (*k*) and (*p*). (*t*) N/A only the conclusion is given (*hint*: move 'therefore' to the front of the proposition and you can see this more easily).

4 (*a*) 'Bank' could mean a financial institution or the area beside a river or lake. (*b*) 'End of life' could mean the final part of one's life or the goal/function of life. (*c*) 'Organ donor' could mean someone who donated a body part or someone who donated a musical instrument (*hint*: the term is ambiguous here because of the context – the Archbishop of Canterbury praises the donor). (*d*) 'Mummy' could mean either someone's mother (probably the victim's) or an ancient Egyptian exhibit (*hint*: the context makes the term ambiguous – the attack takes place in a museum). The phrase 'by mummy' could also be ambiguous: the sentence could mean either that someone's mother or a museum exhibit was responsible for the attack, or that the attack took place in the vicinity of either someone's mother or a museum exhibit. (*e*) 'by statue' could mean that the statue found the car or that the car was found beside the statue. (*f*) 'British left waffles' could mean that British left-wing politicians talk meaninglessly about Ireland or it could mean that the British (military, maybe) left some square pancake-like pastries in Ireland. (*g*) 'Arms' could mean weapons or limbs. 'Head' could also be ambiguous here, meaning either a head of state or a body part, so there are four possible interpretations of the sentence, though not all of them are equally plausible. (*h*) 'Depression' could mean a drop in the atmospheric pressure or a psychological condition. (*i*) 'The right' could mean that Blair is physically leaning further over to the right hand side or that he is shifting his political position rightwards. (*j*) 'More lies ahead' could mean that the Chancellor is facing further challenges or that the public can expect to be told more untruths.

5 (*a*) Before the officers' arrival the two suspects fled the area in a red Ford Escort that was driven by a woman in black. (*b*) Yesterday I was invited to go to the movies. (*c*) When Mary left her friends she was feeling depressed *or* When Mary left, her friends were feeling depressed. (*d*) Often people who neglect their diet die early *or* People who often neglect their diet tend to die early. (*e*) Smith had five pairs of boots as well as a pair of slippers. He lent the slippers to Jones *or* Smith had five pairs of boots and a pair of slippers and he lent them all to Jones. (*f*) Wanted: a bay mare with white socks, suitable for a novice. (*g*) When Jones left the company, it was in a better state *or* when Jones left the company, he was in a better state. (*h*) Glasgow's first commercial sperm bank opened last Friday with twenty men's semen samples frozen in a stainless steel tank. (*i*) A week ago, they were exposed to someone who was infected with the virus *or* They were exposed to someone who had been exposed to the virus a week ago. (*j*) The police would like to speak to two women and a van driver who all fled the scene of the accident *or* the police would like to speak to two women and also to a van driver who fled the scene of the accident.

7 (*a*) No one. Hard. (*b*) Few. Soft. (*c*) Most. Soft. (*d*) A majority of. Soft. (*e*) All. Hard. (*f*) Generally. Soft. (*g*) Almost all. Soft. (*h*) Hardly any. Soft. (*i*) Every. Hard. (*j*) Almost none. Soft.

8 Only (*d*) is *uncontroversially true* as a hard generalisation and you need to use 'No owls'. (*a*), (*b*), (*c*), (*e*), (*f*), (*g*), (*i*) and (*j*) should all be soft. (*h*) may turn out to be true as a hard generalisaion, but it is unlikely that readers (and their lecturers) have sufficient information about UK universities' mathematics departments at their fingertips to determine this. Also, there may be some disagreement about what constitutes a 'department', hence a hard generalisation is unlikely to be *uncontroversially true*.

Chapter 2

4   *Hint*: according to the definition of soundness, an unsound argument may have a true conclusion.

5   *Hint*: review the remarks on pp. 49–50 on the concept of *truth*.

6   (*a*) Valid. (*b*) Valid (*hint*: see what follows from P2 and P3; then see what follows from that proposition together with P1). (*c*) Valid. (*d*) Invalid. Even if no member of the Green Party voted for the tax cut, it could be that people outside the Green Party voted against it as well (or failed to vote for it). So Mr Jacobs could be one of those outside the Green Party who didn't vote for it. (*e*) Valid. (*f*) If every member of the Conservative Party voted for the tax cut, it could be that others outside that party voted for it as well. (*g*) P2 says that *some* of those who voted for the tax cut voted to increase defence spending, but it doesn't say that *all* who voted for the tax cut voted to increase defence spending. So it could be that some voted for the tax cut without voting for increased defence spending; if so, then that group could contain all the Liberal Party members who voted for the tax cut. (*h*) Invalid: to make the argument valid, we would have to add the premise 'Infanticide is not morally permissible'. That premise might be obviously *true*, but until it is actually added to the argument, the argument remains invalid. (*i*) Valid. (*j*) Invalid (!): what follows from the premises is that the *antecedent* of the conditional P1 is false – *namely*, that it is *not the case* that each person has the right to determine what happens to his or her own body. This means: not *every* person has that right. This leaves it open that *some* people might have that right, even if not everyone does. The conclusion, however, says that *no* people have that right. So the premises could be true and the conclusion false. As a further exercise, you might try to construct an argument similar to (*j*) but which is valid. (*k*) Invalid: P1 allows that a regime might be both corrupt and inefficient. (*l*) Invalid: P1 doesn't tell us that only one of those two things could have happened. Compare: if the car has no petrol (gasoline), then it will not start. If the car does have petrol, it doesn't follow that it will start – it might have a dead battery, a faulty starter, etc. (*m*) Valid. (*n*) Invalid: P1 tells you that if a political system is just, then it is a democracy. It doesn't tell you anything about unjust political systems; it could be that although all just systems are democracies, not all democracies are just. (*o*) Invalid: the word 'only' can be tricky. Actually P1 here says exactly the same thing as P1 in the previous argument. Compare: 'Only boys are members of the club' and 'The only members of the club are boys' – these say exactly the same thing, namely that every member of the club is a boy. (*p*) Valid. (*q*)

Invalid: Mr Cleever may have been drunk at the time of the accident, even though his drunkenness did not cause the accident. (*r*) Invalid: in order to infer the conclusion from the conditional P1, we need to know that Constantius' Christianity was genuine, but P2 only tells us that we do not know that it was not genuine; it doesn't tell us that it *was*. So perhaps Constantius' faith was a fraud, but no evidence of that fraudulence has survived. (*s*) Valid. (*t*) Invalid. If no Roman Emperors were wise, then it could be that Marcus Aurelius was not wise, and P1–P3 are all true. (*u*) Valid. (To see this, see what happens if we try to suppose the conclusion false but the premises true. Thus suppose C is false, i.e. that Augustus was wise. Then according to P3 Marcus Aurelius was not wise. Then according to P1, no Roman emperor is wise. But then Augustus, a Roman emperor according to P2, *is* wise! So it is impossible for the premises to be true but the conclusion false.) (*v*) Valid. (*w*) Invalid: P1 says that Mary will be disappointed if *both* John and Susan are late; so perhaps she won't be disappointed if only John is late. (*x*) Invalid: perhaps P1–P3 are all true, but Mary is disappointed for some other reason; perhaps John's being late was enough to disappoint her (P1 doesn't say Mary will be disappointed *only* if both John and Mary are late). (*y*) Invalid: this is disputable, but it seems that P1 tells us that Mary will be disappointed if John and Susan are married to *each other*. Perhaps John and Susan are both married but not to each other, in which case the premises could all be true but the conclusion false. (*z*) Valid.

7 (*a*) False. (*b*) True. (*c*) False. (*d*) True. (*e*) False. (*f*) True. (*g*) False. (*h*) False. (*i*) False. (*j*) False. (*k*) True. (*l*) False. (*m*) False. (*n*) False. (*o*) True. (*p*) False. (*q*) True.

9 Note that each of these admit of more than one correct answer; for example, 'If Hadrian was not great then Trajan was great' is equivalent to the answer given to (*a*), and would be equally correct. (*a*) If Trajan was not great then Hadrian was great. (*b*) If they are not mistreated, then dogs are loyal to their masters. (*c*) If there were any benevolent emperors, then Marcus Aurelius was a benevolent emperor. (*d*) If you do not study, then you will not pass. (*e*) If your dog does not get the ball, then my dog will get the ball. (*f*) If you are not wearing a tie, then you will not be admitted. (*g*) If you are not wearing a tie, then you will not be admitted. (*h*) If my dog barks then your dog barks (or: if your dog does not bark, then my dog does not bark). (*i*) If you drink every night, then you will not pass. (*j*) If you do not study, then you will not pass. (*k*) If you do not study, then you will not pass. (*l*) If the champion does not fight aggressively then he will not win. (*m*) If the ball does not go in the water, then either your dog will get the ball or mine will. (*n*) If Maximin was admired in Rome, then Galerius was not admired in Rome.

Chapter 3

1 (*a*) (A) P1) Most sex crimes are committed by victims of child abuse.
P2) The defendant committed a sex crime.

  C) **(Probably) The defendant was a victim of child abuse.**

(B) Inductively forceful.

(*d*) (A) P1) Most old people have poor eyesight.
P2) No one with poor eyesight should be allowed to drive.

  C) **(Probably) Most old people should not be allowed to drive.**

(B) Inductively forceful.

2 (A) Both are inductively forceful. (B) They could both be sound. If Mr X is a non-homosexual AIDS patient living in Orange County, then still the premises of both arguments could be true. (C) The four premises together do not give us a reason to conclude that Mr X is a homosexual, and do not gives us a reason to conclude that he is not.

3 (*a*) Incompatible. (*b*) Compatible. (*c*) Compatible. (*d*) Compatible (according to our convention, 'some' means 'at least one'). (*e*) Compatible. (*f*) Incompatible. (*g*) Compatible. (*h*) Incompatible. (*i*) Compatible. (*j*) Compatible. (*k*) Compatible. (*l*) Compatible. (*m*) Compatible.

4 Reconstruct it as a single argument; its tree would have three premises pointing separately to the conclusion 'Probably, Lewis is not going to win another gold medal in the 100 metres'.

5 (*d*) (A) P1) If this meat was grown in Scotland, then it is extremely unlikely that it is infected with BSE.
P2) If this meat is infected, then it is very unlikely that eating it will make you ill.

  C) **If this meat was grown is Scotland, then eating this meat will not make you ill.**

(B)   Invalid. (C) But the argument can be made valid as follows:

> P1)   If this meat was grown in Scotland, then it is extremely unlikely that it is infected with BSE.
> P2)   If this meat is infected, then it is very unlikely that eating it will make you ill.
>
> ---
>
> **C)   If this meat was grown is Scotland, then, probably, eating this meat will not make you ill.**

(D)   This assumes that the expressions 'extremely unlikely' and 'very unlikely' in the premises are strong enough to justify the word 'probably' in the consequent of the conclusion.

(*e*)   (A)   P1)   Brazil is more likely to win the World Cup than Argentina.

> ---
>
> **C)   Brazil will win the World Cup.**

(B)   Invalid, and not inductively forceful. (D) The arguer is probably thinking that Brazil is the team *most* likely to win the World Cup, but that could be true even if the probability of Brazil winning is less than one-half.

(*g*)   (A)   P1)   Probably, English football fans will make trouble at the World Cup.
> P2)   If English football fans make trouble at the World Cup, then England may be expelled from the Euro tournament.
>
> ---
>
> **C)   England will be expelled from the Euro tournament.**

(B)   Invalid, and not inductively forceful. (C) However, it could be made valid as follows:

> P1)   English football fans will make trouble at the World Cup.
> P2)   If English football fans make trouble at the World Cup, then England may be expelled from the Euro tournament.
>
> ---
>
> **C)   England may be expelled from the Euro tournament.**

Alternatively, it could be made inductively forceful:

> P1)   Probably, English football fans will make trouble at the World Cup.

P2) If English football fans make trouble at the World Cup, then England will be expelled from the Euro tournament.

___

C) **(Probably) England will be expelled from the Euro tournament.**

(*h*) (A) P1) If the murderer passed through here, then, probably, there would be hairs from the victim on the rug.

P2) But there are no hairs from the victim on the rug.

___

C) **(Probably) The murderer did not pass through here.**

(B) Not valid, but it is inductively forceful.

(*l*) *Hint*: note that 'many' of a given population can be thus-and-so, when most are not. For example, many people have gym memberships, but most do not.

6 (*a*) and (*b*) seem to be inductively forceful; (*a*) is very forceful because the sample looks to be representative; (*b*) seems to be less so, since it is possible that communist systems might succeed in other historical circumstances. Reconstructions should be obvious.

(*c*) (A) This is a bit more tricky to reconstruct. One way is as follows:

P1) The average IQ from among 17 conductors of major orchestras is 17 points higher than that of UK doctors, and 18 points higher than that of UK lawyers.

___

C) **(Probably) The average IQ of musicians is higher than that of either doctors or lawyers.**

(B) This argument is not inductively forceful because the sample is not representative. The relevant population mentioned in the conclusion is *musicians*, but the sample cited in the premise is only that of conductors of major orchestras. These are likely to be among the most intelligent musicians, so it is no wonder that they should be found to have high IQs.

(*d*) (A) P1) Most of the teenagers who have come to me (a counsellor for teenagers) and confessed to taking illicit drugs have serious family problems.

___

C) **(Probably) Most teenagers who take illicit drugs have serious family problems.**

(B)   Not inductively forceful because the sample is not representative. It might be that most teenagers who take illicit drugs do not have serious family problems, and do not do seek the services of a counsellor. The counsellor sees only those teenagers who are sufficiently troubled to seek a counsellor.

(e) (A)   P1)   No English club has won the treble twice.
              P2)   Manchester United is an English club.

           C)   **(Probably) Manchester United is not going to win the treble again.**

(B)   The argument is *not* inductively forceful. For all that the premises tell us, perhaps *only one* English club (United) has won the treble (FA Cup, League/Premiership, Champions League/European Cup). (In fact, that is true; only United has done it – but you don't need to know this in order to see the weakness of the argument.) Thus, even if no English clubs *have* won it twice, it could be that *given* that a club has won the treble once, it is likely to win it again. That is, P1 could be true even though the conditional probability of an English club's winning the treble given that it has won it before is quite high. Note also: it is tempting to think we should add 'Manchester United won the treble once' as a premise, but that statement does not *support* the conclusion, so it is not part of the argument.

(f) (A)   P1)   People who take vitamins regularly live longer than average.
              P2)   Jenna takes vitamins regularly.

           C)   **(Probably) Jenna will live longer than average.**

(B)   This is inductively forceful. If you think it isn't, it is probably because you are reasoning as follows: 'We cannot conclude from P1 that taking vitamins regularly *causes* people to live longer than average, because it might be that already healthy people are more likely to take vitamins (perhaps well-off people tend to take vitamins more, and are healthier because they are well-off, not because they take the vitamins); therefore we can't conclude that *because* Jenna takes vitamins regularly she's likely to live longer.' It is true that P1 doesn't tell us anything about a causal relationship.

But C doesn't tell us about a causal relationship either! Compare: 'Most people with sore throats get a runny nose. Jenna has a sore throat, therefore, probably, she'll get a runny nose.' The sore throat doesn't cause the runny nose, but still the argument is inductively forceful.

Chapter 4

1 (*a*) Scare quotes. (*b*) Appeal to novelty (*c*) Buzzwords ('knowledge management', 'competitive advantage', 'learning culture', 'shared vision', 'common purpose'.) (*d*) Appeal to popularity. (*e*) Smokescreen (*hint*: avoids the question of our moral duty). (*f*) equivocation (over the vagueness of 'most successful'.) (*g*) Appeal to fear. (*h*) Buzzword ('censorship'.) (*i*) Appeal to novelty *or* appeal to vanity. 'Hair management technology' is a buzzword (phrase). (*j*) Smokescreen (*hint*: avoids the question of the alleged threat to democracy).

3 (*a*) Slippery slope. (*b*) *Post hoc ergo propter hoc*. (*c*) Fallacy of majority belief. (*d*) Affirming the consequent. (*e*) False dilemma. (*f*) Conflation of morality with legality. (*g*) Mistaking correlation for cause. (*h*) *Ad hominem*. (*i*) *Tu quoque* (*hint*: it is implied that the well-fed middle classes do not follow their own prescription). (*j*) Perfectionist fallacy.

4 *General hint:* remember that the crucial move when reconstructing substantial fallacies is that of adding the premise (which is usually hidden and operates in all instances of the fallacy) that exposes the fallacy.

(*a*) *Ad hominiem* circumstantial:

> P1) Lecturers are always extolling the virtues of critical thinking.
> P2) Lecturers only have jobs if they have students to teach.
> P3) Whenever someone would benefit from something we should reject their arguments in favour of that thing.
> ___
> **C) We should reject lecturers' arguments in favour of critical thinking.**

(*b*) Conflation of morality with legality:

> P1) It's not illegal for me to exaggerate my skills on my CV.
> P2) Anything which is not illegal is not immoral.
> ___
> **C) It's morally acceptable for me to exaggerate my skills on my CV.** .

(c) *Tu quoque:*

P1) The opposition criticises the Government for spending money on the arts.

P2) When the opposition was in government it increased the arts budget by 200%.

P3) Whenever someone's actions are inconsistent with their claims, we should not take those claims seriously.

C) **We should not take the opposition's criticism seriously.**

(d) Inversion of cause and effect:

P1) Smoking causes lung cancer.

P2) Whenever one thing X causes another Y, an absence of X will cause an absence of Y.

C) **People who do not smoke will not suffer lung cancer.**

(e) Epistemic fallacy:

P1) Jo believes that the Chancellor is doing a poor job. (P)

P2) Gordon Brown is the Chancellor. (Q)

P3) If someone believes that P, they also believe that Q.

C) **Jo believes that Gordon Brown is doing a poor job.**

Chapter 5

1 Except in the case of (*k*), we provide only the missing premises. (*a*) 'You should not marry an idiot', where this is understood as a hard generalisation; or perhaps 'If someone is an idiot, then you should not marry him'. (*b*) Same. (*c*) 'Everyone who likes the Jeeves books likes the Blandings Castle books.' (*d*) 'If Pavarotti sits in that chair, then it will break.' Or possibly add two premises (though this is not specified as an option in the instructions: 'If a very heavy person sits on that chair, then it will break,' and 'Pavarotti is a very heavy person'. (*e*) Possibly a hard generalisation: 'Prices rise only when the savings rate decreases,' or 'When the savings rate does not decrease, prices do not rise'; or a soft one, i.e. 'Usually, when the savings rate does not decrease, prices do not rise'. (*f*) 'If Schumacher's mechanic is not inept, then Schumacher's car will not break down.' It may help in this case to translate all the uses of 'unless' into sentences using 'not' and either 'if' or 'only if'. The first sentence would be 'Hakkinen will win only if Schumacher's car breaks down', or 'If Schumacher's car does not break down, then Hakkinen won't win'. (g) 'Rossini was greater than Puccini.' (h) 'No socialist country is a democracy.' (i) 'If we withdraw the offer, then we carry on with a second-rate manager.' (j) 'If there isn't any wine, then we'll drink beer.' (k) The conclusion – 'Cigarette advertisements encourage people to smoke more' – is not quite explicit. One likely implicit premise is simply the conditional: 'If ads for chocolates encourage people to eat chocolates, then cigarette advertisements encourage people to smoke.' One might think the implicit premise is something like the covering generalisation: 'All ads for a given brand of consumable product encourage people to consume that product.' This generalisation would be too broad in scope, however; it doesn't seem true that ads for toothpaste or toilet paper encourage people to use more toothpaste or toilet paper. Yet the suggested conditional is surely motivated by a generalisation (why should there be a connection between chocolates and cigarettes?). A good exercise would be to find a plausible generalisation (or appropriate scope) that would serve the purpose of the argument.

2   There are many ways in which these sentences might be reformulated; we offer one suggestion for each. (a) The democratic candidate adopts whatever position is most popular. (b) The invasion of Iraq was a huge (large, massive, etc.) miscalculation. (c) If they impose trade tariffs then trading agreements will not be fair. (d) Since beginning to write novels aimed at a young female adult audience, she has earned a great deal of money. (e) However long they attempt to persuade us of their position, we will not be persuaded. (f) Although it is widely believed that shares in Ramsay represent good value, they do not. (g) We will continue our attempts to ban the advertisement on children's television of innutritious convenience foods until such advertisements have been completely eliminated. (h) Mis-takes by doctors contributed to the deaths of 40,000 patients last year. (One might use 'caused' instead of 'contributed to', but one would have to know more of the relevant facts in order to determine which is appropriate.)

3   (a) If you do not release prisoners then there will be no cease-fire. (b) If we do not increase our appeal to women then we will not win the election. (c) All universities allow the most offensive forms of speech (conceivably, this means only that *some* universities allow such speech). (d) Every leaf-blower is louder than every rake. (e) If embryo research is allowed then human cloning will be allowed. (f) Everyone who laughs last laughs longest. Alternatively: for every group of people, the one who laughs after everyone else in the group has laughed laughs longer than anyone else in the group.

4 As is often the case, each of these might be answered in either of several ways. (*a*) No one under the age of 18 can legally purchase alcohol in the UK. (*b*) All scorpions are poisonous. (*c*) Most non-French wines are not overpriced *or* Few non-French wines are overpriced. (*d*) Most oil paintings from before 1500 are either Dutch or Flemish *or* Except for Dutch and Flemish paintings, few paintings from before 1500 were painted in oil. (*e*) Most successful lawyers are good at analysing arguments. (*f*) The blood pressure of any haemorrhaging patient will decrease.

7 P1) Everyone who supports across-the-board pay rises for female academics supports a reduction in the evidential standard for rape convictions.

P2) Mrs Jones supports across-the-board pay rises for female academics.

C) **Mrs. Jones will support a reduction in the evidential standard for rape convictions.**

9 (*a*) P1) Most healthy, young parrots can be trained to talk.
P2) Your new parrot is healthy and young.

C) **(Probably) Your new parrot can be trained to talk.**

(*b*) P1) Most men marry.
P2) Every married woman has, at the time of her wedding, a mother.

C) **Most men have, have had, or will have a mother-in-law.**

(*c*) Since human beings are primates, the scope of the generalisation must be reduced. The argument might be represented in different ways, but however it is done, some implicit premises will need to be made explicit.

P1) All chimpanzees are primates.
P2) No chimpanzee is human.
P3) Bobo is a chimpanzee.

C1) **Bobo is a non-human primate.**
P4) No primates except humans can learn to talk.

C2) **Bobo cannot learn to talk.**

(*d*) Not all countries can be attacked by sea – Paraguay, Laos and Switzerland, for example, are land-locked (assuming that 'attacked by sea' means 'attacked using ships or boats', and does not include attacks by aeroplanes from aircraft carriers and the like). But most countries have a seacoast.

P1)   Most countries can be attacked by sea.
P2)   Any country that can be attacked by sea requires a naval defence.

C)   Most countries require a naval defence.

P2 might well be disputed. Does, say, Equatorial Guinea *require* a naval defence?

12   The conclusion is that same-sex marriage should not be legal. Note that the following reconstruction would be inadequate:

P1)   No deviant sexual relationship should be legally protected.
P2)   The legalisation of same-sex marriage would legally protect homosexual relationships.
P3)   Homosexual relationships are deviant sexual relationships.

C)   Same-sex marriage should not be legalised.

First, this reconstruction leaves out of account the slippery slope appealed to in the last sentence. The point seems to be that the only reason that only heterosexual relationships (between mature persons not genetically closer than cousins) are entitled to legal protection is that others are deviant. Therefore, if homosexual relationships *are* entitled to legal protection, then since they are deviant, *all* deviant sexual relationships are entitled to it. Second, this reconstruction uses the word 'deviant'. But there are at least three possible meanings here, one of which is rhetorically charged: the word can mean simply 'deviating from the norm', which might mean 'not biologically typical', or 'not socially typical'. But it also carries an opprobrious connotation of sickness or unhealthy abnormality, as when we speak of 'social deviants'. The factual basis of the argument can be clarified by eliminating the term.

15   There are just two relevant outcomes here: you draw an ace, or you do not draw an ace. A pack of playing cards contains 52 cards, of which four are aces. So the probability of drawing an ace is $4/52 = 1/13$, and the probability of not drawing one is $12/13$. So:

$$
\begin{aligned}
EV &= (1/13 \times 10) + (12/13 \times -1) \\
&= (0.77 \times 10) + (0.92 \times -1) \\
&= 0.77 \qquad\quad + (-0.92) \\
&= -0.15.
\end{aligned}
$$

The expected value is negative, so you shouldn't accept the wager.

17 The first two sentences are true, but only the second is relevant as a premise. *Hints*: the first conclusion is ambiguous. Interpreted one way, there is a sound argument for it using the second sentence as a premise, but it does not support the second conclusion. Interpreted the other way, it supports the second conclusion but is not supported by the second sentence.

19 (*b*) The conclusion might be 'The stress of modern life is caused by the amount of shopping we do, combined with our not going to church', or something like 'Our lives are more stressful than our parents' lives were because we shop more and attend church less than they did'. Taking the latter as the conclusion, a simple reconstruction might be:

P1) Our lives are more stressful than our parents' lives were either because we shop more and attend church less than they did, or because we work more than they did.

P2) We do not work more than they did.

C) **Our lives are more stressful than our parents' lives were either because we shop more than they did, and they went to church whereas we do not.**

Note, however, that the argument hints at an argument for P1 itself. Since shopping is said to be a highly stressful activity, the arguer might also be assuming that attending church reduces stress.

Chapter 6

1 (*a*) No. (*b*) No. (*c*) Yes. (*d*) Yes. (*e*) Yes. (*f*) No. (*g*) Yes. (*h*) No. (*i*) The argument is defeated for James because he has much stronger evidence that the conclusion is false (in fact, he knows that the conclusion is false).

2 (*a*) Yes. (*b*) No. (*c*)–(*f*) The argument is rationally persuasive for Catherine if we assume she was justified in accepting what David told her. It seems that she was. Jane's case is less clear, but it seems the argument is not rationally persuasive for her because her reason for accepting P2 is not good. The argument is defeated for Mary, hence not rationally persuasive for her. Though she does not accept the conclusion, it seems the argument is rationally persuasive for Anna: her reason for rejecting the conclusion is poor.

3 (i) *Hint*: Remember that false beliefs can be reasonable, i.e. well-supported and justified. The word 'wrong' is possibly ambiguous in this context; does it mean 'false' or 'unjustified'?

4 (*h*) P1) Every educated Roman knew Homer.
P2) Everyone who knows Homer knows the story of Achilles.

C) **Every Roman knew the story of Achilles.**

Suppose X is *any* Roman. According to P1, X knew Homer. Then according to P2, he knew the story of Achilles. So whatever Roman X is, X knew the story of Achilles. So, every Roman knew the story of Achilles.

7 (*a*) P1) If P then Q.
P2) If Q then R.

C) **If P then R.**

(*d*) P1) If a is not an S, then a is a D.
P2) All Ds are T, and a is not T.
P3) If a is an S, then either a is R or a is A.
P4) Every W is either not-A or Y.
P5) Everything that is S and Y is T.

C) **If a is W, then a is R and S.**

We can try checking for validity just using the logical form. We suppose a is W, and see whether the premises tell us that a must be R and S. We know from P2 that a is not T. Therefore from P2 a cannot be a D (if it were, then it would be T, which it is not). Then P1 tells us that a is an S. So we know that a is an S. It remains to show that a is R. P4 tells us that a is either not-A or Y. Let us see what follows on each alternative: first that a is Y, then that a is not-A.

So suppose a is Y. Since we know that a is an S, P5 tells us that a is a T. But we know from P2 that a is not a T. So a can't be Y.

So suppose a is not-A. Then P3 tells us that if a is S, a is R. According to P1, if a is *not* S, then a is D. So a is either D or R. But we know that a is not a D. So a is R.

So if a is W, then a is both S and R, and the argument-form is valid.

Answers and hints to selected exercises

Chapter 7

2   (b), (d), (i), (m), (q), (s), (t) and (z) are indexical. (t) could also be implicitly speaker-relative if it means 'that hurts me', as could (z) if it means something like 'I think this one is better than that one', in which case it could also be implicitly relative to the preferences of the speaker (but need not be).

(g), (h), (l), (o) and (w) are implicitly speaker-relative and also implicitly relative to the preferences of the speaker with respect to food, presidents, beer and music, respectively.

(f) depends on context. It could be both implicitly speaker-relative and relative to the preferences (in respect of climate) of the speaker if she is explaining, for example, why she doesn't want to go to Southern Italy for a holiday. On the other hand, the speaker might be talking about, say, the suitability of the climate for growing a certain crop – Riesling grapes, for instance – in which case the sentence would be neither implicitly speaker-relative nor relative to the preferences of the speaker. Note that it would be implicitly speaker-relative in the sense dealt with in Chapter 1.

(e), (j) and (k) make prescriptive claims ((e) and (j) are specifically moral claims, (k) arguably so). These are tricky. If we take the philosophical view that moral values are relative to the preferences of an individual or to a group of individuals or a culture (the position called *moral relativism*, discussed in this chapter), then we should say that these sentences are both implicitly speaker-relative and implicitly relative to the preferences of the speaker(s) asserting them. If, on the other hand, we take the philosophical view that moral values are independent of individual or collective preferences (the position called *moral objectivism*), then we should say that the sentences are neither implicitly speaker-relative nor relative to the preferences of the speaker(s).

4 A sample answer:

Yes, if I were justified in believing a proposition that is in fact false, there could still be an argument for that proposition that is rationally persuasive for me. This is because rational persuasiveness only requires (a) that an argument be valid or inductively forceful, (b) that I have *good reason* to accept the premises and, if the argument is inductively forceful, (c) that the conclusion is not defeated for me. So providing these criteria are met, the fact that the conclusion is false does not undermine the argument's rational persuasiveness for me. The situation would not change if the proposition were actually true. Apart from (c), which is not relevant to this case, the criteria for rational persuasiveness do not make reference to the actual truth values of an argument's conclusion.

Example

P1)   Jeremy is a nine-year-old boy.

P2)   Most nine-year-old boys like to play football.

C)   (Probably) Jeremy likes to play football.

I have good reason to believe that Jeremy likes to play football because I frequently see him playing football, he has football posters in his bedroom, reads football comics, and so on. In fact, the proposition is false. He doesn't really like to play, he just goes along with it to please his father, a very keen football fan. The argument is inductively forceful and I have good reasons to accept P1 and P2 – I know Jeremy and I have more than a passing acquaintance with the likes and dislikes of nine-year-old boys – so criteria (a) and (b) are met. I have no evidence that should lead me to reject C); that is, I don't know that Jeremy's apparent football fervour is really a front to please his dad, so the argument is not defeated for me. Thus it is rationally persuasive for me. If it turned out to be true that Jeremy likes to play football, the argument would still be rationally persuasive for me.

Answers and hints to selected exercises

■ Index

Index